Ten Thousand Scorpions

ALSO BY LARRY FROLICK

Splitting Up: Divorce, Culture, and the Search for Real Life (1998)

TEN THOUSAND
Scorpions

THE SEARCH
FOR THE QUEEN
OF SHEBA'S GOLD

LARRY FROLICK

M&S

National Library of Canada Cataloguing in Publication Data

Frolick, Larry
Ten thousand scorpions : the search for the Queen of Sheba's gold

ISBN 0-7710-4780-0

1. Frolick, Larry — Journeys. 2. Sheba, Queen of. 3. Yemen — Description and travel. 4. Ethiopia — Description and travel.
5. Turkey — Description and travel. 6. Ephesus (Extinct city). I. Title.

G490.F76 2002   910'.92   C2001-903804-6

We acknowledge the financial support of the Government of Canada through the Book Publishing Industry Development Program for our publishing activities. We further acknowledge the support of the Canada Council for the Arts and the Ontario Arts Council for our publishing program.

All efforts were made to clear permissions for material. Oversights will be corrected in subsequent editions if the publisher is informed in writing.

Line illustrations throughout: Steve Wilson
Typeset in Minion by M&S, Toronto
Printed and bound in Canada

McClelland & Stewart Ltd.
The Canadian Publishers
481 University Avenue
Toronto, Ontario
M5G 2E9
www.mcclelland.com

1   2   3   4   5   06   05   04   03   02

For Adam

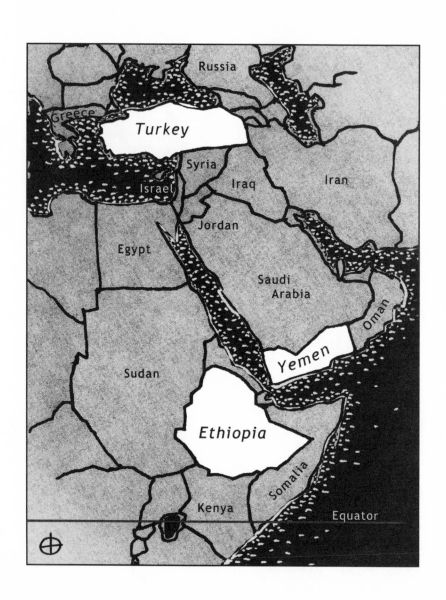

"The man who plays to an inside straight ain't no cardplayer. He's either a fool, or he knows somethin' you don't."
— Johnny Harrison, gold prospector

Contents

Interregnum

Note on Usage

As written Arabic employs no vowels, I have tried to stay consistent, within the realm of reason. Alternate spellings for geographical place names like Axum (Aksum) and Ma'rib (Mareb) abound. I have followed the *Yemen Times* and Oxford usage where applicable, and the authorship of errors is mine.

Introduction

In the early spring of 1996, an exploration crew belonging to Cantex Mine Development, a Canadian mining exploration company, was out doing its daily rounds surveying the tribal lands of Al-Jawf in northern Yemen, working at the edge of its government-licensed mineral concession, when it came upon some odd holes dug into the ground. The two Land Cruisers skiffed to a halt, and the men got out and bent down for a look.

The pits appeared to lead to tunnels. Old tunnels, judging from the primitive stone implements scattered about the sands. Nobody dared to crawl inside. Too many snakes, poisonous scorpions. They contented themselves with poking around; and then, with no more effort than it takes to heft a basket of fruit off a market stand, one of the geologists spotted and dislodged an alabaster plaque, a tablet with curious, ancient letters painstakingly carved on it. Some of the men had seen that script before, in the museum back in Sana'a, the capital.

They recognized the script as Sabean, from the ancient kingdom of Sheba. And now, as they took a closer look at the scattered implements, they realized that the stone bowls lying in the sand were paired with stone pestles, and that ground-up quartzite lay in sparkling heaps everywhere. It was enough. Enough to tell them that the people who had dug this complex of pits and tunnels had been doing the very thing they were doing now: searching for gold. They decided it was time to call the boss.

Cantex was a small British Columbia public company headed by Charles (Chuck) Fipke, the famed extreme geologist who had struck it rich with a huge diamond play in the Northwest Territories, and the Yemen concession was not its only mining play. Listed on the CDNX stock exchange, the company held exploration licences in Greenland and Angola, and other Third World countries were more than willing to entrust its multimillionaire founder with generous mineral-exploration licences in a bid to attract foreign investment. But Yemen was special for Fipke. He loved the land, its hard edges and rock anomalies. It was perfect for a geologist who wanted to break every record in the book. It was the country to which he had returned immediately after his diamond mine near Yellowknife was formally approved by the Canadian government, rushing off as if he could not wait to get into the rough wilds after the months spent indoors at government tribunals and public hearings.

When he heard the news of the discovery of the ancient mine workings, Fipke had dispatched Kelowna geologist John Greenough and his wife, Leanne Mallory, an archeologist specializing in Egyptology, to the remote site. In summer the daily temperatures now reached 120°F in the shade. The two scientists made a preliminary study of the site and concluded that it was likely an Iron Age gold mine, worked by slaves or prisoners of war, and that the resulting bullion might have been exported along the ancient caravan route that lay a few miles away. More than this, they could not say. Again no one dared to enter the tunnels, and they had no licence to excavate.

Fipke was pleased to pose with the alabaster plaque; he and his chief field geologist, Abdul Shybani, held it up for a picture, and it was this photo that had prompted my undertaking three years later. As it circulated, the story of the discovery of the ancient mines had excited its own share of international press interest and, more particularly, provoked renewed enthusiasm for the stock from the Cantex shareholders. Had Fipke done it again? Had he found the source of the queen of Sheba's gold? Nobody did much more than speculate, for Yemen wasn't the sort of country over which an idle curiosity-seeker could muse from the safety of an air-conditioned tourist bus. For one thing, there were no tourist buses.

No, it was necessary for someone to actually go and check the story out. Get in-country, as they say. My brother Vernon, who knew Fipke personally and had written a book about his diamond exploits, had originally suggested we go together to Yemen and write a book about the queen of Sheba's gold mines. He had hung out with Fipke in Brazil, treading up black jungle rivers in the Amazon basin as deep as their chests, exploring for gold. But now he begged off, citing a heavy workload. I was alone in this enterprise. If I still wanted to pursue it.

I had never met Fipke; indeed I had only talked to him briefly a few times on the telephone. Nevertheless, I called him in his office in Kelowna. He told me if I wanted to write a book I could stay at the Cantex villa in Sana'a; it was in a walled compound, and it was safe, with guards and everything. And to call him Chuck. Everyone, staff, even his children, called him Chuck.

From all accounts Chuck was a maniac. He had taken his family for a vacation to Uganda under Idi Amin, that kind of thing. In my copy of the now-famous photo, he appeared to be a powerfully built, stocky man, younger-looking than his fifty-odd years. I saw a moustache, and the intense eyes of a dentist who'd spotted that molar tooth he wanted, there way in the back. I had collected my Yemen visa, my high-UV sunglasses, and a new pair of my favourite walking boots. And the photo, of course. In it, Fipke and Shybani were smiling proudly, holding up the ancient loot as fisherman do, hoisting a trophy bass. The plaque was held upside down.

I had done some reading in preparation for the trip. There were numerous technical problems regarding the famous Biblical account to which all the news reports invariably alluded. For one thing, no queen of Sheba was ever mentioned in any of the ancient inscriptions of Yemen. And more, these records were dauntingly extensive, for there were three times as many Yemeni written artifacts as all of ancient Egypt's and Israel's put together. Did she even exist?

Secondly, between the civil wars of the 1980s and the previous government's strict interdictions, most of Yemen's artifacts had either been looted or were locked away in storage, and what was available had never been properly examined by scientists. The real history, as opposed to the national myth, was largely a great gaping blank, not least of all because inquiries into its pagan origins were not a high priority for the devoutly Muslim nation. Who, if anyone, was an authority on the subject?

And lastly, and perhaps most tellingly, even the old myths about Sheba did not concur. The queen was the subject of some fairly intense patriotic idealogies, part of the fabric of opposed national identities and national destinies that defined politics in the Middle East. Anybody stepping into this field had to be careful on that score alone.

There were no less than four myths about the queen of Sheba, each with its own sources and tradition. In the familiar Biblical account in I Kings 10: 1-13, the queen brings King Solomon a tremendous caravan of gold, which would place her reign about 975 B.C. In the Holy Quran compiled after A.D. 650, the queen walks on a mirrored floor laid out by the king and is fooled into lifting up her skirts, thinking it is water. In Jewish medieval tradition, the queen is a pagan temptress on a par with Lilith, the arch-seductress. And in the national epic of the Ethiopian Orthodox Church, the queen is the founder of the great dynastic line that ended in 1975 with Haile Selassie, bearing the son of Solomon after the king took her to his bed by guile. How to reconcile these disparate views with an undateable alabaster plaque and some granite mortars that had seen better days?

The country was oppressively hot in summer, and dangerous throughout the year. Politically motivated kidnappings were common. The best time to go was after Ramadan, the month of fasting usually observed around late December. People I talked to about the impending trip gave me "the look." And then they quickly talked about something else. This general reaction contributed to my increasing sense of unreality about the whole thing. Each day before my intended departure date I studied the headlines of the English-language *Yemen Times* on the Internet. Every day a car bomb was going off somewhere in the country. That, or there was a hijacking. They always seemed to get the guys responsible, and the guys always seemed to look exactly the same as the last ones. It was like *Alice in Wonderland* with guns and beards. Terrible car-crash statistics too. And then, without fail, it was January.

Now the date of my departure had arrived.

Here I was, where this passive and idle curiosity had got me: at the point of no return. Now it was no longer a story, now it would get real very fast. I was thinking again about the plaque they found in the desert. Al-Jawf, they said, in the north. Tribal lands.

They had given it to the museum, and now nobody could find it. It was lost. All they had was the photo and a garbled translation. Every third word, a question mark:

> Sa'd Ibn de Abyat dedicated to [?] yagraw the bronze statue,
> thanking [?] for protecting his servant Abi Lat Sa'ad [?] visit
> to [?] of di Tagraw.

That was it. My whole trip. This was what it came down to. An alabaster plaque, illegible with cracks, dedicated to a god. And the name of the god, broken off . . .

Interregnum

The night I left Toronto for Yemen, a cold sloppy rain pelted the city. People stooped uncertainly in the miasma, congealing in bus shelters, half-blinded by the effluvium of late winter. Inside the travel agency, I ran into Katrina Keown, the eighteen-year-old daughter of a friend, and her chum Cian. Cian was a tall girl with freshly cut hair and dark eyes that noticed everything. They were off to Central America. Three months.

Travelling light, they said.

"Three months? What kind of luggage are you taking then?"

"Just this."

Cian held up one of those loose African string bags, the kind European hippies used to flaunt. I looked at her and she looked back at me. They asked me questions. I wondered if she could tell I got dizzy just from looking her way. Later I phoned my brother to say goodbye.

"All she had was this string purse, I swear to God."

"Jesus," he said, getting into the story. "Eighteen, huh?"

"I told them about you getting it on with that girl from the Bader-Meinhof gang in Belize. And about Victor leaving a trail of green poop all the way back to Mérida. They laughed."

"We should have married hippies," he said, fierce all of a sudden. "Me and you."

"Maybe you can't marry a hippie," I said, trying to get philosophical.

"Tall, was she?" he went on, ignoring my concept. "Slim?"

"As tall and perfect as ever."

Silence for a moment. Then:

"So it's still out there, eh?" he said, a voice full of wonder.

"Oh, yeah," I said. "It's still out there, all right."

It was still raining when the cab arrived. The cab driver was a Somalian, who said he was Ethiopian even though he was born in a Somali-speaking village.

"Boom-boom," he explained, meaning the war. I admired his huge mane of tufted hair without saying anything. He drove well. It was still raining.

"What are you writing book for?" he asked.

"Gold," I replied.

"Ah, gold. In Yemen?"

"Yes. They find gold in rocks. They must take it out with a factory, though," I explained. "Not like the old days, with rock hammers."

"We have gold in my country too," he said proudly.

"Yes?"

"In the east of Ethiopia. It was like this: Lightning hit the earth, bang! All these black stones, the people found them. They rubbed the black stones and – "

"Gold?" I nodded.

"Gold." He shot me a quick look. His fingers splayed over the pink, leather-wrapped steering wheel. "My friend, he bought a lorry, to take the black stone out, you know."

Gold is where you find it, I told myself, watching the meter measuring off my trip in forgone lunches. "And did he get it?"

"Too many problems, down there."

"Boom-boom?"

"Boom-boom," he agreed. "Always the boom-boom."

At the airport I watched the planes lumber through the rain, trying to make out the name of my DC-10 *painted in fancy script on the nose cone. Marie-Claire?*

No more time for reading; the announcement came. The passengers stirred. We shuffled forward into the hollow mouth of the gate.

PART ONE

Ma'rib

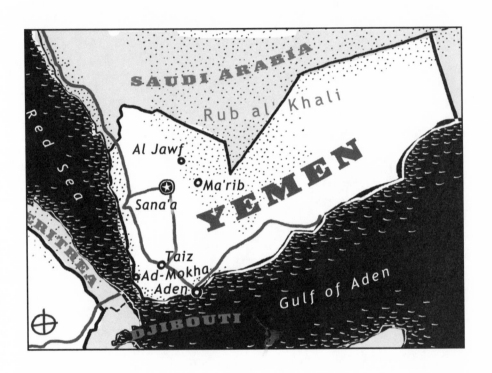

Chapter 1

The Flight of the Mad Cow

From the air, Yemen resembles an indolent tyrannosaurus that has curled up in a bed of hot sand for a million centuries, his jaws open wide to Rub al-Khali, the Empty Quarter, the great yawning desert to the east, and his clawed feet tucked neatly against the heat-flattened Red Sea in the south.

Tonight I am flying Lufthansa, and the *Tyrannosaurus rex* of our aircraft's final destination shows on our television monitors as a cartoon landform in volcanic cherry red, a creature of legend and myth, snoring blissfully away along with our catatonic passengers. His sand bed is neon yellow, the surrounding sea a phosphorous green. The screens artfully suspended above our heads are not content with showing us pretty pictures. No. We must have our facts too. Statistics follow the cartoon maps. Digital readouts of wind speed, outside air temperature, altitude above sea level, and time to destination monotonously follow each other in Arabic, German, and English, imperial alternating with metric. We've just left Cairo, and we are now three hours and forty minutes from final debarkation. The temperature appears. From the throbbing darkness outside I try to imagine what −45°C air temperature feels like, without success. A minute later it's the same in Fahrenheit, −45°F, a number I recognize from home. We've got a Saskatchewan winter up here at 28,000 feet, although the equator is just down the block.

As for the plane, it represents itself on the screen (or its trip computers do) as a red arrow moving east, droning down across the scaly neck of the T. Rex. Droning, droning, ever so slowly but certainly, burrowing into the heart of the rock-beast, the ventral spot marked *Sana'a* . . .

I can hear a mantra in the hum of the engines, maybe several mantras. I can feel it in my bones, a sustained, semi-holy feeling, composed of a slight but irrepressible terror and a giddy resonance caught between being and nothingness. Fourteen hours of straight flying so far, and I've almost had it. *Yum'hum, humm hum.* I want to believe in my mission tonight, really I do.

Jetliners are the flying cathedrals of our age; it seems so obvious to me now from where I sit. The harmonic pitch changes, a choral crescendo that hits its full stride now that we've reached cruising altitude, 45,000 feet or 13,500 metres, take your pick. Now the trip-screen tells us just how dead we would be, immediately outside the vessel. An unbelievable −108°C brushes past the black port-window, and it's getting even colder. The wind velocity hits 450 km/h and, according to the digital clock, the hours I thought we'd gained on the stopover in Cairo are now lost to another time zone.

So, despite the endless flow of numbers, it's still midnight where I sit. Midnight, like it's been for hours. I am thinking about Chuck Fipke, about the guy who routinely makes these fourteen-hour flights overseas and must have accumulated enough AIR MILES by now to get to the moon and back.

So this is his regular commute to the office?

I was the only one who chose beef on the flight into Cairo. The shadow of the Mad Cow has fallen heavily over Europe; everyone else chose the chicken. When I made my selection, the flight attendant gave me the certain eye. Trying to decide, I suppose, if I was a hero or merely another fool from America. In this age of major decisions at mealtime, the lines get so easily blurred. The beef was tough but the sauce tasty, and I ate like a wolf, although I wasn't hungry. Who knows what kind of food is available in Yemen? And how do I feel now?

Okay, I guess.

Tired, but watchful. Unlike me, Fipke is famous for his ability to sleep on airplanes, to grab his power naps even in buzzy little alpine helicopters without any heat. People told me he could work on only two hours' sleep a night, that he could turn his brain off and on like a light bulb. That he could do an eighteen-hour day slogging in the Yukon bush, in a leech-infested swamp, in a catastrophically hot desert. Then go home, wash up, and be ready for dancing an all-nighter at the disco, cantina, or whatever passed for the local party-scene headquarters. He had come out to Yemen in 1994, made his deal with the government, got forty thousand square kilometres of prime rock-land in the west for his company's exclusive mineral conces-sion. Rented a nice villa in town. The only problem was, he had to fly to Dubai to party, in the United Arab Emirates two thousand kilometres away. There wasn't much to do in Sana'a except go to restaurants with the Cantex boys. That, and work.

The story was, they had found gold. In their concession. The details were a little foggy, I was not clear on the facts, and the fortunes of gold exploration companies since Bre-X were altogether a dicey thing to predict. The Internet did not help either, for there was a huge gap between what the Securities Commission regulators coldly permitted and what the speculators' chat-rooms warmly encouraged in the way of disseminating information. The Cantex stock had spent most of its life as a penny stock, hovering between ten cents and a buck, depending on the mercurial mood of the True Believers and the liquidity demands of the Big Players. The official corpo-rate announcements did not help either. These were filled with a technical language that had to be decoded like the editorials in *Pravda* during the Cold War.

The gist of it was, there was lots of gold in recoverable quantities ready for leaching, a cheap acid-based process that anybody with thick rubber gloves and a face mask could learn to operate. Low-tech. And how much gold? Lots. Only it was the kind of gold that was invisible to the naked eye, the kind that was measured in parts per million, not the hefty river nuggets that brought millions of dreamers to old California.

Chuck Fipke had come out to Yemen precisely *because* he was sure the story of Sheba's gold mines had to have some basis in technical fact. That, and the fact that the geology of the Arab country was identical to the state of Nevada's. Nevada was now chockablock with silver and gold mines. And nobody had taken a good, hi-tech look at Yemen's geology until now. The country was opening up. Fipke would be ahead of the pack.

Just how far ahead, that was the big question.

From up here at 13,500 metres, it all seems pointless to me. This question of first and last, this eager optimism and visionary opportunism. Look at those sketchy strands of dim lights, the deserted coasts. This is not a frontier, but the old, *old* world below us. As we skim and skiff and ski-bob over the humdrum airpockets and queasily fly across the golden filigree of the lonely Arabian coast and over the ship-strewn Red Sea, I try to recall the long flight so far. The flight of the Mad Cow. What sticks in my throat is this uncanny sense of flying directly into the past. Especially that slow descent into the mud-city of Cairo at night. Decaying old Cairo, flat and prickly Cairo, with its spear-shafts of blue-green light I knew to be mosques. Needle-sharp and ever-potent, those cold prickly-lights were the only things to pierce the flat immensity of the rotten old delta.

And here we are and here we are and here we are, the old whore and bride of death itself now safely behind us, except perhaps in our dreams. Cairo the Unbidden, Cairo the dank delta repository of Mother Africa. Cairo the charnel house of desire, wrapped in her fetid dreams and putrid smoke. But where were the forbidden sun-seeking pyramids in that flat endless expanse of walled warehouses? There were only fields of winter mud, and no light.

Now I remember how the western sun broke through the right side of the airplane at dusk, suddenly transfixing us all with gold light. We the passengers, we the elect, given our new faces of pure gold. And me, at 45,000 feet, thinking, At last! Feeling blissful that this stained-glass row of windows was almost perfect, this cathedral ship had painted our faces with the near-fatal colours of the spectral sky, gamma rays and ultraviolet.

But here I am again, suddenly back in my narrow little crypt-seat. In the dark of this old midnight that will not move an inch. So I am watching a movie with Bruce Willis, glued to my monitor, although Sana'a is less than an hour away now, although there is much work to do. I am watching the film without earphones. Now Willis gives out a scream of frustration I can hear even with the sound turned off and my headset stuffed safely in the pocket in front of me.

Originally I thought the smart brunette across the aisle (she with the dancing eyes and chic suede boots, a real French *madeleine*) was getting off at Cairo with her ensemble of Gucci and Prada bags. But she didn't. She is still here. She is going to Yemen too, it seems. Now I imagine her the spoiled daughter of the minister of the interior, heading home for the holidays from London. Or from Paris, more likely, with quart bottles of Opium for her friends, clinking away in that matched set of bags . . . flying alone into an unruly land.

The crowd at the departure gate back in Frankfurt had proved unruly as well, ignoring the blonde attendant's instructions, regarding her with studied disdain, as if she had already debauched herself by appearing in public without a head scarf or black drapery. "*Pleeze.* Only za first three rows!" The passengers milled and mixed and commingled in happy regard for each others' joyous proximity, a lusty mob of Turks, Adjerbanjis, Egyptians, Yemenis, all eager to get home, and more tribes arriving by the minute, all seemingly out of *mittle-Europa* nowhere. It proved too much for the militantly modern Fräulein, this influx of non-queuing clans from the suburbs. She yelled, tried to shut the gate, make them line up. I turned to examine a young guy with a brushcut and black turtleneck sweater, a French version of Bazooka Joe. He was reading a paperback novel, *Savoir Dire Non*, his head sinking deeper into his turtleneck with each turn of the page. A Marlboro smouldered away in one careless hand.

"You guys ever get tired of being European?" I asked him.

He looked up at me, shrugged, and turned the page.

Meanwhile the blonde attendant retaliated against the nomadic throng by rejecting various items of their luggage as too big for carry-on: aluminum coffeepots, boom-boxes, red plastic rocking horses. The chic girl with the suede boots barely looked up; I remembered that about her, with approval. She merely pushed her bangs off her forehead and continued to flip through *Vogue*. A page every ten seconds.

Yes, I thought for sure she would be getting off in Cairo, but here she was, still on the same flight, idly flipping through fashion magazines as the lights of tiny ports on the distant shore of the Red Sea twinkled dully. I watched her as a scimitar moon rose in the east, the elliptical suggestion of another world for a whole civilization to contemplate in profound and apparently intentional silence. For who knew about these people? This civilization? This clear night on that lonely shore with so few lights, so much vastness?

Chapter 2

A World by Men, for Men

January 2001 has not been a good month for Canadian Mountain Minerals (Yemen) Inc. The shares of Cantex Mines, its publicly owned parent company, have dropped to a low of twelve cents, wiping tens of millions off the value of a widely held stock that had reached its new highs only last fall, when all the excitement about the new gold deposits in the Yemen concession had been at its peak. The true believers, those who had carried the stock faithfully for five long years, couldn't understand what was happening. The subsidiary company had done its job in the desert, a fantastic job. Canadian Mountain prospecting teams had found gold in Al-Hariquah, nickel in Suwar, loads of other stuff too, what they call heavy anomaly. Enough heavy anomaly riven throughout its exclusive forty-thousand-square-kilometre Yemen concession for not one, but two damn mines! At least! Fipke had done it again, the reports said so! And the geophysicals and the core samples and the independent assays all concurred too. The drill sites were posted on the company's Web site; anyone could look it up, see for themselves what was happening. The topographical maps and the three-colour stratigraphics and the cross-hatched overlays told the story.

Here was the CMM concession, a big square chunk of territory that began some dozen miles northwest of Sana'a. But suddenly Falconbridge, the Canadian-founded international mining conglomerate, the big player that had eagerly optioned the Suwar site and painstakingly performed its own drilling program – to the gleeful hush of Cantex investor anticipation – had announced they were not exercising their option. They were letting it expire.

They were pulling out of the deal!

"The country is too unsettled for sustaining business interests like ours," was the company's stated position.

Was it the spate of kidnappings, the troubled aftermath of the pernicious civil war between the north and south? The civil war between North Yemen and the communist People's Democratic Republic in the south had formally ended in 1991 with a union the north soon came to dominate. Secessionists in the south, centred around the port of Aden, proclaimed a new Democratic Republic of Yemen, which was quickly crushed in 1994. For the last five years a general peace had been restored for the first time in decades. The central government headquartered in Sana'a was strong, and it had the support of the bulk of the population.

Or perhaps Falconbridge was spooked by the Aden ship bombing? The USS *Cole* had been bombed at harbour, with the loss of American personnel. Or was it the constant spontaneous dementia, like last week's hijacking? To the surprise of the blundering kidnapper now rotting in a local prison, the American ambassador to Yemen was on board with a full security entourage when the hijacker pulled out his one-shot pen gun and threatened to blow everyone to bits with a nonexistent bomb.

The *Yemen Times* had reported that Jaber Ali Satir was able to smuggle his pen gun on board because airport security, while realizing that he had set off their metal detectors, considered it just a local flight, so they did not bother to find out what was triggering the alarm. Five minutes after takeoff, Satir climbed into first class, kicked the male flight attendant "in the thigh" to demonstrate his newfound authority, pulled out the pen gun, fired it off, and bungled his opening line: "I am dead – but I will bomb this head!"

This rhyme didn't make any sense in the original Arabic either, so the crew must have realized Satir was a crock from the start. The Air Yemeni pilot told him that, while he sympathized with his position, he was running low on fuel. The crew, as the *Yemen Times* reported, knew immediately his bomb claim was suspect, because the bag he was waving about was too droopy to contain anything heavy; sure enough, it proved to contain only a pair of socks and a towel. And a doll. This was Satir's big ticket out of the country: a droopy bag of socks and a doll. He ordered them to fly away as far as possible. The pilot concurred.

They would fly as far as they could on the available gas.

They landed inside the country. As the crew leaped to overpower Satir, using a fire extinguisher to hose down and then batter him into submission, the ambassador escaped with the passengers in business class by hurtling down through the forward exit. The ambassador's security staff hustled them away. Economy was left clueless in the rear; they knew only that someone was getting beaten to a pulp up front. The *Times* also reported that pen guns were a speciality of the local gunsmithing town of Jeyhanda, fetching forty dollars American in its scandalously open gun market. Satir had spent the last of his foreign earnings from Saudi on his little weapon; he was broke and getting desperate for action . . . for something.

The acts of such solitary maniacs were a staple of the local press. Maybe it was this highly publicized stream of desperate men that had scared Falconbridge off? It couldn't be a question of the mining *results*, these were obviously too good.

I had read all about Satir's deranged exploits in the free guest's copy of the newspaper in the hotel in downtown Sana'a the morning of my arrival. I had seen nothing of the city the night before, as the taxi from the airport careened through empty, darkened streets and past police checkpoints. From my seventh-storey window in the morning I had the impression of a bustling city of white low-rise buildings stretching off into a series of brown, dead-looking hills. On the main thoroughfare below I could see at a glance shiny black Mercedeses, and men pushing bicycle carts loaded with hay. The usual mix of sixteenth- and twenty-first-century lifestyles, meeting in a clamorous city of a million people.

My plan was to travel with the local Cantex people into the rough back-country. See for myself how these virgin mine sites stacked up, and compare them to the old ruins that, I knew from my readings, lay close by – as the crow flies. Or, as the caravan treks. I would be happy to congratulate Fipke on finding Sheba's mines if that's all he'd got for his years of effort.

At eight-thirty sharp, Iqbal Jailani, a mining consultant and operations manager for CMM, met me at the hotel lobby. A pleasant and serious man in his early forties, he anxiously apologized for not meeting me at the airport the night before. He was of Indian extraction, yet he ordered breakfast in rapid-fire Arabic and appeared completely at home as he led me out into the street and escorted me through the old Sana'a market, a walled jumble of stalls and shops that began only a few hundred yards from the hotel.

The bright daylight hit me like a new blade. I tottered around behind Iqbal, fending off the overbright desert glare of the old city as best I could, absorbing only the vague impressions of a fantastic creamy maze. The plastered white buildings were smooth, overdone. Vanilla icing. They seemed to be inhabited exclusively by cheerful little men with pearly teeth and black eyes, and I contented myself with snapping a few desultory pictures and wondering privately where all the famously veiled women were hiding.

I felt myself getting dizzy quickly, and almost pitched head first into a fruit stall after tripping on a chunk of thousand-year-old cobble. Iqbal watched me recover myself with apprehension.

"Be careful now," he said. "Please watch where you step. This market-place is *very* old." As if its age had proved my undoing. I was unaware that the capital was twenty-two hundred metres above sea level, and this jaunt of ours was comparable to taking a hike around the high slopes of the Rockies. Thin air, and motorcycles ripping up over the sidewalks every-where. We stopped for a mid-morning snack in a little café. Over superb coffee and toast with real-tasting apricot jam, Iqbal politely asked me if I would be able to proofread the paper he was to give to the mining commu-nity in Dubai that coming weekend. When I told him I would be most happy to oblige, he seemed to relax for the first time that morning. The sharp, achy smell of burning charcoal made me ask him what the workers were doing in the adjacent stall.

"Making handles for the big knives."

He meant the jambiyas, the curved daggers everyone except ourselves proudly sported, stuck in their belts. I asked about the economy of this trade. How many ceremonial daggers did a man need? Were they like silk ties or shoes, matched to the occasion? Did you trade up as you made the grade towards village elder? Why were some men walking around with empty dagger sheaths?

"They may have pawned their knives," Iqbal replied evenly. "I'm not sure." He got up and plunged into the crowd once more.

I followed. Beyond the section where the knifesmith laboured were the blacksmiths, who forged iron hammers and picks and great hooky claw-things with nothing ceremonial about them whatsoever. Hand-hewn wooden handles lay heaped in piles, sturdy farmers' tools ready for cus-tomers. It appeared that a great deal of farming in Yemen consisted of simply grappling stones up from the ground. After the tool-quarter came the roasted peas, spices. Orange carts and mango-juice stands. The flash of colour and kaleidoscopic market life went on and on, street after crumbly fantastic street. After more than an hour's worth of tour commentary, I was growing tired, despite my initial excitement. Iqbal's beaming face was disappearing fast into the final colour of beige, a sustained blur at the centre of my vision.

This souk was no market set up for the tourist trade – we'd passed only three Europeans in the last two hours – this was the sixteenth century, *la comédie humaine*, in full dress and all its theatrical chaotic voluptuousness, something last experienced by the generation of Shakespeare and Marlowe. High drama and low comedy, sacred and profane, mixed together higgledy-piggledy.

In this street theatre, you could see how easily one's daily public life could take on a brilliant, improvisational quality. I watched as a young guy sputtered up in an ancient motorcycle, an English bike that might have belonged to T. E. Lawrence, looped a lazy figure-eight through the adoring crowds, dismounted nonchalantly, ordered himself a meal with a hand gesture, chewed abstractedly at his plate of fresh lamb's liver, stared keenly at nothing, frowned at something only he saw, flicked his red-checkered headdress back into the morning-glow, and tossed the empty plate back at the waiter. He was as self-possessed and enigmatic as a hooded falcon or a narrow ledge of granite. Then he was off again.

Brum brum brooom.

Here was the Arab of midcentury fiction, the enigma of French novels. The man who cares for nothing, who has a thousand moves and no position. Has this character something to do with the shifting alley-light of the souk? How might such a character exist in countries ruled by insurance and traffic lights? The narrow passageways were redolent with oddly familiar scents and echoed with the sally of voices, background music for a thousand colourful vignettes, all immensely satisfying to behold. Here was an old man, magnificently striding by like a mountain prince, with the face of a golden eagle, holding his perfect granddaughter's white hand. Now he was lifting her, high out of reach of a shower of flying sparks from the blacksmith's. Suddenly jealous of the camera's power of appropriation, I put it down, and kept the image to myself.

"Now we will drive to the Cantex villa," Iqbal announced. Our morning tour was over. We got in a banged-up Toyota Land Cruiser. None of the seatbelts worked. I held on to the roof handle.

Iqbal sped down a series of one-way streets to a residential area dominated by walled embassies flying obscure flags. Sana'a was bigger than I
anticipated. I thought of the hijacker again, of his performance in first class.
How he must have envisioned that supreme moment, when he finally got to
fire off his climactic shot from the spy weapon, a prop purchased with
careful forethought from a street market just like this one. Perhaps this was
the company's real problem: How were they going to do business in a
country that didn't need alcohol, that didn't need the bliss of the momentary lapse, the customary blowouts we needed to expunge the programmed
claims of an overweening reality – because it was already drunk on the
giddy accelerations of such momentous occasions?

We arrived at a concrete-block wall and a steel gate: the Cantex villa. A
guard poked his head through a slot and pulled a lever. We drove through,
and he shut the gate quickly behind us. Then he smiled a shy hello at me.
Piles of rock samples sat in shipping boxes in the walled courtyard. I asked
Iqbal questions about the numbered rocks, but he preferred to talk about
the house. The building was leased; a local millionaire owned it. Iqbal took
me inside for another tour. The four-storey house was made of dressed
limestone over concrete blocks. It was cool, with cavernous hallways that
ended in locked doors, and *takhrim*, simple stained-glass widows, gleaming
everywhere. I peered at a geological map pinned to the wall. The house was
an odd cross between a church and an office. Stone floors, and little furniture. There was no one else around. Iqbal said he had work to do, but he
would be back to the villa soon to pick me up for lunch.

"I hope you like Yemeni food?"

I nodded, watching the uniformed guard close the big steel gate behind
him as he drove off. The guard smiled at me from the shade of his little
guardhouse. I smiled back. The midday sun was bright out in the courtyard.
I stood uncertainly on the flagstone paving for a moment, gawking at the
loose heaps of discoloured rocks. These were all carefully numbered. A-234.
K-118. I picked one up, hefted it. The guard watched me. I put it down. The
sun was getting stronger. I went inside the villa. Feeling drowsy, I made
myself a coffee, using mineral water from a fresh case of bottles, and thought
long and hard about heading off into the desert with Chuck Fipke. He was

due to arrive later in the week for a fieldwork review. Iqbal had confirmed it. I thought about the line, the line between what's stupid and what's bold. Maybe I was getting stupid too. That's when you don't know the difference. And worse, no longer care, because you're not going there any more. Yes, here we are at that fine line between stupid and bold . . . once again.

I took my coffee and looked around for a radio, magazines. Nothing. I would have to amuse myself. I found an overstuffed chair in a hallway by some empty desks and put my feet up. I recalled an odd story I had heard the night before, and its unanswered questions now nudged at me in the stony silence of the empty villa.

When I had arrived in Sana'a, I'd met an American in his early forties named David, who was standing by himself in the grotty little airport hallway. Sports jacket, good shoes, private-school haircut. We'd shared the battered taxi into the city centre. A tanned tennis player clutching a tita-nium laptop to his chest, he said he worked for the World Bank on various water-irrigation projects. Over tea in the hotel, ordered at two in the morning from the sleepy staff, Dave was happy to unload his big secret on me, the attentive stranger booked into the next room.

After years of plugging away on aid projects in India and Sri Lanka, he was finally getting ready to quit the bank. More: David was happy now, because finally, after being a widower for two years and at the ripe age of forty-five, he had fallen in love. Mind you, he was feeling guilty too, because of one thing. His new girlfriend was the wife of his good friend. And now that couple was getting a divorce.

Oh-oh.

"Don't they stone you for doing stuff like that out here?"

I was joking. But still.

"But they were never compatible in the first place," he insisted, looking to me for understanding. "Soon as she left him, five years of migraines dis-appeared overnight!"

He now looked to me for sympathy. My tea was weak. We were alone in the deserted hotel lobby, at almost 3 a.m., decompressing after the long flight.

"That's something," I nodded and went on in a neutral tone. "I guess all the good women are already taken. You've really got no choice but to take someone else's."

"They weren't compatible," he repeated. "A nice guy, made lots of money, but the sex wasn't there. One thing led to another, she got him to go to a therapist, a counsellor, and after a while they broke up. I was just there," he grinned. "And with us, the sex was amazing."

He shook his head at the wonder of it. Good sex at his age with someone he knew all along. No bar-hopping for him. The luck of it.

"Did she tell the therapist she was seeing you?"

"No," he stroked his gingery beard. "The counsellor just made it clear how incompatible they were. . . . Of course, since those amazing first months, we've slowed down a bit. To tell you the truth, I'm kind of glad to be out here, heading up another project."

Another flash of guilt went by in his eyes, this time going in the opposite direction.

"So what are you going to do when you quit this business?" I asked him, meaning his water-irrigation projects.

"You've heard of Steve Levine, the relationships guy? He's like, into the tantra of relationships; *that's* what I'm going to get into. Like the troubadours, you know. They really got into this whole love thing too, except that I can't find any good books on them."

"The French troubadours from the twelfth century, you mean? Courtly Love and all that?"

"Yeah, I looked them up on the Internet. All there was, was one book. But I had it already."

He signalled for the waiter, and we said goodnight.

Men away from women like to talk about women, I reflected now. And you couldn't get farther away from women than in a place like Sana'a, where all the service jobs I had seen so far were performed by men. There was no discernible nightlife, either. On our long midnight trip in from the airport, Dave and I had seen nothing stirring. Only the checkpoints, with young soldiers in burnooses checking out our cabby's ID with flashlights. Where were the million people hiding in the gloomy, blacked-out city? Nightlife was a phenomenon endemic to Western society, to Modernism; it specifically designated those hours when men and women were free to walk informally through the streets and chat each other up spontaneously, a temporary social loosening fuelled by alcohol, and essentially it was a response to the high-stress demands of industrial labour. They do not appear to have a nightlife here, that was clear. We're machine-centred, and they're not.

The irony was – and it had been immediately apparent to me that first morning, sitting in the café with Iqbal, watching the street life in the souk unfold – that I came to do a book on a mysterious queen who may or may not have existed, to a country that was among the most male-centric in the world. A land where women were so invisible as to be nonexistent. This country, where I had seen maybe three local women so far, as against five thousand men, had supposedly given birth to a powerful queen of Sheba, the equal of King Solomon? Scholars were divided on the historical under-pinnings of the Biblical account, some even maintained that Solomon himself was a complete fiction, a product of the wishful thinking of outcast Hebrews, and that the queen of Sheba was even more hopelessly so. But then what was the point of her story, which was amplified in the Quran more than a millennium later?

Had the country's culture changed that much over the last three thou-sand years? Where were these powerful, regal women? As if to answer my question, two women in black chadors had come up the street as we finished our tea, looked in the window of a tiny dress shop, and disappeared inside. I had the impression of a black-curtained reality, a glimpse of tat-tooed fingers placed on the doorframe. The dresses on the blank-faced window dummies were frilly blue frocks. Fussy feminine.

The sharshaf, the black robes and veils of the Yemeni women, are not really clothes at all but street armament, portable tents marking their immediate space as private territory, and the Yemeni men appeared all the more relaxed for this, enjoying what remained of public space for them-selves. As far as I could tell, the competitive tension that the presence of sexually available women usually arouses in men was nowhere to be seen. All these men, eating and laughing in the fast-food joints around us! The constant need to compete (Was it the same for women, I wondered, this compulsive sexual tension?) dissolved in the fraternity of good fellowship. How would the boisterous lads get along if women in tight tank tops were suddenly plunked in their midst? I wondered.

The local women must be tenacious and wholly self-assured in their own sphere, I told myself. For they, too, possessed their private space, exclusive to themselves. Outside the family, their common sphere appeared nil. The women had their separate gates to the household compounds, separate afternoon qat-chewing parties, called *tafrita*, where liberal use of the amphetamine-style herb loosened the barriers to social fellowship, all resulting in a strong sense of female identity and community. I had spotted several eight-year-old girls, deftly rolling plastic water barrels down alleyways, or skipping by careening trucks in the old city. Hard to imagine that they grew up to be housebound prisoners of a stifling male empire. They, too, must belong wholly to their world. Wherever it was. Somewhere far from the prying eyes of the *farangi*, the foreigner, with the camera.

A car honked twice outside the steel gate, and the guard ran to let Iqbal into the compound. Did I want to try a local restaurant? Sherbani's was a ten-minute drive, and when we parked Iqbal had soft words and a few coins for the little boys wiping down windshields outside the restaurant. The customers were all male, of course. Long tables with freshly printed cellocovers, waiters screaming orders to the cooks, a high desk up front where the jolly mustachioed owner perched and surveyed the action and spritzed his departing customers with lemon water.

"You like lamb? You like fish?"

"I like everything," I admitted, surveying the enormous heaps of coiled Yemeni bread that came steaming out of the kitchen. They were baking bread for lunch! Within seconds a waiter plunked down dishes of chopped fresh vegetables and a clear broth soup for starters, and stood at attention waiting patiently for our orders. He was sweating freely from the exertion. The din in the room increased dramatically as more customers piled in, and the other waiters began baying to each other like hounds lost in the woods. We could hardly hear each other.

"I'm sorry, no beer," Iqbal explained. "Pepsi okay?"

"Fine," I grinned. My childhood preference for soda pop with my meals had finally met with social approval. "Excellent! Make that two bottles please."

The meal arrived in a few minutes: roast leg of lamb, a liquid halvah, a creamy hummus enlivened with heaps of fresh green coriander, a fat grilled sea bass the size of a chicken. "You need a fork?" "It's okay. I'm fine without." Mad rushing all around, general hilarity. Tear off the blackened *khubz* bread and dip it in, fabulous, my ears are buzzing, I'm getting high off the food, dribble the fresh limes into the lamb soup, soak up the salt-dried lamb with the vegetables, scrub a piece of sea bass with the lime rind and wash it down with the cold, sweet Pepsi, cut with a whole lemon, and then start all over again. Iqbal is talking about Canada and America and how he applied for immigration and that he's doing it for his children; they want to go to good universities and his sister is a doctor there already.

"Ah, good luck, but you will never ever eat like this again," I warn him. The food is a revelation. It is fresh and real and brilliant and my body is coming alive as if it's been pickled until now in chemical preservatives, gone stiff with unmet hungers. This is what they ate in the Bible, I tell myself. This is what they meant by a feast.

Iqbal's face has fallen. He knows this to be true. He has been to Canada to visit his sister in Montreal. Five times. In winter.

Young men in beards now bring us juicy red shards of watermelon, bunches of tiny sweet bananas, a dish of liquid brown syrup.

"Honey," he says, cheering up at the sight. "Wild, from the mountains. You dip the bananas in, like this."

We double-dip and triple-dip and I still can't get enough. The sweetened fruit is like a drug in my mouth. "It's fabulous," I manage to say.

"No sugar added," he explains.

It's the most off-handed comment he makes, and it says everything. About our society, at least. Now the long tables beside us are littered with heaps of bones, fruit rinds, bread crusts. A big mess. The waiters run and pull the table covers up, bagging the whole heap, dishes, pop cans, and all, and joyously begin to sweep the floor. They're happy to be working in a place so lush with the royal life of the senses. I pick at the bones of my sea bass, trying to drag out the experience, already hoarding my pleasures like a good northerner.

Iqbal tells me that he studied mining engineering in Cairo and Hanover, Germany.

"So what is your favourite place," I accept a proffered toothpick, "in the whole wide world?"

"This is," he says. He introduces me to the owner, who comes over holding his young daughter up in his arms like a trophy. This is a world by men, for men, I tell myself. Mr. Sherbani invites me to take pictures in his kitchen, where spouts of gas flame and ancient iron ovens roar over the hoarse cries of grinning T-shirted men. Sweat runs down their temples. They laugh at my camera. The lunch hour is almost over, and they are exultant.

Chapter 3

Meet the Blackhawks

The next morning Chuck Fipke arrives at the Sana'a villa in the cold dark before dawn, outfitted in a three-quarter-length black leather trench coat, buttoned tightly up to the high collar, and closely attended by an entourage of six or seven men of diverse hues and sizes, all bearing sidearms and daggers. The clamour of their boots on the marble floor wakes me. I lope out of my bedroom to join them; Chuck and I are the only ones without weapons. He looks like a U-boat commander with a multinational crew, or perhaps the captain of the Blackhawks, the Cold War bomber squadron coming alive from the pages of the 1940s comic book.

"Don't come too near me," is the first thing he says to me. "I've got a really bad cold."

Despite the chill of the desert dawn, Chuck is sweating like a pig. He coughs, a low, guttural, dangerous sound, the Bengal tiger grunting in pain, and although I've seen lots of pictures of him they don't convey anything of the man. Larger than life. It's as if a loaded camera follows him around the room, locked on a dolly. He turns, and in profile Chuck now looks like my Uncle Oleh, playing the part of General Rommel in a local production.

"Those Chinese, hey?" he wheezes. "They've got these flus going around, too many people over there. We're defenceless."

"You need a lime toddy," someone says. Ahmed Mossen, Chuck's driver, a large black man and a ringer for boxer Joe Lewis, is dispatched to round up some fresh limes for Chuck's hot toddy. The other half-dozen men press up close, jostling to be first at the Boss's elbows as he proceeds up the marble stairs two at a time to the central inner office. Without further discussion he begins to examine a large coloured map on a glass table placed under the watchful eyes of President Ali Abdullah Salih. Even the portrait of the President seems to follow closely as Chuck's thick forefinger traces wavy mineralization patterns down across the heavily marked-up map, stopping at something he refers to as a *hot spot*.

I yawn, watching the proceedings from the edge of the room, drinking bad instant coffee. It's about five-thirty in the morning. They seem to be planning the upcoming field expedition for maximum manpower impact. I look out the window. Another cloudless day is breaking over downtown Sana'a. The sun is just starting to top the mountain rim encircling the old city. Already it's heating up in the villa, but Chuck keeps his leather trench coat buttoned – as he will for most of the day.

Among his attending staff this morning are the effusive Iqbal Jailani, the office manager and my guide of yesterday, of Indian descent but a Yemen national, since he was born in Aden; the serene and confident Abdul Shybani, head geologist, whose picture I had already studied, since he was the one holding up one end of the missing ancient plaque in the photograph; the large and quiet driver, Ahmed Mossen, born in Ethiopia but now also a Yemen national; Abdul Razzaq, another Ethiopian-born driver, who allegedly had married two or three times although barely thirty; and Ahmed Mossoud, a swashbuckler who might have stepped off the set of *Lawrence of Arabia*, and who carries a 9mm pistol tucked discreetly in his belt.

Then there is Chad Ulansky, a twenty-six-year-old Canadian geologist from Kelowna, B.C., in a surfer shirt and nylon tearoffs, who has popped up out of nowhere. His name is perfect, it fits him like the body shirt. If they had their comic-book nicknames, Chuck would be *Ruger*; Iqbal, *Dr. Atchoo*; Mossen, *The Moose*. And Chad, *Chad*. The Blackhawks, as I said. Ready for action, right out of their D.C. war comic from fifty years ago.

"And this here is *another* hot spot, hey?" Chuck is running his finger down a further transparency, this one coded with a dozen colours in bright felt marker. I gather from their eager nods that a hot spot is a mineral site with exciting test results.

"Yeah, we looked at that," Chad says happily.

"How come we didn't see any samples at the lab?" Chuck turns to Iqbal.

"They're here, waiting to be shipped out," Iqbal says unhappily.

Chuck looks at him. Everyone waits.

"They're still here?"

"Yes, I – "

"Why are they still here, Iqbal? What did I say? I said all the samples have to go out as soon as they are documented. Everything but the gold. Isn't *that* what I said?" He looks around the room for confirmation, stopping at me. I find myself nodding in agreement, even though I don't really know what they're talking about.

"Well, they were before my time. I was saving them to put in the next shipment, to save money on the transportation costs. There's a block charge, and Fred said – "

"That's an excuse. I've got a whole book of excuses." Chuck held up an invisible book to the group, letting them all see it: Chuck's Invisible Book of Excuses.

"That's not what I *said*, was it? I said *as soon as* they're documented. Out they go! You fucked up, Iqbal, didn't you?" Chuck is nodding at his own question, and everybody begins to do the same. "Now they are still sitting here. It's a fuck-up. What good are they doing, sitting in box crates in the yard? You tell me."

"Well, I'm sorry, it was the other one . . ." Iqbal mumbles away, publicly chastened.

"You always have someone else to blame. You're just like me. Except nobody can blame *me*, because it ends here."

"I'm sorry. I take responsibility."

"Next time," Chuck puts a finger in his ear, "listen, okay? *All the samples except the gold.*"

He shoots a glance at me, to see if I caught the moment. I did. Everyone takes a deep breath. The air has been cleared. The Boss has arrived.

Now they get down to work.

It's clear that Chuck is unhappy with the Falconbridge pullout. I find a copy of Falconbridge's fifteen-page memo, dated December 15, 2000, lying on an empty desk out in the open like a bad penny nobody wants, and I sit down to peruse it while the other men scurry around the office to find more charts, hustling to align them properly on the big glass operations table.

TO: Joseph Dutton / Chuck Fipke
FROM: Nick Fenner / *Falconbridge Exploration*
Fieldwork was suspended October 22nd due to safety concerns and the inability of the UTEM crews to carry out surveying due to ongoing deliberate loop breaks by the local populations in the work area.
Potential to host a World Class Nickel Deposit remains.

Conclusion: Potential still remains to recover an economic
      sized sulphide deposit of Falconbridge Target
      Size. It is important to complete geophysical
      surveys . . . this will only be possible if a suitable
      working environment can be established.

"So I guess Yemen is a bit of a hard sell," I suggested to Chuck at my first opportunity, waving the memo like a red flag.

"It wasn't Yemen that was the problem," Chuck replied evenly. "It was Falconbridge."

"Falconbridge? I thought they had good results," I objected. Although they were smaller than Inco, they had cash available and were looking for action. And Fipke's company needed a strong partner to develop a mine, always a capital-intensive job. "Aren't they loaded?"

"They've got the *money*, but they're getting fat, and slow."

"So they're not worried about the local politics here?"

"Most of their management is South African. Now, that's kind of a tough place for business. Way worse than here, hey?" He watched for my reaction through his 1980s aviator-style glasses before he went on.

"It's the wives, hey?"

"The wives?"

"Sure. Their main guy's got small kids, an' his wife doesn't want him out in the desert for months at a time."

"I see." I thought of my own wife at this second, a flash of guilt as I enjoyed the 25°C morning and the prospect of another big lunch ahead. "So it's a *cultural* thing?"

"It's like this, see? Personally, there are diamonds in Angola, and gold. It's great, but I wouldn't send my guys there, too dangerous. *I* would go there myself, but I wouldn't send my guys there, right?"

I understood. It was all relative, this mining-in-the-big-scary-world business. The danger was always there, and Chuck Fipke understood that better than anyone too. But being a guy who wasn't afraid of bandoliered rebels didn't exactly make him the best stock salesman around town. Not for a play like Yemen, either. Chuck Fipke telling you that a place wasn't really dangerous was like a pro boxer telling you that the tenth-round punches didn't really hurt.

It didn't mean *you* wouldn't get hurt.

I put the memo down and drift over to the big glass table for a closer look at this mineral exploration business. I can see the transparent cell-overlays are done to a scale of 1:50,000, and they are each about three feet by four feet. This morning we appear to be looking at a region of Al-Alayyah. The name is affixed to a corner of a transparency, but whether it refers to the political region or is the geologists' chosen code name, I cannot decide. Anyway, Fipke is famous for deliberately giving confusing names to his exploration sites, to throw off the competition. Needless to say there are no towns in this Al-whatever — only wiggly concentric rock formations with an array of neon colours marking the intensity of the minerals to be found there.

"The blue spots are weakly anomalous," Chuck says for my benefit, "and the red ones are really hot, hey." There appears to be plenty of red, so clearly the trouble isn't with the rocks.

"What's hot *mean*, exactly?" I ask him.

"Seven ppm or more," Chuck replies, "and we're getting more than that everywhere out here."

Seven ppm. I work it out. Seven parts per million.

It doesn't sound like much.

"But this stuff *is* gold, isn't it?"

"Now we're looking for PGE, platinum group of elements. Palladium and platinum, they're *in* now. We go for what's in, hey? Gold goes up, it'll be in again, now it's down. We've got lots of platinum and palladium. . . . We've got some good copper, nickel up *here*, little spots. There's something really hot *here*; the red, copper, nickel, cobalt, it'll be in the follow-up, hey?"

We all nod, mesmerized by the maps that promise so much red *hotness*. Chuck goes on.

"We don't mind finding either massive sulphides, copper nickel cobalt, do we?"

"Uh-uh." The group nods as one.

At the opposite end of the fashion spectrum from Chuck's Uberkommander outfit, Chad has now returned in his daytime gear after a quick shower. He sports aqua Teva hiking sandals, ultramarine Second Skin shorts, and wraparound Oakleys with orange lenses. Junior extreme geologist, I figure. Chuck gets on the line to the B.C. lab, a company in Kelowna that does all the analysis of the Yemen rock samples for Cantex, using several patented techniques he invented. Chuck says he is looking for listings that are missing from the office.

"What exactly are listings?" I whisper to Chad.

"Spread sheets of findings with exact latitude and longitude," he replies without hesitation.

"Maybe we'll go out today. I'm feeling a little better," Chuck announces when he gets off the phone.

"*Yesss!*" Chad jubilantly smacks his fist into his palm. Then he turns to me. "For Chuck, getting back to work always makes him feel way better."

"Have we got any pink markers? Pink is my favourite colour!" Chuck's feeling jovial now. "And get me oranges, fresh ones, we need oranges for my throat. Can you make sure someone goes out and gets them?"

The group stirs and gets to work. The phone starts ringing. Faxes pour out of machines set up in different parts of the big house.

"You want oranges?" Abdul asks him, to make sure he wasn't kidding.

"Yes, and a girl too!"

"What?" This brings Abdul up short.

"A girl. I'm feeling a little better now."

"A girl?"

"Make it *two* girls, I'm feeling a *lot* better. And I don't like pink, I was just kidding. Get me a yellow marker, I hate pink. Even if pink shirts were in, I wouldn't wear them. It's a colour for poofters."

"So what's on the agenda today?" I ask Chuck pointblank.

"In Suwar, we would find strong copper, nickel, cobalt, and nickel in the valuable ore, and we're capitalists not communists, so we go where the money is."

He waves his palm over the maps.

"I see. Suwar, the Falconbridge site. With the nickel and other stuff."

"Before we weren't doing platinum and palladium. But now we are, hey."

It is clear to me this morning that Chuck has changed his focus. Gold is out. Instead the new talk is about *gossans*. I turn to ask Chad about this unfamiliar word, but he's gone.

At lunch in the dining room downstairs I got another chance to talk to Chuck at length about the recent Falconbridge fiasco. Everyone back at home wanted to know what had gone wrong, and now it appears the company is leaving the gold where it is for now, on the glass table inside those concentric rings marked with red spots, and focusing on something more exciting than mere gold. With platinum and palladium both trading at record levels around eight hundred dollars American an ounce or more, and workable deposits rare in the world, this seemed like a practical strategy.

Over fried chicken and tomato salad, Chuck expanded on his theory about the difference in cultures between South Africans and Yemenis, and how the executive wives didn't want their men to be out here, working alone in the desert, etc. The actual incident that triggered the pullout, according to Chuck, was this: A Cat driver at the Suwar site was accosted by a local neighbour, who fired a gun in the air, in the direction of the Falconbridge rented villa. The Falconbridge consultant then climbed up on the roof, found what he thought was a piece missing from the stone lintel, and claimed the shooter actually hit the building. As he intended.

"Fred overreacted. These local guys? They fire shots in the air like we yell out of cars, hey? Plus, he really screwed up. We go have a meeting with the minister of mines, and Fred asks about legal title to the lands, hey? And they explain to him how it's a three-way council with the village people included, like arbitration, with a tax at fair market value, and he goes, 'Oh, but I talked to a lawyer here and I got a legal opinion, and it's a lot more complicated according to my commissioned report.' Like that's a big deal, right? And they all just look at him. He doesn't get it that the lawyer just wants a couple months' work out of him, hey?"

Still, Chuck acknowledges that Cantex has made mistakes. Big ones. They've spent $10 million Canadian so far on their concession, some of it not so wisely. He draws me a picture on a napkin, and then stabs it repeatedly with a felt pen.

"We've just got to resample this area again, right here. See? Once, we got these hot results right here, really hot, so we kept going back and spent $300,000 on the area, didn't resample, and the only thing that tested hot was the original sample, nothing else, we kept changing back to the original sample. Only it turns out the typist made a mistake in the readout, transcribing it wrong, hey, and there was nothing there."

This was ordinary human error, hard to avoid in its entirety. But there were also mistakes of policy, mistakes that showed the inexperience of the company in dealing with tribal politics.

"We laid the loop, hey, for geophysical, in Suwar, and someone came and broke it. So we hired one of the guys as security. We had more breaks and hired more guys as security and, of course, if a guy wanted a job he knew how to break the wire, hey? At one point we had seven hundred and fifty security guys for a four-mile loop of wire. Not all at once, mind you, over time, but we'll never make that mistake again, bribing guys not to break the equipment."

But there was a bigger issue than management policy.

Strategy. I questioned the whole enterprise, to see if he could dodge the big ones.

"What about the whole idea of gold in Yemen in the first place, Chuck?" I asked coyly. "The price has been going down and down, the banks are selling bullion, and you've spent years perfecting your craft at finding diamonds. Wouldn't your investors be just as happy if you went off and discovered another *diamond* mine?"

"Well, you know," he put his stockinged feet up on the desk (his leather coat was still on, and buttoned tight), "at this point we've got to ask ourselves, 'Hey, what are we here for?' I mean, we've got a lot of investors, and frankly I don't want to disappoint them. If it weren't for them, maybe we'd be doing something else. See, the point is, I'm in it for the learning curve; you can't keep doing the same old thing. Sure, I'd like to find a diamond mine. I'm not rich, hey?"

Chuck has made this complaint before, and I've always taken it with a grain of salt. For a guy who paid his ex-wife a whopping $120 million in a highly publicized divorce settlement only last year, he's got to have *something* left.

"Let me tell you: I owe $98 million, and I'm paying it off, right. Out of the diamond mine, but I still owe it. And the government, they're too much, hey? I wanted to exercise an option, for $2.4 million of shares, and you know what my accountant says? After paying taxes on the deal I get $123,000, and after the brokerage, and commissions and legals, I get less than $100,000. Out of $2.4 million!"

"Sounds like you need another accountant."

"No, he's good. It's the government, hey? They owe me $2 million cash for a write-off; they acknowledge everything was done legal and yet they *still* refuse to give me my money. Here, at least the government sticks to the deal, and the tax deal is good, flat tax rate, royalty, they let Canoxy – a Canadian oil company – keep the money they made here, in oil, but at home, the government has these tax surprises. You go into a deal on something, and next year they change the whole tax law again and you're screwed. They are not pro-development, so in some ways it's easier to do business here in Yemen than in Canada."

Still, the maps and the cataract of colour overlays and symbols give the chartroom the appearance of a last-pitch, all-you-can-eat smorgasbord at a failing restaurant, make it look like the boys are hunting for something, *anything*, that will pay their bills and allow the company to regain its investors' trust.

"Chuck, you've got copper, you've got gold, nickel, cobalt, zinc, lead, gold, platinum, palladium. You've got everything here in those numbers except silver," I point out the obvious. "There doesn't seem to be any *focus*."

"We've got silver, too, in a number of sites."

"Well, oil and gas is sexy. But who really cares about nickel and copper *in Yemen*? Why would a big Canadian company like Falconbridge even want to bother?"

"I'm not an oil-and-gas guy. But while copper is not doing much these days, nickel is big. Falconbridge has only got a seven-year supply left. After that, if they don't find something else, they're screwed."

"Seven years? What happens in seven years?"

"They could have made the worst corporate decision of their history. If they don't secure another mine, they could disappear overnight."

I nodded. Huge companies like Kinnecott Copper had disappeared because of a single political decision. Allende's Chilean socialist government nationalized its once-thriving copper mine. It could happen.

"And maybe it's all for the best, they don't really understand the situation here at all. We got BHP looking at the site, they're really interested, probably they'll pick it up. Plus I'm going to the mining conference to give a paper next Sunday, maybe I'll get some Arab money interested."

"Broken Hill Properties, the Australian company?"

"Mm." Chuck looked down at his charts, musing about the prospect of financing an operating mine with capital from such an unconventional source as the Gulf Arabs. As if reading my thoughts, he continued.

"We're capitalists, hey, not communists. We're in this to make a few bucks, hey?"

Still, Arab money for a heavy-metals mine? It doesn't seem likely. Was he grasping at straws? BHP, well okay. The Aussies might take a run at anything juicy. But conservative oil sheiks? This task needed industrial vision.

"Would they have any interest in running a metal operation? Aren't they strictly oil men?"

"The Saudis have a gold mine going in Saudi Arabia," Chuck countered.

"You think they would be interested in Al-Hariquah?" Al-Hariquah was where Cantex had found its highest concentrations of gold, a 3.5-kilometre-long gold anomaly based on an ancient volcanic dyke. Located in the southwest of Cantex's forty-thousand-square-kilometre concession, this was the hot find that had so excited the investors earlier in the autumn.

"We estimate the gold deposits there to be worth $1.5 billion, at current values."

By *current*, Chuck meant "historically depressed" prices. Gold was off around $260 an ounce, making a lot of mines and potential sites chancy if not unprofitable to develop, and who knew what the future would bring? I pushed the point.

"Do you think the Yemenis would welcome a Saudi-owned gold mine in their country?"

"Money talks," Chuck fixed me with a look.

"How much money do you need to set up a gold mine?"

"Well, the more you spend, the cheaper the final product is, once you've got your capital outlay figured. What you do is a feasibility study to show that, if you spend x dollars, your production cost is y. And if you spend 2x, what's your production cost, with different market prices factored in? We spent $932 million just to get the diamond mine open, for example."

"Wow. So if you go looking for the money to open a gold mine, you need to raise that kind of cash?"

"No. It'll be a lot cheaper. In the magnitude of $100 million or so."

It was emerging that Chuck had two responses to Falconbridge pulling out of the whole option agreement. One was his new emphasis on finding PGEs – the platinum group elements. And two was his newfound determination to hunt up an unconventional source of funding for the mine from Arab sources. If the Canadians had had a failure of nerve, so be it. He wasn't going to let that stop him from starting a gold mine in the desert that would rival anything back in Red Lake or Hemlo, Ontario.

Thirdly – and was there always a thirdly with Fipke? – he was not going to let Falconbridge walk away from their deal and potentially commit hari-kari without a fight. My next question provoked a sharp retort:

"I thought that the *force majeure* clause would cover their situation, a legal out. You know, acts of war, terrorism? That was in the contract, was it not?"

"*Force majeure*, bullshit," he snorted. "A so-called bullet in the villa wall? Suwar is not *force majeure*. And the guy who fired that shot, hey, he got three years for doing it, so they got a real justice system in this country. So the *force majeure*, if that's what it was, is *over*. They got to come back to the table."

Chuck had yet another problem with Falconbridge's decision. They had committed to spending $1 million on their feasibility study, and the final estimate of their cost figures, which he believed to be accurate, fell short of that level.

How short?

"Let's just say it's not only the figures, it's what they spent the money on too. They're not officially out of the deal yet, until we agree that they are out."

This discussion seemed to enliven him for the day ahead. Chuck got up to work with Abdul Shybani, his chief geologist, analyzing the latest charts and making decisions on the upcoming platinum-group sampling program. I went outside to check on the weather.

Today was exactly like yesterday. Clear skies, no clouds. Around the perimeter of the walled courtyard the magenta shrubs were in full bloom, and nimble, big-eyed birds of morning were in full song. Chad Ulansky, the junior extreme geologist, was checking core samples and looking over the motley collection of anomalous rock specimens that had accumulated since his last assignment in Yemen, months before. Since then, he had been out in the field in Russia, and back in South Africa, working on his Ph.D.

Chad told me he had got the call from Chuck to head up a six-week field trip only a week ago. Now he was blinking at the bright desert sun and the effects of the sudden time change and the long flight from Pretoria, South Africa, late the night before. While I hadn't seen him arrive, he too was staying in one of the rooms located somewhere off in the multifloored villa. He reminded me of a young Mel Gibson with a demonstrable taste for endless grunt work. I watched him hump the rock samples around the courtyard, eager to get at a *really* interesting one. Although he was Canadian, he was enrolled in university in South Africa, doing his doctorate on the geo-chemistry of diamonds.

"Lots of guys in the field I know won't come to Yemen," he admitted when I asked him about Falconbridge's decision. "See, it's not just Fred, whether he was overreacting or not. It's the public perception that's the problem."

"You mean all the locals carrying guns and knives?"

"That too, but for instance? One of the guys had a car that another local liked, so he just took it, a Jeep-thingy, and he fired in the air when they came to retrieve it and wouldn't give it up. We had incidents. Another time we had soldiers hired and the villagers didn't like armed men on their land, so they surrounded them with their own guys and told them to get lost. You have to be cool and know how to handle the situation, or you're screwed. Some of our guys just can't flippin' take it! And their wives don't like them being here either. *Me*, I like it here."

"What about your girlfriend?"

"Oh, she'll come around. She's got to."

"She's South African?"

"Yeah, and believe me, compared to the situation in South Africa, this is a cakewalk. That's the number-one murder capital of the world, plus 25 per cent of the population's got AIDS down there. Pretty soon the mines are going to be feeling a pinch for workers, they're losing so many to AIDS."

In truth, Chad looked as if he was happy to be working for Chuck again. An extreme-sports athlete, he had won the Namibia Eco-Challenge the previous September, a gruelling 250-kilometre run through the deadliest desert in southern Africa.

"It's the MRI Desert Challenge, and it consists of a 20K beach run; a 35K ocean paddle – shortened this time because several people almost drowned – then a 15K mountain-bike run; 8K running across sand dunes; a 50K mountain hike; and a 95K run across the Namibia desert. Plus a scramble up a mountain. Over thirty-two hours."

"Sounds insane."

"Oh, it is."

"What's the best part of being here? The fieldwork?"

"Well, you're outside all day, you get a good night's sleep, and you're carrying thirty- to forty-kilogram sample-bags down the mountain after
hammering them out. Then you see *one more sample* . . . Shit, you say to
yourself, should I get that sample?"

"And?"

"And then you realize, it's another couple of kilos, and it means that
you'll be that much more in shape for the next ultra-marathon. So you
squat and bag it."

I stared at him.

It appeared that Chuck had managed to recreate himself, without
benefit of sex.

Chapter 4

With Rock Man and Abyss Boy in the Gold Fields

"**M**ay Allah keep you safe in your journey," the black-hooded woman told us from the slurry of the roadside as we started our descent from the highway, two hours' drive northwest of Sana'a. From three thousand feet up, the Wadi Qataba was a long, ashen smudge snaking through green files of stacked hill-terraces. This wadi was a bone-dry riverbed, like many we had passed today. It would become green for only a few months when the June rains fell. If they fell.

With a few rials tossed out the window for luck, we started down. Abdul Razzaq's last job as a driver had been escorting the big boss of the Sana'a constabulary around the town. He seemed careful and competent enough, downshifting into the steep exit, but then who knew about the other guy lurching up the hill in a maelstrom of road dust?

There was space for only one vehicle on this goat-track to the Absolute, and the innumerable switchbacks made it seem likely we would encounter more opposing traffic halfway down. No guardrails here, of course, just the sheer slices of raw geography. The valley floor appeared in the distance as a patchwork Eden, a safe haven, until you realized that, even if you did make it down there in one piece, you still had to come back up the same way at some point. And the only way for our convoy of Land Cruisers lay through this tight track. "Perdition Lane," I mumbled to myself.

I was clinging to the outside of the rear seat, getting tossed about, thrown repeatedly against the same broken armrest, while Chuck Fipke slumped beside the driver. He had exchanged his Berlin trench coat for a Jungle Jim safari jacket. Judging from the heap of peels at his feet, he was on his tenth or eleventh orange.

"Great stuff, hey?" he inclined his head, apparently referring to the cosmic view outside.

"Yeah. Who built the road? The Chinese?" I tried to concentrate on getting facts instead of the imminence of our final trajectory.

"No, we built it. Yemenis," Abdul turned and smiled proudly. I noted how the road kept disappearing over his shoulder with gut-churning alarums, while Abdul Shybani, the head geologist, and Chad, the extreme runner, hung loose in the seat beside me, ignoring the quaking pitches and motor stumblings. This was their daily commute to work, I realized. Hanging to the foreskin of the sky by the grace of Allah! Earlier, out from Sana'a, driving through a tableland of blue sky inhabited only by God, His tiny farmers, and their sprinklings of mini-goats, I speculated on what the large kites floating mindlessly overhead might find to eat out here.

Now I knew: roadkill. And by that I meant stuff killed by the road itself, by the sudden whiplashing absence of it. A moment's inattention was all it would take to feed these vultures a juicy multicourse smorgasbord. Another grinding switchback (Had they checked the brakes recently? What about the bald tires?) and a huge shard of basalt thrust itself into full view on the left. It soared over the edge of the three-thousand-foot cliff, a lonely sentinel. We approached a low overhang of the same glittery beige rock without slowing a jot, and even semi-comatose Chuck made a joke of ducking low as we scraped by underneath.

"Looks like they ran out of dynamite right here," Chad commented.

"Tertiary," Shybani observed. "Basement rock. Hard to blast."

We passed the plinth on the right.

"I always wanted to climb that thing," Chad sighed.

"You go. I'll snap the pix." I closed my eyes to the violent plummet.

It always came back to this place, didn't it? No matter what I did in my life, what year it was, or how many books I read, here I was again: once and forever on this death-defying road, just like the last time, a suicidal romp that was only good in the end for a few wide-angle snaps. (Was it the *altiplano* of Bolivia? Mount Hagen in New Guinea?) Like I never left it, like this Third World shrieking roller coaster was the *only* reality, and the rest of my fleeting life just a screen-saving fiction. Back to this fantastic view I was too nauseated to take in, back to these angry trapped thoughts of what a bloody dumb way to die, mangled in a promiscuous heap of hamburger with people you scarcely knew, getting your eyes pecked out by all-too-eager foreign ravens, the clinging bits of rusty Land Cruiser making it impossible for them to pull your body out in one piece. My mind so good at imagining its own vacuity, this helpless vertigo.

Always I find myself here, back at the edge of some nameless unforgiving mountain, a tight little spot that would look good if I survived it and remembered to bring along the polarizing filter. Always the brink at the precipice. Hello, Nameless Gorge, here we go again.

We got down. The chalky white wadi floor smelled like burnt toast, a hot and phosphorous moraine, baking away in the flat sunshine. Except you could see that the dry course kept to a sinuous, habitual presence, that it was not the spare change of a passing river, cast out by a one-time event. The line between the green banks and the grey riverbed was too sharp, etched hard. Something ferocious had come this way. Something regular and with great force. The big rains fell in July, feeding this wadi and all its brothers. The wadi was sleeping now. Rustling trees sighed along the banks, their shiny dark leaves evidently poisonous, since the goats were careful not to touch them, selectively pulling out dry twigs with their shuddery purple lips instead.

"Yeah, over there." Chuck spoke quietly, but his tone had changed. I'd heard that tone before. Deer-hunting with my late father in the fall. It meant the game was afoot.

Fingers on the safety now, lads.

Razzaq pulled the vehicle over into the semi-shade of a forlorn eucalyptus. The other truck, the one with the guards in it, pressed close behind, but Chuck was out the door and off before they had a chance to display their hardware and check out the local colour. Shybani and Chad followed him, ambling down the little wadi that followed the big one like a baby follows its mother. They were heading for a rusty excrescence they called the Big Anomaly. I wobbled out of the Toyota and took a few tentative steps in their direction, but they'd disappeared. Eight seconds had elapsed since Chuck last spoke.

"They're geologists," Razzaq smiled, seeing my irresolution. "Want an orange?"

We sat on the rocks and listened to the musical ululations of unseen children echoing across the hills. *Tinkie tinkie weewee waaaaah!* It sounded like someone playing toy pianos with the reverb on full. Animals blatted at each other in the thorny wayside. I amused myself by trying to analyze the difference between sheep and goats. Why had Noah taken on two such similar creatures? And why had men persisted in herding them both, and in such great, if diminutive, numbers all over the faltering landscape? Some

of the goats (sheep?) gambolling in the nearby scrub were as tiny as chihuahuas. What possible economic value was a goat the size of a mini-pizza? Skin and hooves included. How would a marketing consultant move these runts in an ad campaign?

First, drop the word *goat. Chevre de pays, Origine de Wadi Qataba.* And drop the word *meat* while you're at it. Frenchify the cuts, *fricassee, roti,* etc. Make up a new word, but don't tell anybody it's invented: *Chevretec.* Too generic to register a trademark? "From the naturally wild plateaus of Yemen comes our delicately flavoured, low-fat *Chevretec Leans.* Grill as you would any lean cut, drizzled over with our authentic *Memories of the Souk*™ Rosemary Grillade. And enjoy with a warm coil of President's Choice™ Unleavened No-Fat Chorib-Style Bread!"

I was getting hungry. Razzaq was rummaging through plastic bags of groceries, looking for lunch possibilities. Some skinny, dusty herdboys had collected around the armed drivers, peppering them with questions. The drivers lounged in the shade, relaxed and happy, watching Razzaq as he took his own sweet time slicing the tomatoes. Chuck and the other two geologists might not be back for hours, who knew? It was a big world out here, in the middle of the Cantex concession. They were getting paid, and lots more food sat waiting in the trucks. Oranges, two kinds, oatmeal cookies, Arabic Pepsis, cases of an orange drink in a garish tetrapak called Orange Drink, bread rolls, cans of tuna from Thailand, green hot peppers, white onions, fresh garlic cloves. The village boys all respectfully deferred to the oldest among them, a fuzzy-lipped adolescent who clearly wielded his authority with the long switch he stroked through the air like a sufi dancer. I watched a girl about six dare to make her way down the steep hill path. When she came too close to the strange men in the trucks, the boy-leader picked up a stone and drove her off with a practised hurtle and a sharp imprecation. She jumped back in the nick of time.

Poor little thing, I shook my head. She ignored the bite of dust at her feet, turned and haughtily stalked up another footpath, her green-golden rustic's dress glowing in the afternoon sun, leaving behind the after-image of a princess from some lost folk tale. Bilqis and Her Brothers.

Bink, bink, bink.

Distant clinking. Chuck and the Blackhawks had started chipping away at the brown rock-heap with their pointed little hammers. So this was Yemen. The sky, the rocks, bleat of goats, and the hammering.

For the rest of the afternoon the process would be repeated on other interesting anomalies: a grey mountain, a black mountain, and finally a curious pearlescent slab of white stone that got the boys really excited. They ran up to it in a flash, Chuck as always unwilling to let any of the gang beat him to the crest. He had to be the rock man. It was growing late, noticeably cooler now in the shadows, and when they disappeared into the gorge, I decided to follow with my camera, less afraid of these wastes now that it was soft twilight. I was trying to get all three of them into my viewfinder, but they kept popping up and disappearing like shooting-gallery rabbits in the fading light. Rock Man and Abyss Boy, with the Grey Ibex loping on ahead. Shybani, the local, had managed to beat them both.

I caught up with them on a depression at the top of the gossan. From up close the stone had the appearance of a giant Greyhound bus that had frozen solid seconds before crashing, and the boys were banging away at it with all their might. Shybani was in the lead, with Chuck in the middle and Abyss Boy bringing up the rear. I took a snap, three dots in geology heaven, and then turned my attention to the birds that twittered and cooed in the rustling trees overhead. Doves startled each other in the swaying branches, fluttering madly about and settling down to conceal themselves anew. Footpaths looped everywhere, and animal droppings were strewn about. Two types, clearly distinct, a mound of round, hard pellets versus ploppy bits of matted dung. Again, the sheep-and-goats question. Birds enthused over my presence as I strolled along a raised dike of gravel, stumbling over rocks that my heavy new hiking boots were determined to dislodge. The rocks kept winning.

It was evident that the whole wadi valley was one large rock-farm. Everything on the valley floor had been cultivated, moved around, fussed over for centuries. Generations of rock-rollers and gravel-diggers had dedicated themselves to making the smallest marginal improvements, an ankle-high stone wall here, a tiny scrap of cleared pasture there. To what end? Innumerable terraces had been painstakingly moulded from the valley floor right on up to the high wastes at the edge of the mountain ridge. Only the sheer granite masses overhead had been left unscathed. Everything pushed at the edge.

I came to a fork in the path.

Here they had deposited several dozen large boulders, they of a thousand years ago – or last September, perhaps. The stones were arranged in a formal little cannonball heap, granite bombasts that must have weighed five hundred pounds each. Why? A diversionary dike for the day when the flood waters, the *sayl*, broke upon the land again? Or was this device the play of a local aesthetic, pretty work for work's sake?

Under the courteous trees of evening, the boys were now taking turns whistling and throwing stones at their small flock. It didn't take eight boys to chastise fifteen goats. It didn't even take one, and yet each lad had his own special language and customs when it came his turn to push the minuscule flock along home. Some preferred gravel and whistles, others clicked and hissed, and one boy spoke to the wee beasties in the trancelike whisper of a fallen angel still wiping the dust off his knees. I passed a dry wall of stones about five feet high, dividing nothing from its brother. That's what it was to be a farmer in Yemen, I realized: inventing uses for the tertiary and its kin.

First the stones.

⚘

It was well after dark when we returned to Sana'a. We ordered in, this time, from Sherbani's: another feast of broiled red *crib*, fish from the Red Sea, lamb joints in fresh curry, roast chicken, tomato salads, liquid hummus with coriander, and platters heaped with big oranges and little bananas. Chuck came down from his wash-up, looking exhausted. He had climbed four mountains today, with a bad case of flu and no sleep for the last two days, except for that head-bouncing nap on the way back from the wadi. Yet the food revived him.

"Unusual anomalies," was his only comment about our day. But you could sense his excitement as he heard out the expanded commentaries

from Abdul Shybani and Chad. They too had never seen such unusual formations. PGE, PGE. The phrase studded the after-dinner conversation like a
mantra. Over coffee I ventured to say that I had taken photos of them
working the last mountain, and how curiously slick the frozen agglomera-
tion looked to me.

"Platinum group elements, being a metal, are deposited with the sili-
cates at the earlier, higher extrusions," Chuck explained. Their chances of
getting hot readings from the new sites were good, all three concurred.

"So Al-Shybani was jumping around like an ibex," I continued, inclin-
ing my head at his distinguished grey hair. "He was way ahead of you guys
at one point."

"What do you mean?" Chuck stopped peeling his banana and looked
up sharply.

Oh-oh. I'd forgotten how competitive he was. A momentary lapse,
fuelled by the good grub. Nothing for it but to go forward.

"Well, from my angle down below it *looked like* he was first, you were
second, and Chad third."

Chuck responded immediately.

"Well, I was behind Al-Shybani because I knew what I was looking for."

"Then I guess Chad was behind you because he *really* knew what to look
for," I said pleasantly.

"He was behind me because he was still getting his bearings," Chuck
countered.

"I don't know, Chuck," I decided to chafe him. "When you're in the middle
of the pack like that, it's pretty hard to claim you're first about anything."

He chewed on this a bit.

"My job's simple: I got to get Chad here in shape. He's been slowing
down on account of thinking of his girlfriend. Already I can see that he's
stumbling around on the rocks, thinking of her."

"I'll be okay in a few days," Chad said apologetically.

"She give you a hard time for leaving like this and coming out here?" I
wanted to know.

"Mostly just the short notice. Chuck just called me up, told me to get out
here last week."

"You just be careful now," Chuck's eyebrows began telegraphing. "You know how it is with the local women when you're out in the field, if you don't focus on work."

"Yeah I know, Chuck," Chad rolled his blue eyes heavenward.

"A two begins to look like a ten, hey?"

"I know, I know." Chad nodded vigorously, hoping to fend this off.

"Next thing you know, you're getting off the plane and introducing the mirror-breaker to Mom and Dad as the new bride, right?"

"That was like Louis's story, huh?" Chad turned to me. "Louis was the field geologist working for Chuck in Zambia."

"We barely got off the plane in Lusaka," Chuck rolled his tongue about in his cheeks, "and we hear this great roar coming at us, and we look up, and there's this black tidal wave, a tidal wave of women, hey? And as they come at us, you can see a white flash of teeth moving right across it, and the first one that reaches Louis, well, guess what? He marries her!"

We laughed heartily. Nothing funnier than the inevitable justice of stupid sex.

"So he brings her back to Canada, hey? And the first thing she does is clean out his bank account. Yeah, yeah. She was the first one in the tidal wave to reach Louis, hey. Poor guy never knew what hit him."

"What about *your* girlfriends, Chuck?" I said. "Where are *you* meeting them these days?"

"Oh well, you know. I was in Brazil, hey, not too long ago. And I go to this nightclub. And there's like hundreds of women dancing, right? And me. Tall blonde, she's a ten, right. And some American guys are talking to her and she's being polite, so I go and get a ticket for a drink, and we start to dance. God, in Kelowna I'd be arrested for dancing like that!"

"You still seeing her?"

"She calls me from different places, hey. Barcelona, Italy. She's a model, travels all over. I swear that's the problem, hey. You get two people, they have different lifestyles."

"So the perfect woman for you would be a sexy female geologist who loved the bush, huh?" I was being sort of serious. Chuck looked at Chad and they both grimaced at this.

"Angie? K. T.? I don't think so." Chad shook his head.

"Who are Angie, K. T.?" I asked.

"Women geologists who worked for us." Chad furrowed his brow.

"What's the matter, not sexy enough for you guys or what?" I said.

"Nah. Not them. Oh, they're okay," Chuck mumbled.

Chad explained.

"You're out in the field on a project and she's out in the field, working for somebody else, right. So you can't talk about your findings. She's working for a possible competitor too. So there's this great big wall that's always between you. So what's the point?"

"Besides, there's too many other women out there." Chuck's eyes twinkled.

"So what's a good number to have going?" I inquired of the table.

"I kinda like the number ten," Chuck laughed.

"So do you have any trouble juggling them?" I reached for my notebook. "These woman, I mean?"

"Hey. I don't want you to write about my girlfriends, hey. Get me into trouble." He fixed me with one greenish-brown eye.

"On the contrary, Chuck. In my experience, after you reach a certain critical mass, girls like it when you have a lot of other girlfriends. It brings out the competitive spirit in them, as long as you're honest about it, and don't try to hide it. Then they just think that you're a real hot catch, simply because *other* women think so!"

"You think so?" Chuck chewed his banana reflectively.

"Of course." I knew my logic was unassailable. "I know a couple of guys, *players.* Used to be *playboy?* Their girlfriends know exactly who the other women in the guys' books are, they don't hide anything. It's all in the open."

"You think it really works that way?"

"Sure." I told them about my friend the ex-rock-promoter, how he went on the road with the band and got a taste of celebrity, how by the end of the tour he said he would get an erection just from looking at the population sign as they drove into their next gig, knowing that a certain percentage of women in town would be there, lined up outside his dressing room. That very night.

"See? There's a world of difference between being an ordinary schmo and a celebrity, right? You think any woman holds it against Julio Iglesias that he publicly admits he slept with more than two thousand women? In fact, they *love* him for it!"

I looked encouragingly at Chuck and rested my case.

"I still don't want you to write about my girlfriends," he said, only less emphatically this time.

"Well, Chad," I said. "How's it feel to be out in the field again?"

He stopped loading up his bowl of corn flakes, and thought a moment.

"The food here is great. That makes all the difference. Last week? I was in Russia, three weeks total. They fly you in by helicopter, drop us off in the middle of a Siberian swamp, brown water, tons of mosquitoes. We're wading around, and they just dip the pot into the swamp and haul it up. Tea time. So mealtime comes and they begin pulling out this white soggy stuff from plastic bags, and I go, Great, cheese, I could go for that. But it wasn't cheese."

"Well, what was it?" Chuck was clearly enjoying this account of misery and deprivation, and watched Chad with approval.

"Pickled fat. Pork fat. That was it. Three weeks of nothing but pickled pork fat washed down with brown swamp tea!" He scooped up a tremendous heap of corn flakes and, *presto*, another pound of cereal disappeared into his wiry cyclist's frame in about ten seconds.

Chuck went off to check on the condition of his "oil ministers" suit. He was leaving for the Persian Gulf on the next available flight, early in the morning. I asked Chad what his best competitive event had been, so far.

"Well, I won the eco-challenge last month . . . but it wasn't like anybody *cared.*"

"Why not?"

"Well, this girl from Namibia got like huge amounts of publicity before the race. She went around telling everyone not only was she going to be the top *female*, she was going to *win* the race too!"

"Uh-huh."

"It was like she was the only contestant. The radio, the TV, newspapers. All gave her tons of promotion. So during the sea-kayak event she capsizes, telling everyone that there were ten-metre waves. Ten metres, you know how tall that is?"

"Size of monster homes," I murmured.

"You get that during a *typhoon*, for God's sake. Then these two other contestants fish her out and she capsizes *again*. So they change the rules of the race *after* I finished my set, saying that the sea was too heavy. Then we're doing the run through the desert and she gets *lost*! For twenty-four hours! She started to see a Bushman woman in the veldt. With a baby! She tried to talk to the woman, ask the way, but the woman disappeared."

"Hallucinating?"

"She began peeing in her water bottle."

"She what?"

"Peeing in her water bottle. For drinking. That's the end, eh? She lay down in her cleanest clothes and resigned herself to die. Then of course someone found her."

"So you won the race and she won the competition," I nodded.

"I know, eh? She got a full page in all the newspapers and I got one line at the end: 'The race was won by Chad Ulansky of Canada.'"

Chapter 5

Tales from the Rock Palace

In the black of the Sana'a pre-dawn, Chuck Fipke got ready for his investor presentation in Abu Dhabi, on the other side of the peninsula in the United Arab Emirates. He was flying off this morning with his manager, Iqbal Jailani, to snag Arab investors for his Al-Hariquah gold project. Al-Hariquah was the gilded star of his Yemen concession, and the easiest site of all from which to extract bullion. Dig, crush, leach, and pour. A few tens of millions would do it; the technology was basic. Between packing and reconfirming his upcoming drill program, he spoke lovingly of his two current passions: racehorses and Bo Derek.

Bo, a familiar sex-icon since her hit 1980s film *10*, had been lolling in the VIP circle at the Kentucky Derby when a thoroughbred trainer introduced her to Chuck, asking them to pose for a picture with the winning horse. Reggie Jackson was there too, but the owner considered Bo's equine caress far luckier than Reggie's, for Jackson had recently petted a horse that went on to lose its next race, and at the Derby you don't fool with such things. At forty-two, Bo had been a widow for three years and, according to Chuck, she was still a knockout.

"She's an *eleven*, hey!" He shook his head in wonder as he poured himself half a cup of honey, then topped it with fresh lime squeezings. I took the opportunity to ask who he could see playing him; his biography, *Fire into Ice* – after making number one on the Canadian bestseller list the previous summer – had been optioned by a well-known British director/ producer for a feature film.

"I don't know," he said coyly, knocking the bright-green sludge back in one shot. "Who do *you* think would be good?"

"I dunno," he replied. "Maybe I should ask Bo."

Maybe I should ask Bo. Was I a great straight man or what? How's that for a line from a boy off the prairies?

"That's *one* way of finding out what someone thinks of you," I commented. "If she says Danny DeVito, you could be in real trouble."

"Well, I think she likes me," Chuck went on. "She danced with me at the Derby Ball, and Reggie danced with my date. I think that was fair, hey?"

"Morning, guys," Chad greeted me as he strolled into the kitchen in yet another brilliant Patagonia ensemble, peacock and crimson ripstop nylon, and headed straight for the honey jar. He made himself the same lurid green potion. I knew then that my Tilley stuff had to go.

৯৫

That afternoon, after Chuck and Iqbal left for the Gulf, Chad and I drove to the Rock Palace of Wadi Dhahr with Ahmed Mossen and Abdul Shybani. The Dar al-Hajar is the famous Yemen landmark an hour's drive north of Sana'a, a gaily decorated little citadel perched perfectly if precariously atop a yellow sandstone cliff. Built as a summer home as recently as the 1930s by the Imam Yahya, it appears to grow directly out of the ancient rock, an aesthetic intention common to all of Yemen's indigenous architecture. This strong local building tradition is thousands of years old, so if the queen of Sheba did have a palace, it is likely that many of the refinements to be seen here were used in her palace as well. These might have included: deep, full-season wells, creamy plaster fretwork, multiple storeys kept cool with breezeways, and narrow arrow-windows.

Today the Rock Palace was perfectly situated as a spot for newly married couples to celebrate their nuptials. They usually did this every Thursday with a healthy fusillade of AK-47 fire, a volley directed towards the stone bluffs so as to avoid injuring the neighbours. The immediate area was filled with these fantastic formations of yellow sandstone, alien grotesqueries lifted straight from the cover of a 1950s Clifford Simak sci-fi novel, *Alpha Centauri Sunrise* or some such. As we pulled up into the parking lot, I couldn't decide if this abstract aerie was more Outback or Nevada, as desert tableaus go. Either way the scene was heavy with ancient vibes, spirits seemed to hover in the canyons. A convention centre for djinns, spirit-dwellers of the wastelands.

"This is for you. Is okay." The cheerful youth held out a loaded AK-47 as soon I disembarked from the vehicle. He pointed to a distant scab on a mammoth outcrop. For an American dollar, I could have my way with this nasty discolouration, teach it a lesson.

I looked around, half-expecting to see the police descend and snatch the weapon away from the *farangi*, but there was only a small knot of grinning onlookers, awaiting proof of my manhood.

"*Peeeowwhh!*" The limestone blight a hundred metres off exploded in a cloud of white turtle-dust.

"You shoot like Yemeni," the bullet-seller said, taking back the gun.

"I bet you say that to all the boys." I handed him a hundred-rial note. It was worth the dollar.

The palace itself grew straight out of the pillow bedrock, a white ginger-bread fantasy, equal parts dune-mirage and fat lumps of sugary plaster, all apparently smoothed over by devoted hands. "My wife would love a place like this," I commented to Chad as we puffed up the dark winding stairways into rooms lit by ruby-coloured *takhrim*, the stained-glass window crescents. "Twelve storeys and no yard." The *manzar*, the attic with the great view, was always up another flight of stairs, but the view was perfect when we eventually reached the high tower, a grand vista of hills and more rock palaces and wobbly intricate roads, too many details to absorb with one pair of eyes. After we toured the palace interior ("This is mother-of-Iman's room, this is mother-of-Iman's bathroom, this is where Iman go to be alone . . ."), we had a look at the grounds. A giant baobab tree hid several guards perched high in its thick branches. The guide invited us to peer into the deep household wells.

Here Abdul and Ahmed grew visibly uneasy. One pit plummeted two hundred metres into the earth, and the other apparently sank below four hundred. Was it only djinns who inhabited these subterranean corridors? Or did the local geologists have other reasons to fear such chasms? Over glasses of black tea in the courtyard, Abdul told us a strange story about these traditional wedding grounds, the ochre flatlands visible across the wadi.

"This happened to a man I know. One day he came to this place, for a family wedding, and a bullet fell from the sky in the head, here." He placed his hand over his left grey temple.

"He fell down, and was sick. Then he would not get better. He was like a crazy man for three years. Then one day another in the family was getting married, so again he comes to this place.

"Bang! Another bullet falls from the sky and hits him in the head, but this time it was the other side."

Abdul now placed his other hand on his right temple.

"Again he falls to the ground. But this time, when he gets up, he is well again!" He searched our faces, seeking from us a sign that we comprehended this event. A happy miracle, yes, but a deeply mysterious one too. I watched a brilliant blue-and-mauve lizard scoot over the smooth limestone wall. He seemed to be taking his cue from the *oud* music playing over the loudspeakers.

"Well, I have a story about a wedding disaster too. And it also happened to someone I know personally."

"Please tell us," Abdul cupped his hands around his glass of tea and studied my lips. Chad examined the azure lizard through his telephoto camera lens. Ahmed nodded encouragingly. It was clear Yemenis loved stories.

"Once there was this woman I know, her name was Ellen. Blonde hair. She got married, twenty-two years old. So for her honeymoon – you know what that is, the new couple goes on a holiday? No mother-in-law? – she and Bob went to an island in the Caribbean, where they took an apartment with a kitchen.

"Ellen goes to the bedroom and begins unpacking, and her husband goes to the kitchen to make coffee.

"Suddenly she hears a terrible crying sound, '*Ugh! Ugh!*' from the other room. She runs to the kitchen, and sees Bob wrestling furiously with the stove, dragging it across the floor, trying to pull it from the socket. He's white in the face, making terrible cries, '*Ugh! Ugh!*'

"She realizes: Bob is being electrocuted! He can't let go! The electricity seizes him like a bear! She quickly takes him and drags him back, breaking the connection. He falls to the floor like a dead man.

"When he comes out of the hospital, he screams at her, 'I don't know you! Get away from me, you *kitchen-woman*!'

"For two years she tries to help him get better, but he refuses to look at her, so they divorce.

"Some years go by, and she learns that her husband is working again, and he is getting married again too. Then she learns the end of her story with him: for her husband has married a blonde woman, age twenty-two ... and *her* name was Ellen too!"

"And did she marry a Bob also?" Abdul quizzed me anxiously.

"No, she never married again. She was afraid to."

The two men nodded with delight.

I looked at Chad. His mouth was open.

"True story," I confirmed to him. On the way back to the Land Cruiser we passed men selling qat by a spring, washing the ubiquitous bundles of leaves for market. Qat is a national drug habit that is Yemen's curse or blessing, depending on your existential politics.

"You like to try this?" Ahmed inquired politely.

"No, no," said Chad. Too quickly for my taste.

"Yes, yes," I said. "Come on, it's supposed to be good for your endurance."

"It's not *physical* endurance they're talking about," Chad muttered to me. "It's *sexual*, and where I'm going I won't need any of that."

"Really?" I said, wondering how I missed this prescription in my preliminary reading. Ahmed bought three washed bunches of leaves for twenty dollars American. They looked like any dark variety of a household tree for the contemporary living room, benjamina or what have you. Shiny and modest in their deportment. Not nearly as sinister as the fang-toothed hemp weed or the voluptuous red poppy.

Chad was anxious to visit the souk in the old city, to procure some personal supplies for his upcoming field trip. He expected to be in the field for most of his six weeks; Chuck had put him in charge of working the Suwar site – and perhaps the new Wadi Qataba if the sampling worked out – with one of the four field crews. But first he had to secure warm clothes. The Suwar site was above seven thousand feet and at night the temperature dropped to 3°C.

We arrived at the old market in late afternoon. The secondhand-clothing sellers had their own enclave within the old city, and kept their wares nicely folded inside rustic wooden wheelbarrows, items that decorators one day soon will be shipping back in containers marked For the Trade Only.

"This is rather fetching, don't you think?" I pulled out a red-and-white Tommy Hufinger. "Or do you like this Perre Cartin better?"

"That one looks like a knockoff of a knockoff," Chad said, putting it to his chest.

"I think it looks good with your red Patagonias," I said enviously, determined now to buy myself the whole regalia at the first opportunity.

"How much?"

"Three hundred," the young man in the Nehru jacket replied immediately.

"Jeez, it looks new," I said, rubbing the collar.

"Hey, look at this one!" Chad grabbed a green pullover from out of the bin. I hadn't recognized a single label, but at three dollars American apiece for semi-new, who cared? I bought a black-and-white checkered shirt with the famous jockey embroidered on the pocket, except he looked more like a guy riding a motorcycle, waving his gun in the air.

After deliberating over his prospective purchases for what seemed like an hour, Chad went with the white Tommy X and a grey number with no logos, saying he was tired of sporting logos. All his competition clothes had six or seven sponsors stuck all over them, screaming at the world as it went by.

"In Canada, you can't get anything. But in South Africa, you just call them up and they say, 'Sure thing, how much do you need?' It's crazy!"

"Maybe you should organize a new event," I said, eyeing the qat with anticipation as we got back in the truck. "Something like a 1,000K run, all desert. What did you say your favourite race was?"

"The Cour de Sables," he replied reverently. "The sand-dune race. It's fantastic, your feet sink in, there's no traction. It's like running in a dream for hours. Literally."

"How 'bout the Cours des Thornes? You know, where you have to race through cactuses and so on, bleeding like a sieve? Take blood supplies with you."

We were both feeling relaxed after our shopping expedition. Chuck had spelled out his directions for his heir apparent for the next six weeks, and with a plastic bag full of leaves waiting, I had my work cut out for me too.

"The one race, you know, it's like run, pluck the shirt off the thorns, run, pluck, run, pluck." He nodded.

"That kind of describes Chuck's life, hey? Except change a letter or two?"

֍

Like all the houses in Sana'a, the Cantex villa was equipped with a qat-chewing room, but this was normally kept locked. The furnishings consisted of a long row of heavy cotton futons pushed against the walls, and covered with Turkish carpets and plumped with little pillows for your elbows. Ahmed gave the branches to the Somali cook "to prepare," and she returned a few minutes later with trays of cold bottled water, Pepsi, and the qat leaves, washed and trimmed.

"You chew red leaves at the top," Ahmed instructed, demonstrating. I looked around for a spittoon, assuming that you ejected the remains after chewing. Chewing, however, is a misnomer. You're obliged to swallow, but I suppose *eating* qat has a less sociable ring to it. The leaves tasted like peanuts. The buds dissolved in the mouth quite easily, with little mastication.

I took another piece. Ahmed looked on approvingly. Chad watched warily from the other end of the room, as if Ahmed and I might, at any moment, turn into drooling fiends. No effect so far.

I ate some more buds.

No effect. I looked at Ahmed. He had not been transformed into a sinister Malabar slaver. He looked relaxed, thoughtful. I wondered what he thought of Chad and me. Chad was nervous. He kept tapping his water bottle with his finger, making the hollow space at the top resonate in a high-pitched drone. Outside, the muezzin began calling the faithful for the six o'clock prayer. It sounded like music, but a music that wasn't going anywhere. It was just *there*.

I chewed a whole bunch of tips, determined to finish the bundle, and tossed the twigs down into the basket as Ahmed had done, with a little flourish of dismissal.

And reached for another handful. Still no reaction. Heartbeat the same, maybe a mild intensification of colour, but then it was sunset and the room was flooding with golden light anyway. Chad had calmed down somewhat, realizing we weren't leaving him behind for the House of Manson.

"How is it?" he said.

"Just a slight tingle in the mouth."

"Try the water. It taste delicious with qat," Ahmed advised, leaning back.

He was right. It was delicious. I couldn't stop drinking it, although my mouth was scarcely dry and I was not at all thirsty. One bottle disappeared, and then another. I felt calm, ordered. Evening was coming. I was ready for the descent of darkness, the slow, easy passage into the inner world.

"So is it doing anything to you?" Chad asked breathlessly.

"Not yet," I told him. "Not yet."

"You like it?" Ahmed inquired.

"I feel calm, yes. It's nice," I obliged him. The soft leaves were rather agreeable. I enjoyed popping them into my mouth; it was one of those useless actions like smoking that is pleasurable precisely because it offers up the undervalued satisfactions of downtime.

It was when Ahmed said we had to pick up my film at the shop before it closed that I realized I had been affected by the qat. I didn't want to move. I wanted to sit here on these Turkish carpets and do nothing but think or talk. Chad, however, was off like a shot to his room, even though it was my film that awaited us. I looked after him.

"The store doesn't close until eight," I called out.

Over the course of the next three hours, it came to me that there were three distinct phases of the qat experience. The first phase was a sense of engagement in the people around me, an unshielded impulse to inquiry and rapport. I had found myself looking directly into Ahmed's face, searching his expressions from six feet away. Chad, at the far end of the room, was the object of a more impressionistic examination.

The geologist was tense, as if his body was barely held in check, and he had to be restrained from jumping up and running away. Running, and running.

Ah, the flip side of the quest for physical attainment, I realized with a flash of insight. It simply becomes harder just to sit still! As if the athletic body, released from its normal domestic habits, finds its own mind and begins telling the one upstairs, Hurry up, hey? We gotta go!

This stage of outward empathetic pleasure and colloquy lasted an hour or two, and was followed by a sharp internal readjustment, in which I realized the depth of my own moods. Next came a moment of dislocation and slight anguish, that I was alone, then a second phase of introspection and abstraction took over. I thought of the ordering of facts and their relationship to each other, as if I were investigating the structures of my mind, with the emotional colourings of the previous stage now replaced by a cool indifference to such things. I was sere, the world was what it was. My breath came even and untroubled, and left that way. That I was essentially alone in a city of a million people, half of whom bore long daggers and automatic rifles, no longer concerned me.

Outside, the muezzin again called the faithful to prayer, this time a sweet, importuning wail with enough embellishment at the upper registers to show that even muezzins were individuals seeking their own ascendancy in skill and reputation. I followed the voice that was floating above the city. The traffic was a distant, idle aggregation.

The dominance of acoustic public space by the religious order was the supreme achievement of the Middle East, I concluded that evening. Yes, we in the West had once surrounded ourselves with the sound of church bells, their ringing had once marked the sure passage of the day into matins and vespers. I wondered about the Greeks and Romans. I could not recall anything about the public sound-effects of those inventive civilizations. Surely the mechanically minded Romans were capable of dominating their own airwaves with some powerful state music?

"It's getting late." Ahmed got up to go. "The store will close soon."

He left, and, with Chad still working somewhere off in the villa upstairs, I was alone in the qat room. Now I realized how fascinated my body was by its own presence in space. Fascinated and captivated by its paradox of object and sensation. It was with difficulty that I lumbered to my feet and followed Ahmed to the truck sitting in the courtyard.

Twice during that short trip to the photo shop we came close to causing an accident. We almost hit someone when parking. Then Ahmed nearly backed into a passing truck that was clearly visible, inching its way along behind us; I was watching the impending intersection with clinical interest until it occurred to me that Ahmed's peripheral vision had gone on an extended leave of absence.

"Stop!" I yelled, breaking my Olympian indifference. I began to turn my mind to the statistics of road deaths in Yemen, horrendous by any standards. The precipitous landscape was a major factor, of course. But still, you saw truck drivers tossing leaves out the window and stripping their branches at the highest passes. You had a choice. You could do like Chad, and freak out at all the puffy-cheeks coming at you. Or you could chew along with the best, and smile at the abyss whenever it came up and said hello.

When we returned from the photo shop, the third stage of my qat experience made itself known. I felt a vague, unsatisfied longing, which I initially took for boredom. I began searching for something to occupy my thoughts and picked up some old copies of *Wired* magazine, which a long-departed executive had brought over. Heavy mothers, I commented, as I hefted them to a couch. I lay down and began flipping through the endless ads for more peripherals and boring software services, glamourized by big-budget photography and endlessly clever copy.

"Too bad you're all screwed now!" I smirked at the epicene claims and headlines, patently ridiculous in the light of NASDAQ's recent bust. "Keep cool, the New Economy is Hotter than Ever," promised some fool back in June 2000. "Growth is a Commodity!" screeched another halfwit in September. I flipped and flipped. Men stood in front of their little metal boxes. I flipped.

More men, more little boxes.

Ah, here we are.

A photo of a woman.

Actually, her calves only. With a tattoo of a laptop on her ankle.

I studied the picture for a long time, contemplating the creases in the heel of her instep. Four hundred pages, and that's it. Useless issue.

I picked up another edition, November 1999. Ah, excellent.

A Thai or other Southeast Asian woman, standing by a pile of business books. I liked her because she looked real. Pink silk blouse, gold silk pedal-pushers. Was her name really Elisia Singstock, or was that just the software she was touting? She had big hands, Miss Elisia did, and thick big lips. I couldn't take my eyes off her hands. She was covering her breast with the book in her hands, but I didn't care, her lush big lips and hands were enough for my inquisitive senses to feast on, and I was transported into the erotic realm.

Was this mania the result of one womanless week in Yemen? Was the sudden deprivation of all female allusion eroticizing my imagination unmercifully? The dark eyes in the veil, the female outline glimpsed under the chador – were these making my feverish sexual imagination work overtime?

Or was it the qat?

The next day I asked Ahmed, "So, what do people say chewing the qat is good for? The stomach? The headache?"

"No, they say it is good for the woman. It make you happy to be with the woman. Happy, and not for a little while."

Chapter 6

What Cry, the Fabled Hoopoe?

The next morning Chad Ulansky packed up his titanium 18-speed or 36-speed or 72-speed bike, whatever speed it was, shoved it into an orange vinyl shipping crate, and dragged it up to the roof of the Land Cruiser. ("It's not my good one," he said. "I left that at home.") He and Abdul Shybani were off for a week of showerless camaraderie to the giddy hills of the Suwar nickel site.

"What do you know about the old gold-mine ruins? The tunnels that Cantex discovered in Al-Jawf?" I asked him, getting nervous now about the prospect of investigating the distant archeological site in the face of the company's pressing needs for instant and hard exploration results. "Got anything on that?"

"The pits that Leanne Mallory looked at in Al-Jawf?" Chad was noncommittal. "The geology up there was perfect for hand-crushing. Vein gold, quartzite. From what I saw, they seemed to be following a gold vein until it ran out, just like they did in South Africa before the Europeans came."

"What about the idea that it was the queen of Sheba's original mine, that it supplied King Solomon with all his talents of gold? Was it big enough to justify long caravans of one hundred and twenty donkeys?"

"Depends on how big the donkeys were, I guess."

"Did it look to you like it was a major industry, or what?" I prodded.

"You can't say what they took *out*. You can't tell from a *hole*. The ore must have been fairly rich though, because we're talking about *visible* gold back then."

"As opposed to invisible gold."

"Believe me, there's lots of that around. Especially out here."

I thought a moment. "Would there *still* be gold up there at those old ruins?"

"Of course. You take out what you can see, or what you can recover economically, depending on the concentrations. Either way, it's gold."

"So they *could* have extracted a ton or two, before they exhausted it?"

"There's one way to find out," he said as he tossed some loose sleeping bags onto the Toyota's roof. "Gold has a specific signature, depending on where it's from. You get some gold from the old mines, get a reading on its exact signature, the specific mix of impurities, the proportionate isotopes, etc. Then you compare that to the stuff in museums, the ancient artifacts. If it has the same signature, you know exactly where the gold originally came from."

We shook hands. The gate guard waved them out. Now it was our turn. I threw my little pack into the second vehicle.

We were headed down to Taiz towards the coast, to meet with a young classical Arabic poet, Mohammed Al-Hakimi. Al-Hakimi's collection of verse, *Madness Ports*, had won him the 1998 National Poetry Competition and the title, Poet of Taiz, from the ministry of culture. No small endorsement, as Taiz was the centre of literary activism in Yemen and its traditional refuge for scholars, writers, and artists. I wanted to meet Al-Hakimi because of an article he'd written in the *Yemen Times*, surveying local folklore in the manner of an Arabian Grimm brother:

"The Sayad is a beautiful woman who comes to you, but if you look down and see that she has donkey feet, then she will disappear and you will know you have been visited by a demon."

It was Wednesday about 8:30 a.m. when we set off under the same flawless sky that had hung breathlessly over the city since the day I arrived. Blue, cool, and austere light, with a constant temperature hovering in the mid-seventies. Ahmed Mossen was to be my driver and a new Abdullah was to be my security man. Ahmed was originally from eastern Ethiopia and had come to Yemen at age thirteen with his war-refugee family. Partly because of his resemblance to boxer Joe Louis, he gave the impression of a solid heavyweight who knew which side was up, and where his strength ultimately lay. Taciturn, with good instincts.

This Abdullah wore a suit jacket and business shoes. In general appearance he was more of a Turk or even a Hungarian, with his quick blue eyes and citified, European manner. Paradoxically, Abdullah spoke almost no English, and it was up to the heavyweight to translate anything that came up. We got in the Land Cruiser and drove a block and came to a full stop in the middle of the road.

"What are we waiting for?" I essayed a question of my new companions after five minutes spent examining the steel red-and-purple gate of the walled house before us. Save for the two-tone paint job, it was indistinguishable from the other steel gates fronting the street for blocks.

"The gun," Ahmed said.

"Oh yes."

A man let himself out of the steel gate and held out an automatic pistol to Ahmed. He looked at it, pulled out the magazine and counted the bullets, and handed it to Abdullah.

"Good," said Abdullah.

We were off.

Taiz lies about 260 kilometres south of Sana'a, on a well-paved but extremely narrow highway designed by German engineers. It sloped to the coast, and the drop in elevation is almost seven thousand feet. The trip would take us about four hours one-way, considerable faster than the return, because it was downhill all the way out. From the first hairpin turn, Ahmed pushed the tires to the farthest limit of their specifications.

Eeeeeekkk!

The scenery might have been breathtaking, but I could only snatch glances from the corners of my fear-paralyzed eyes.

"I think I could use some qat."

"You like?" Ahmed turned to me long enough to miss the next Z-bend coming.

"No, no, later. It's okay." I gave him a toothy rictus.

The Toyota was equipped with a selection of handgrips, and I eventually found a combination that kept me pinned to my seat. There were no seatbelts, but then did I really want to hit the bottom, three thousand feet below, caged in the wreck? Or did I prefer being tossed out the window somewhere nearer the top. Say, where that battered pickup was lying down there, stripped and rusting?

Eeeeeekkk! Eeeeeekkk!

Another twist and dipsy-doodle.

Oh those diabolical Teutons and their fiendish *funkengrooven*! No guardrails, of course, we've already established that. Palaces everywhere, plopped down on the hills and ridges like so many Monopoly hotels. Money must have gushed through here at one time. That, or the Yemeni were the most spectacularly inventive home builders in the world. Lonely little forts and aerie hideaways topped the summit of every big rock. Crevices and concourses going nowhere. Charlie Manson would have been much happier here than in Death Valley. This place was perfect for a maniac into harems and nocturnal meanderings. More to choose from in the way of mayhem.

Eeeeeekkk! Eeeeeekkk! The tires smoked and squealed as we defied the statistics of suv rollovers and hurtled towards our final destination, the green lands in the south. Yes, Yemen had its green spaces, I could see that now. Trees and everything, a happy blur. We passed an accident, still smouldering, two vehicles with smashed windshields where the foreheads of the occupants had met them in strict obedience to Newton's Third Law. Count them: two cars, four shattered red bull's-eyes.

Eeeeeekkk! Eeeeeekkk! Welcome to the ride that will never end; time has stopped, replaced by sheer momentum. We hurtle down through the valleys, the sons of gravity and their many plunging offspring, down down down into subvalleys and undervalleys and the rest, as if the land was a skyscraper you could only see a few storeys at a time, and the bottom a sickening haze coming up at you far too fast.

Eeeeeekkk! Eeeeeekkk!

"Good, yes?" Abdullah shouted into my ear over the squeal of the tortured tires.

"Yes. Beautiful," I said, trying to relax my grip on the window stanchion. Cowardly *farangi*! Got to hold our side up. To pass the time I began to count the dead dogs on the side of the road. Four . . . five. Six.

All full-sized canines too, about the size of border collies, their short coats either yellow or black-and-white. Neither the distant vultures nor the swooping kites seemed much interested in this available offal. Too much largesse? I counted thirteen corpses before the trip was over, averaging one per fifteen kilometres.

"Why so many dead dogs?" I asked Ahmed.

"From the night. The truck drivers hit them."

"You'd think they'd learn to be more careful," I said.

"They drive fast, after they chew the qat," he explained.

"Oh." I'd meant the dogs. How could they not get it, see the lights coming and not know they signified instant obliteration? Or were they chewing qat too?

Another corpse, mashed, still fresh. Yemeni dogs were either the stupid-est in all dog-land, or there was a scientific explanation for this wholesale slaughter. The only time I'd ever seen anything like it was in Louisiana, up near Baton Rouge, where the cretinous locals shot anything that moved from the windows of their pickups.

"So, you're married," I asked Ahmed when we finally reached the central valley and the sight of flat water calmed my nerves a little.

"Yes, twice."

"You have two wives?" Shybani had said something yesterday about how you put four Yemeni wives into one room and, unlike Western women – who could not, as was well known, be happy in a room even alone with *themselves* – the Yemeni brides would get along famously with each other! This sounded rather far-fetched to me, this latter, something outside my experience of human nature. But then I suppose there was *nurture* to con-sider here also.

"Only one. First one, she go."

"Why?"

"She don't like the city."

"And did you have to pay dowry for your wives?"

"Pay, yes."

"How much?" I wasn't sure if this was a polite question, but I would soon find out. They had the pistol and the side of a very desolate road if I transgressed some basic tribal law.

"Two hundred thousand rials."

In other words, about two thousand dollars Canadian, or fifty bucks American.

"Is that a lot?" I pressed on with my Nosy Parker fieldwork.

"No, is not so much. Is cheap." He fiddled with the radio, but nothing came on except static.

We passed another accident, this time a milk truck that had decided to transcend the limitations of a workaday existence on the road and make for the empyrean blue – but luckily for the driver, the rear wheels had stuck fast to the soft red earth of the shoulder. The land was looking more fertile. Maybe all the highway gore.

"Why cheap?"

"A woman from the country, she cost maybe one million, three million, rials. Because you take her away from her family, you see? She do not like the city. And also, you must give presents. Many sheep, for the wedding meal. Also much qat, for the party, and sometimes gold for the women." He looked briefly at me and went on.

"My wife was educated. From Cairo. She works as a nurse. So she don't cost so much. A girl from the province, she not like to come to the city. It is a shame for her. So she cost more."

"I see," I nodded, although I didn't get it. Still, it was clear that, here in Yemen, people seemed to prefer living out in the country. While I had noticed one discreet shantytown of tin-roofed shacks near the Cantex villa, it scarcely covered more than two small city blocks, nothing like the wretched outskirts of Rio or Bangkok that I had witnessed on my other travels. This worldwide phenomenon of rural peasants flocking to the city, looking for new opportunity, seemed not to obtain here. Did the impulse for such migrations fly in the face of stronger social values? Out in the Yemen countryside you were one with your *clan*; and what did *that* feel like? Impossible for me, the dwindling atomistic product of far too many technical revolutions, to ever imagine. I could see it everywhere, this vivid tenacity with which these people clung to their land. Every crevice to the highest hill was painstakingly terraced, every summit crowned with elaborate, multicoloured stone houses, every house glowingly maintained as the sacred keep of some clan.

Gradually my eyes grew accustomed to the dazzling light of the low plain, and began to connect the dancing dots. Shattered rocks and enormous clumsy boulders marked the path of past upheavals and earth-reversing catastrophes. Sinister black cones appeared on the horizon, resolving themselves into a long march of volcanoes.

"Do you get earthquakes here?"

"Yes, once maybe sixteen years ago. But not here. Far."

It grew palpably warmer. Trees gave way to silvery sagebrush of some kind, and dust devils spun across the dry plains. Impressive rocks the size of apartment buildings brooded alone in the flats. Southern Yemen looked for all the world like the bleached California gulches of my televised childhood: there was the big boulder that the Cisco Kid and Wild Bill Hickok went riding by every Saturday morning, firing chrome six-guns over their shoulders at the edge of the screen. This was the American Southwest, populated by thirteen million scrawny desert farmers with a penchant for risky architecture and a profound talent for survival.

The highway shoulder hereabouts was used as a marketplace, with stalls set back only inches from the constantly humming velocity. Honey-sellers, cheesemakers, fruit vendors, and peanut-growers saluted us with their wares. A little lean-to sat every four hundred yards, its proprietor importuning us with sharp shouts, despite our accelerating pace. Their cries were lost in the distance, only to be followed by fresh barrages that also failed to slow our passage. For some reason the carrot-vendors had chosen to swarm around the military checkpoints, and they held out their scrubbed vegetables with the air of men who had made a good deal on their leases. The soldiers asked Ahmed who I was.

"*Canadesi*," he replied. "Oil Ministry." He handed over a copy of the internal transit visa with my name on it, and we proceeded onwards with a salute and a friendly "Goo morning!"

♦❦

We reached Taiz by lunch. The city was clustered around the sides of a huge, dizzying ex-volcano I renamed Mount Vertigo. The local name was Jubal Sabim. Motorcycle riders sat idling in clusters at the city's intersections, revving their engines and admiring each other's rigs. The city was bustling with people far more heterogeneous in makeup than their northern cohorts back in Sana'a. The riders wore a variety of headgear: hats, caps, scarves, everything but helmets. The prolix street life and variegated skin hues suggested the south in all its lax complexity, eternally opposed to the dour preoccupations of the north.

We took rooms in the Al-Ekhoh, happy to be out walking again after the road trip. The lobby of this older hotel was lifted straight out of a 1940s Hollywood musical, *Blondes of the Casbah*. A set designer's idea of mysterious bazaar-luxe. Overstuffed, armless red leather club chairs, luridly tinted chandeliers, carved wooden shutters and aimless screens blocking the hallways, altogether an unconscious air of retro-fantasy and postcolonial torpor. My friend, the cutting-edge nightclub owner Johnny K, likely would have sold two good waiters for those fat sultan's chairs alone. The poet Mohammed Al-Hakimi and journalist Farouq Al-Kamali met us there for tea.

Mohammed did not look like his photo, I told him. At twenty-eight, he was tall for a Yemeni, with a visionary's eyes burning behind amber sunglasses. He swooped down into his chair with the controlled restlessness of the high-wire acrobat. Like he'd spent a lot of time "up there."

"What English authors do you like?" I asked him.

"George Orwell, for his *Animal Farm*, and also Charles Dickens, *Great Expectations*," he said without hesitation.

"Why so?"

"George Orwell was honest, Charles Dickens too, about the conditions of the people. And you?" He gave me a good-humoured poke in the arm.

"I admire Orwell very much," I told him. "But people in my country no longer have the time to read Dickens."

"You have published books?"

"Yes."

"You are lucky. The ministry told me yes, maybe tomorrow. That was yesterday. Still they will not publish my book."

"How much does it cost here to publish a book? Like your poetry?"

He calculated. "Maybe eighty thousand rials."

"About eight hundred dollars." It was exactly the same cost to put out a simple chapbook at home, which meant that it was at least four or five times more expensive here, judging by the cost of living. Our hotel was twenty dollars a night, and gas was twenty-five cents a litre.

"Would you recite one of your poems for me?"

"Yes, of course."

He recited four verses of one of his love poems in English, and I was immediately struck by the inherent musical value he rendered the consonants; in effect, he was producing a percussive composition, using his voice the way Rachmaninov or Satie did with the piano. At every second line, he effortlessly replaced the developing harmony with a controlled but unexpected octave change. He also drew out the hidden diphthongs in ordinary English words like "perplexity" and "source." Classic Arabic poetry is usually four or six stanzas and evokes aural sensations over visual imagery, marking a fork in the road we took the other way with Wordsworth and Keats. His recitation gave me a shudder, because it implied a whole hidden dimension beyond ordinary speech, a dimension we moderns had taken pains to forget. The influence of Arab poetry on the West cannot be over-estimated. When Dave, the World Bank official who had discovered the troubadours in his middle age, was singing the praises of romantic love, he was responding to a tradition that began with the Moors in the eleventh century. Such poetry marked one of the highest peaks of civilization.

I told Al-Hakimi I was moved by his recitation, and he agreed to provide me with three or four copies of his work translated, by fax. Farouq, the journalist, who was also in his twenties, was less fluent in English but had distinguished himself in my eyes by producing an up-to-date and reasonably scholarly article on the origin of Bilqis, the traditional Yemeni name for the queen of Sheba. Neither the Bible nor the Quran holy books mentioned her name, or her exact country of origin. It was almost certain that Sheba was coeval with the historical kingdom of Saba, whose domains began just north of Sana'a. The only woman referred to by name in the Quran was Miriam (Mary), the mother of the Prophet Jesus. It had taken me this long to get my bearings on the subject, and here I was now dealing with a living tradition, an oral legacy, and the stuff of newspaper accounts. The queen Bilqis was something like Paul Bunyan, a blend of life and art. But what lay beyond it?

Farouq apologized that his article had been flawed by a computer program that transposed all his B.C. dates to A.D. Apart from that, he stuck by his basic research. Bilqis was what they called her, although I knew that this name belonged to a real princess *circa* A.D. 300, a much later dynasty than the reign of the original Biblical queen. Both men carried cellphones and demonstrated computer literacy, and I was impressed by how this high-tech knowledge fit like a faceplate over an essentially medieval culture.

Farouq's long piece in the *Yemen Times* in the week of my arrival was mere happenstance, he said. The queen of Sheba was not a regular feature of the paper, a possibility I had originally considered, given the importance of the folklore of Bilqis to their nascent tourist industry. Hotels and tour excursions were designed around the ruins of the kingdom in the country-side north of Sana'a, especially near the town of Ma'rib with its famous dam. Wasn't this tradition the major tourist draw, I asked. No, they claimed, the ever-hardy German trekkers were the biggest fans of the country, followed by members of various development and archeological teams. If anything, both men seemed reluctant to say anything more on the subject of Bilqis than what was in the published article, as if the subject was not an entirely serious one, but something more fanciful.

"People don't have a desire to *prove* these tales from the past?"

"No, mostly we are hungry for news of the country," Farouq insisted.

I took the cue and went forward. "I find it remarkable that Jaber Ali Satir was caught, interviewed, tried, interviewed, convicted, and interviewed again, all in a week or so." I wanted to know what they thought of this hijacker who had dominated the headlines with his pen gun for weeks now. "You journalists go straight to the prison and ask him questions?"

"Yes, it is the normal thing. To ask questions of such people and to print their answers. The government lets us do this."

"He got fifteen years' imprisonment for hijacking the plane. Not death."

"Yes. Some say it was too lenient, that it encourages hijacking. But we think that the court saw the man had no plan, and was disturbed."

Indeed, Satir's defence gave four wildly contradictory reasons for the hijacking to the paper. Farouq listed the man's justifications.

"First, he said he attempted the hijacking because he wanted to go to Baghdad, as he admired Saddam Hussein. Then, he said he did it to express his resentment against the Border Agreement between Yemen and Saudi Arabia. After that, he said he wanted to hijack the passengers for ransom. But in the third session of the trial, he said he was fed up with living in Yemen and did not have a job to support himself. He had come back from

Saudi Arabia. He paid three thousand rials for the pen gun from Jehanah [the gun market] just to show off and he decided to hijack the plane one day before."

The last explanation was the most consistent with the plotless plot, as hatched. It made me wonder how many other incidents – like that critical rifle shot at the Suwar villa of Cantex – were the consequences of a kind of postal workers' syndrome endemic to the country, rather than the nefarious schemes of an international cabal of jihad terrorists. More importantly, who would be in a position to judge the difference between madness and conspiracy? We in the West had been assaulted by electronic technology and the pace it surely exacted on us, but still there were jobs and a social cushion for most. We had sufficient comforts and outlets to absorb the shock of the new, while Yemenis had no two hundred years of industrial preparation time. Even their so-called *white pollution*, the plastic bags that littered the streets and suburbs, showed the woeful inexperience of a people dealing suddenly with intractable garbage. This new stuff was not like the fruit rinds and clay jars of past millennia, was it? The modern world was also proving itself intractable.

And modern local madmen like Jaber Ali Satir were extremely important for the journalists of the *Yemen Times* to understand, for in his flight from law, a truth was revealed, a truth about the impulses of an age no one truly understood. Satir's fiasco was absurdist theatre brought to life. A bungled ultimatum, *The head will be dead!* The clownlike finale, with the crew's fire extinguisher sprayed in his face, and then the final indignity – no execution. That was for serious crimes only, and what acts could be serious in these mad times?

No, fifteen years instead. More of the same idiocy.

๛

That night Ahmed, Abdullah, and I met with Mohammed Al-Mujahed, the general manager of the Tourism Authority and the man responsible for protecting Taiz's cultural heritage. I was determined to examine the local folkloric aspects of the story of Bilqis, and he seemed to be the one to ask. In the Quranic account, there is a lengthy setup to the actual meeting of the queen and King Solomon, including some inexplicable business about a bird messenger. In a dark little editorial office of the *Yemen Times*, off a grubby sidestreet, I asked Al-Mujahed about this hoopoe, the name of the bird identified in the Quran as the messenger that alerted Solomon to the imminent arrival of the queen of Sheba. I wanted to know everything about this presumably indigenous avian go-between. What cry, the fabled hoopoe?

"Yes, yes. *Hoot hoot!*" he cried out gleefully. "*Hoot hoot!*"

Al-Mujahed drew me a picture of a bird like a blue quail with a four-pronged crown on its head. I had never seen its like before.

"What colour was this bird?" I asked. This question ignited a sharp debate within the group.

"Yellow!" pronounced Al-Mujahed.

"Black and blue," insisted Ahmed, who claimed to have seen the bird personally back in his boyhood home in Ethiopia.

"How big was it?" I demanded, and received pitched answers ranging from "Like this!" (sparrow-sized) to "No, like this!" (pigeon-sized).

We bade goodnight and descended the dark staircase of the shabby office building, past sleeping bodies laid out like question marks on each landing, no wiser as to the significance of the bird in the ancient tale – other than a general agreement that it cried "Hoot hoot!" at the top of its little lungs.

Chapter 7

Winter and Compunction

We returned to Sana'a the long way around, first west to the Red Sea port of Al-Mokha, a collection of half-ruined buildings famous in the nineteenth century for its export of mocha, fine Arabian coffee. Then we headed north along the coastal road. The trip that had taken us four hours south now took us almost ten hours going north, for we had to traverse two terrific mountain ranges to the west of Sana'a, and, at twenty-five hundred metres, the second traverse, through the pass of Manakah in the Haraz mountains, proved an exhausting climax to a nerve-racking ascent of hairpins and disappearing shoulders, a jaunt that made the trip out pedestrian in comparison. Ahmed leaned on the horn and kept tight to the outside shoulder as we rounded the bends; Abdullah slept soundly in the back seat. The sun fell behind a ragged jigsaw of rapturous peaks, as I snapped a few blurry shots out the window, for there was no place to stop. Or time.

"Pretty wild road," I commented.

"*Dangerous* road," Ahmed said quite unnecessarily. "Many people killed." He made a planing motion with the back of his hand.

82

"They fall off the road?" I wanted to know.

"Trucks come at night and shine the light in eyes, and they cannot see the road any more."

"How long until we reach Sana'a?" I asked, eyeing the setting sun like Lon Chaney in *Revenge of the Wolf Man*.

"Not long," Ahmed said, and braked hard for a band of ghostly goats. They had materialized on the cliffside at the last second, and now scattered themselves like living pylons across our course. Ahmed twisted and turned the truck, and called out something to the goat herder. I looked back as the dusty scarecrow shook his crook at us.

"What did you say to that man?"

"I called him a donkey. Not the animal – him," Ahmed grinned.

"Where's he going anyways?" My voice was flat and dull, the freshness of the mountain air was cancelled by its lack of oxygen.

"He go same place as us: Sana'a."

"Sana'a! He's taking his goats all the way to the city by foot?" I looked at the impossible asphalt ribbon disappearing into the thin air above our heads. Miles yet to ascend. And night coming!

"These ones are special goats. They eat dry mountain food. Good for tasting."

"How much does he sell them for?"

"Good one, he gets maybe seven thousand rials, ten thousand. More if there is holiday."

"And how far does he walk? From his house? Altogether?"

"Maybe one hundred kilometres. Maybe more."

"Amazing. And how does he eat, how does he find water?"

"He finds, where he goes." Ahmed saw the beginnings of the first village after the pass of Manakah, Sulnal-Aman. "Abdullah!"

Our security man stirred in the back seat. As a greasy dusk settled on the dismal mountain village, he jumped out of the truck to buy three *rubtas* of qat for fifteen hundred rials from a squatting vendor in his teens, the price of a pair of rep-house film tickets back home. He passed a handful of bush over to Ahmed and the road straightened out of its own accord while they chewed the miles away. Sana'a's outskirts appeared in the twilight, a desert fantasy of pink gabled strongholds taken from the dreams of sleeping Normans, and multiplied endlessly over the valley plain.

৯৶

The next morning Iqbal Jailani, Chuck's office manager, returned to the Cantex villa in triumph from the Gulf, holding his charts and core samples high for all to see. He removed his sunglasses, and stood proud in the court-yard, the Achaean home from Troy.

The trip had proved a resounding success. As he unloaded the truck, Iqbal grew jubilant, feverish, even bellicose as he recalled their adventure.

"Oh, yes, it was wonderful! Mr. Chuck Fipke, he is not the man he is in the office, no way! He is great, he talks so strongly, and everybody listens! His friend the millionaire, very important investor from Vancouver, Mr. Steven, he flies in his own plane to Abu Dhabi, just to be with Chuck!"

"And you, how did your own speech go?" I inquired politely.

"Perfect, wonderful!" Iqbal turned impatiently and barked out some orders at the staff. "I need you all inside! *Now*, not later!"

This was a man not to be trifled with; no, now that Chuck had left for the Maldives, he was in charge. And letting everyone know it, *pronto*. He turned to me once again.

"Now, Chuck and I discussed your program on the airplane."

"My program?"

"Yes. What you will do every day."

"I see. Good. Well, I am planning to go to Ethiopia, follow the story up to Axum, the Sheba on the other side of the Red Sea."

"No, no!" Iqbal shook his head impatiently. "That is not the program!"

"No?"

"No. Mr. Chuck Fipke, we met the sheiks, the most important men. They are coming here to Sana'a. You must finish your program here first, then go off as you like."

"That's fine," I said, trying to go with the program, though I didn't know what it was yet. "So, you talked to some investors?"

"Oh, yes." Iqbal's face split into a beatific smile. "Very big, very strong. Oh, Mr. Chuck Fipke! And they loved him on paper too! He is so great. They asked me questions about the mining law of Yemen. They liked it."

"How many men were there in the audience?"

"Maybe five hundred."

"And in suits?"

"No, only me and Chuck Fipke. And Mr. Steven. They all wore *gebaya*, the Gulf robes."

In an instant, partly from the electric undercurrents in Iqbal's voice, partly from an account peppered with incomprehensible sheiks' names, it struck me: Fipke was playing for big stakes again. I could sense the vast numbers looming behind the frayed diction and semi-hysteria of Iqbal's tale. Thirty-five million dollars, sixty-five, a hundred, two hundred. American greenbacks, of course. It was raining, yes, although the sky was intemperately blue.

I pictured Chuck in his bespoke suit, leading them through his coloured charts and numbered rock samples. Falconbridge wants out? No problem. Here were five hundred Gulf investors in dashikis and dark glasses. His gold site in Al-Hariquah needed a strategic partner. Chuck Fipke would simply go where the money was – the money and, more importantly, the ambition, the drive.

How was that for lateral thinking? Not bad for the prairie boy from Edmonton with a mild stutter and a decided preference for humping stones with the guys over the office politics, hey?

Maybe I should ask Bo.

The Saudis, Iqbal explained, already had one gold mine operating in their own country. It was close enough to the border of Yemen to pique their interest in his project. And everyone knew the story of the queen of Sheba, here were the core samples to prove it. What was another mine for big guys like these, right next door? They knew the operation; and, moreover, they knew that, if Falconbridge was out of its depth here, then the Arab investment community would jump at the opportunity to diversify its holdings. All it took was for one to say yes, others would follow.

"There is no question," Iqbal concluded, "that if Suwar and Al-Hariquah had been found in the Yukon or the Northwest Territories, we would have a big mine there now."

I wondered aloud if the Arabs who made their money in oil would be so quick to diversify.

"It was very good," Iqbal waved his hand impatiently. "Oh, Mr. Chuck Fipke!"

He shook his head, his eyes glistened. Then his pupils turned hawk-bright as he spotted a miscreant fumbling with the sacred core samples. He barked out more orders, chased everybody out of the villa, and left for his home in the suburbs and a fitful rest. I was left completely alone in the big house for the first time, alone except for the nearly invisible security guard chain-smoking in the concrete guardhouse. Before he took off for the field, Chad had asked me if I wanted to hear "Fred's Favourite Song."

"You mean Fred the Falconbridge guy, who freaked out about the bullet in the air? The guy who signed all the directives?" I responded.

You couldn't help noticing them. The signed memos were plastered everywhere, on the walls, on the desks.

> TO: All staff:
>   No one gets paid without submitting time
>   sheets unless they get left in the field after

the job, in which case we will be flexible.

– CCMY Office Management

"Yeah," Chad flipped the switch of the Pentium® III and skipped through thirty software programs.

"Here it is." The file said simply, "Fred's Song." I waited. A familiar tune came through the tinny speakers. Otis Redding's 1965 hit, "Dock of the Bay," rang out in the near-empty office.

Chad turned to me and grinned. I started to laugh. We joined in.

"Waaaasting time, oh oh oh!"

We both laughed hard; Fred's misery was as palpable as a brick. I didn't tell Chad, but I once played that same sad song myself, over and over again too, when I was stuck up in a fire tower in the bush by Red Lake, Ontario, for the summer of 1965. My first job in the field.

Now everyone was gone, and I was alone with Fred's ghost.

The villa was silent, except for the fax machines that spat out paper occasionally, and the surge protectors that sounded long irregular bleets, audibly tracking the random voltage fluctuations of the city's power grid. At any moment after 6 p.m., the lights could go out. People cooking their suppers strained the system intolerably. I had arranged pairs of candles throughout the marble hallways in readiness for the blackouts.

One fax was from Al-Hakimi; he'd sent me the poems and a copy of an interview in which he'd stated, "When I start writing, I feel I live in a world that is full of leisure, conceit, beauty, and charm." Asked what the uses of poetry are, he stoutly replied, "Poetry is needed for the sake of poetry itself."

Wordsworth could not have said it better. By contrast, the articles in the two leftover copies of *Wired*, which I had been flipping through, seemed demonically inspired. Crass means to a horrible end. The November 1999 issue contained an interview with one Dr. Michael Persinger, a professor from Laurentian University in Sudbury, Ontario, who conducted experiments to find God in the disturbed impulses of electromagnetic brainwaves measured in his human subjects. More, Persinger was actively trying to sell his technology – which allegedly induced visionary experiences – to Hollywood. A virtual and final synthesis: God and Mammon.

Talk about a *core sample*. This article measured just how far down the road we'd gone in our Western obsession with high technology. Outside, the muezzin called the faithful to prayer from their afternoon qat parties. It was 6:15. A light rain scattered drops like pearls on the dusty streets outside. Al-Hakimi asked, "Can anyone deny . . . the unpleasant winter that we are passing through on a large scale today?" I looked at his first verse, and tried reading my translation aloud in the local manner:

> Completely adrift, we're made for surrender,
> Made to bow low, to a lower pretender
> Yielding up, all that we're given,
> Grateful for the Show, they call *Forgiven*.

> *Winter and Compunction,*
> *2001*, Mohammed Al-Hakimi

Arab intellectuals like Al-Hakimi still believed in Arab ideals, still believed in God. A few days before, someone had showed me an article from the Internet, about two intrepid Yemeni explorers who took off in 1998 on camelback to visit the entire Muslim world. Indonesia included!

Why camels?

"No wild animals will attack us with a camel in camp," they told a reporter in Egypt, citing a widespread folk belief.

Their trust in traditional values, including the incontestable supremacy of the camel, the natural friend of man, was profound.

Now, with a few weak bleeps, the power was expunged in the villa. Darkness fell. I looked out the window, but there was little to see except other walls. I walked carefully through the marble halls, striking matches and inhaling the sulphur fumes.

"It's not that we in the West don't believe in God," I muttered, flipping again through *Wired* in the candlelight, losing my place in the flickering dark now that the electrical system tried to correct itself. I waited. The villa lights went on, then off again.

I sat where I was, watching this battle between lightness and dark. Oh, we too believed in God in the West; it's just that we don't love Him so much any more. Not since the Machine first proved stronger than Love in 1914. We who had experienced the full brunt of the Machine in two world infernos were full of dread. Can we be forgiven for holding the Machine in such terrible awe, for giving it God-like powers to save us from ourselves?

Another article in *Wired* made this clear, the diabolical pact we had made with technology. In it, Koolhaus, the Dutch architect celebrated for his unbuilt projects, decried modern architecture for creating more *junkspace*, his term for the dead-air limbo of mass-transit escalators, jejune airport terminals, and the meaningless "shopping experiences." Koolhaus proclaimed that the junkspace created by the Western technical imagination was even more horrible than the physical assault on nature evident in the Amazon, evident everywhere. What was the suburban sprawl of places like Singapore and the Pearl Delta, where towers designed on Mac computers shot up every week, against the absolute dead end of Planning & Design? Maybe Third World slums were okay, Koolhaus argued. Maybe the antiplanning of barrios and squatter markets and slums was only a healthy resistance to (sneer) Modern Architecture. Maybe rock-bottom slums were okay, more real.

Art itself had gone through the same crisis with Dadaism, and then effectively disappeared, except as a specialized language nobody actually spoke. Was the same to happen to all we held dear? Was the anti-Islamic bias of the West directly related to the fear they were simply waiting for us to collapse under the dead weight of our own malaise, our failed experiment with the Machine? The way Russia had just collapsed? Was Russia the black canary of the West? This End-of-the-Millennium dread was everywhere in popular culture. And the Frankenstein cycle of consumption seemed to move uncontrollably, with a life of its own.

Well here I was, stuck smack in Koolhaus's envied Third World. Every day in Yemen I had been obliged to drive through the most ghastly shantymalls on the outskirts of the towns. These "suburbs" contained roadside stores made from rotten tarps and old tire walls. Greasy bits of refuge had been cunningly fashioned into an outlet for car repairs or welding, and thousands of plastic bags caked the scummy soil. There may have been an infinite progression going from the old man with the rusty wheelbarrow selling oranges to the shiny Skoda dealership in downtown Sana'a, but the bottom economic tier was a cracked and desperate slough of misery. Some welders' shops were so blackened with soot and filth they looked like cancer-factories, and I had to force myself to take photos of them. Was I looking at Charles Dickens's London – or the future of all humankind?

To calm myself I picked up a copy of the one book I'd brought with me, a collection of short stories by the American expatriate Paul Bowles, who had lived in Tangier, Morocco. Bowles's stories depressed me further; and more, enraged me. In one, an Arab boy exchanged his soul with a cobra and then bit two villagers to death before his head was sliced off with an axe. In another, a travelling European professor of linguistics was kidnapped by Bedouins who sliced his tongue off, and then made him dance like a bear with bells attached to his collar, solely for their amusement. In a third, a leather merchant's son was taken from a caravan, robbed, castrated, sodomized, and *then* has his throat slit. But the robber was himself captured and dropped in a hole, where the cycle repeated itself. The stories seethed with self-hate, and cultural mortification.

The linguistics professor allows himself to be delivered to Bedouins in the dead of night. A wealthy foreign tourist submits to her Mexican kid guide-rapist. The plot-climax is always the same: A street urchin finds truth in the sudden strike, the savage blow. Bowles uses his ferouche heroes as simple mirrors for the allegedly fearful, cowed, and inauthentic society of the West. This was his wishful thinking on the subject of power, class-reversal, and social revenge. In his stories we will submit to our true masters, the wretched dispossessed, but truly authentic ones.

I began scribbling out a counter-story, "The Hundred Billionth Hamburger." It was about an illegal immigrant who gets turned into a cheeseburger, which then only gets half-eaten before it is unceremoniously tossed by a tweenie watching her diet.

No wonder I felt so crummy, I told myself. Sana'a was almost seven thousand feet up. No oxygen. I put the notebook aside and blew the candle stubs out.

Chapter 8

Inside Straight to Ma'rib

The next day began with the screaming. High-pitched tremolos struck the villa walls repeatedly, bouncing upstairs, where stray shafts found their way into my room. I listened carefully. Not Arabic. English, with an Indian accent. Iqbal, the office manager, and someone else, a woman.

"You will do no such thing! I'm in charge here!"

"He telephoned first, and it was reasonable!" The woman retorted.

"If you do not understand this, it will be the very last time! You will be fired! No second chance!"

"It is my job! How can you tell me this?"

The tirades belonged to Iqbal and to Mira, the Indian-born office bookkeeper, who spoke no Arabic. They were screeching at each other in English about Falconbridge.

I stopped trimming my beard in the sink and examined my face for more signs of ruination while I listened.

"That was highly improper, *not* to inform me!"

"They were his *own* papers!"

"How do you *know* that!"

Their breathless twitterings had a formal, orchestrated quality, like those of a long-married couple who knew the rules of the game even when the game was Off with Your Head. It was the same whether the topic was the best way to cook rice or how to get Rajid to settle down with a suitable wife: The Bombay Froufrou. Mira had come here to Sana'a directly from India, taking advantage of local opportunities for educated women to work in professional offices. Was this domestic pitched battle with Iqbal the flip side of public Indian decorum? Probably.

After the screaming subsided, a dull silence prevailed downstairs.

Ahmed told me later that morning what happened.

"Dennis from Falconbridge came after the office was closed to get some papers. She let him take them without telling Iqbal, who was away that day."

"And what papers were these?"

"His personal papers, from the Falconbridge office. But she should have told Iqbal. She did not call him, so he knew nothing."

In the subdued aftermath of this scene I grew worried about my promised trip to Ma'rib. The nationwide local elections were now in full swing and the countryside was getting more than usually restive. The power base of Yemen's national government was centred in Sana'a and its adjacent provinces. Tribal clans ruled more or less autonomously in the dusty north and the east of the country, and these clans fought for every inch of advantage with each other, with the federal troops sometimes acting as peacemakers, sometimes as the enemy itself. I had seen the headquarters of the national government, a heavily fortified and barbed-wire-wrapped compound that from the busy roadside appeared to be a private city within the city. And the region of Ma'rib, with its great antique stone dam that had fed the Sabean civilization for generations, was at the outermost ring of this central command. Now Iqbal became preoccupied, vague, and gave me contradictory assurances we would be leaving soon – Thursday, Tuesday, then tomorrow. Tomorrow? I could not believe it.

"Sharp at six o'clock!" he looked at me sternly, the very image of the subcontinent paterfamilias. "Don't be late, we have a long program tomorrow!"

At seven the next morning I stared at Ahmed Mossoud, my designated driver, and Ahmed stared back at me. This was the Yemen-born Ahmed, the swashbuckler from the movie lot. No Iqbal.

"Can you call him again?" I asked.

Ahmed nodded and pulled out his cellphone. For our outing he was attired in full desert-parade kit – white headscarf, white gown, lime green belt, and brass-handled jambiya, a 9mm pistol, and an AK-47.

"You look like Ahmed of Arabia," I told him. Iqbal turned up a few minutes later and immediately began rummaging through the office, opening drawers, throwing papers in the air. He could not find my internal passport papers, which were urgently needed. We would be passing a dozen military checkpoints today on the road to Ma'rib, since most of the ruins were at the perimeter. There were more drawers to open, but the key for them remained missing. A hurried phone call, and Ahmed was dispatched by taxi to fetch the missing key.

Two shaggy fellows I had never seen before slunk out of the guardhouse and cached their weaponry and gear in various locations around the interior of the Land Cruiser. Ali and Mohammed, brothers. Loose bullets were carefully inspected. I understood this was to be a three-AK day. The reason for the tension was clear. The region was not wholly secure. My stomach slid earthward as I watched them loading the ordnance for our trip. Ali, the older of the Squint Brothers (they had identical droops, but in reversed eyes), pulled out several magazines full of greasy new cartridges and the brothers lovingly bound them up with elastic bands, as if they were expecting several *exchanges* of gunfire and not just the odd, demonstrative volley. The state elections were proceeding as scheduled, with a daily body count as reported by the *Yemen Times*. Each day brought a few more shootings somewhere in the country. The usual revenge killings between the tribes were now exacerbated by the naked struggle for political power.

Chuck Fipke, I knew, remained indifferent, if not immune, to all this political discomfort. Angola was difficult; this was nothing. Well, if not nothing, then something to be expected. Chuck came and went on his own schedule here in Yemen, as he liked, and I knew he had telephoned from somewhere in the Maldives to instruct Iqbal on the details of this trip the night before. Chuck was on good terms with the national government; he had his audiences with the President, and the cabinet had encouraged him to succeed in his mining endeavours. He had his deal, a signed one. A gold mine, a big nickel mine, would have meant a ringing success for the country, never mind a good platinum or palladium strike.

But Chuck had learned from all his foreign business dealings that you could not march into an outlying territory under an armed convoy of federal soldiers and expect the locals to greet you with joy. No, you had to keep a low profile. Be prudent, but not provocative. This was a balancing act, and I was left to wonder if three AK-47s were going to strike the right balance today.

We headed straight north out of the city and a monumental sky opened around us, impossibly blue and bright at six thousand feet. Sana'a had no weather, it seemed. Every day here was the same day in the endless eyes of heaven. We stopped at a faultlessly clean restaurant and breakfasted on the traditional traveller's meal, a plate of fresh lamb's liver accompanied by toast, with black tea in glasses. The boys kept their guns with them in the restaurant at all times. By eight-thirty we had left the city outskirts, crossed the first military checkpoint, and descended into open country.

"Iqbal, is that a volcano I see?"

"Yes."

"It looks very black and very fresh."

"Not so fresh."

"How old is it then?"

"One million years ago."

"Exactly?"

"More or less."

"Look, there's another one."

We were speeding through a whole valley of charred volcanos, one after another. The ground for miles about was laden with coal-black basalt, churned up from the lowest plutonic depths.

"If they are so old, how come they're not weathered at all? They look just like Stromboli in Italy, except for the lack of smoke."

"It is desert, no rain. Everything stays the same in the desert."

We passed limestone quarries and belching kilns used for making gypsum. Iqbal pointed out a mountain range to the east and said, "There's ZincOxy, they're doing good business."

This was a British company, a successful mining operation. Their story was similar to Cantex. A British prospecting team had found the lumps of cast-off metal that ancient silver miners had rejected, and had had them analyzed. The lumps were loaded with zinc, lead, and nickel, and led the prospectors right to the source of the new mine.

This north highway, built by the Germans, Iqbal said, was a narrow madacam ramp with sharp gutters leading straight through the volcano range. From its elevated design, it appeared the engineers expected violent rainstorms from the region. A dip in the plateau now; we were snaking downwards into a low plain, and passing a stream of truck-tankers coming the other way from Ma'rib's Hunt Oil field. Commercial shantytown malls began springing up, far grimmer than anything I had seen in the south, with foul road debris piled into rotten little walls and sagging roofs. Dank, oily holes in the dirt. Impossible to know what they were selling, if anything. Koolhaus would have been proud. It was a pointed reminder that the per-capita income of the country was three hundred dollars a year. Signs of vast underemployment were everywhere. Hundreds of men sat around in groups of ten or more at these roadside cesspools, neither selling nor buying, often not even talking or looking. We stopped to get more photo-copies of my transit visa at a relatively ordinary copy shop. One clerk, a youth about seventeen, was carefully stamping envelopes one by one, while another boy stood at his elbow, watching his every move as if he was learn-ing something. Our trifling custom was likely the most productive hour of their day. I saw another man sweeping the litter from the office grounds when we stopped for gas. He was bent low, using a tiny hand whisk, some-thing we might use for brushing spiderwebs out of the boat at the cottage. The steady wind off the plain blew everything right back at him. It was pointless. All pointless. A yellow dog slumped in the shade of the corroded pump seemed to know it too. Futility reigned here. Passing oil trucks snorted clouds of black diesel into the air, their only apparent contribution to the local economy. The yellow dog got up out of the way of the coming whisk, moved, and sagged down again in the gritty dust a few feet away. Where were the refinery workers with their loud new clothes and brassy good cheer? More, where was their *money*? Nowhere.

Inside the vehicle, Ali carefully rubbed at his weapon with a clean white cloth. His brother Mohammed slept in the third seat, and each time we lurched around a switchback his machine gun fell over and hit the metal floor behind my ear with a sharp clang that woke up everyone but him. How good were the safeties on these guns? Did they have safeties?

More army checkpoints. The cut of the soldiers changed subtly, growing by degrees from the foxy-faced five-footers near Sana'a to these strapping, mustachioed provincials with the bold braggadocio to their step. Every second lieutenant among them offered a variation on the theme of Saddam Hussein. Was the resemblance intentional? My sense was yes.

Saddam had stood up, and remained, unbowed.

Pure desert, the floury white stuff of legend, began spilling out of the horizon in dribs and drabs. Now you could see the intelligence of the German road engineers at work. They had built the highway along the very edge of the basalt extrusion, and no sand dunes came nearer this road than a few dozen metres.

"You like desert?" Ahmed asked.

"I was expecting it to be hotter," I said, happy to be on the flats now, and free from loose guns crashing by my ear.

৪৬

We reached Ma'rib by eleven. Barbed-wire gates guarded the entrance to the ruins of the old dam. We were five men in a desolate countryside, yet I knew there were people about. We were exposed, walking out here in the open, and this feeling gave our actions a curiously theatrical quality. The sleepy soldiers at the gate told us they got five visitors a day. Our arrival had doubled their tally.

Here was one of the ancient wonders of the world, and I wandered alone through astounding ruins in the company of two small boys who held up alleged local antiquities for sale, gently whispering their prices whenever I glanced their way. Ali and Mohammed followed close behind me. I stepped over tumbles of hand-hewn blocks of granite and limestone that were three thousand years old. We were sauntering over what had once been the southern sluice gate, a complex that might have stood eighty feet high. The older Squint Brother aimed his gun at a passing kite overhead, and I sent up an urgent prayer for the bird's life, but he failed to shoot.

He wasn't about to fire at all. There were too many other men with guns nearby, men who would have considered it a provocation.

We know that this huge ancient dam was built and in operation after 1000 B.C., perhaps by 800 B.C. Also, that its technology was based on smaller predecessors, conceived near the beginning of the so-called Iron Age – what Greek classical writers refer to as the Heroic Age and roughly contemporaneous with the Battle of Troy. But we don't know if this technology itself was conceived and designed as a strategy of the earlier bronze culture. If it was, it would not only make it a greater technical feat for its age, but also raises profound questions about the origins of the Iron Age itself. What was the significance of feedback loops, critical economic mass, population densities, and so on, to the inexplicably accelerating pace of technical innovation at that time?

At its height the stone dam controlled the runoff waters of Wadi Dhana, a large seasonal riverbed, irrigated more than twenty-five thousand acres, and supported the fifty thousand people of Ma'rib, a tightly knit community living in close proximity to the major incense trade route running from Oman to the Mediterranean Sea. As we had seen today from our truck, this trade route essentially followed a narrow defile that skirted the flat edge of the hostile desert on one side, and the jagged highlands on the other. Today we had oil, zinc, and lead ingots. Yesterday, frankincense, alabaster, honey, and perhaps the fabled gold, from the mines a hundred kilometres to the north. In other words, the highway and the old caravan route both repeated an age-old settlement pattern. The physical reality of this intermediate zone between stony desert and mountain massif suddenly made sense to me. After our morning journey along the highway, I took the opportunity to compare it to the old trade route shown on maps, a trade route that had previously seemed like a ridiculously indirect perambulation. Now it appeared a pragmatic necessity.

Two things had contributed to Ma'rib's destiny as the traditional home of the queen of Sheba: international trade, made possible by Ma'rib's key location on this narrow lip between mountain and desert, and the lush local agriculture, made possible by the great wadi dam and its attendant technologies. The Sabeans were able to export flax for cloth, sesame, date palms, sorghum (a kind of wheat), grapes, and peas, enough for both trade and local consumption. They were able to do both because this dam, and other smaller ones like it in the area, irrigated their crops throughout the sunny year (like a natural greenhouse). Even more importantly, perhaps, the social structures necessary to construct and maintain such grand public works ensured a cohesive, educated, and motivated community, generation after generation.

The Sabeans' technical innovations were not obvious on a visitor's casual inspection of the extensive ruins of the dam, piles of dressed stones stretched out for hundreds of yards in all directions, but their ambitions certainly were. Only the two ends of the twenty-two-hundred-foot dam now survived, now each about fifty feet high, because the half-mile centre had been blown away by a final watery cataclysm in A.D. 570. Archaeologists have found incontrovertible evidence that the dam had been rebuilt under various Sabean rulers many times in its history before this end date; like politicians everywhere they needed to take credit for any additions made during their reign. In Saba, this self-promotion took the form of stelae, or inscribed stone slabs, from the Greek word for a gravestone or dedicatory tablet. These tablets were often affixed to the base of the constructions they honoured (where they could be easily read), and it was such a stela that the Cantex crew had found in the north, near Al-Jawf. That stela had originally been affixed to a local temple to a pagan god, not to a dam.

The date A.D. 570 is highly suggestive, for this was the same year the Prophet Muhammed was born, and his era marks a watershed in world events. At this time in Europe the Saxons had begun invading Britain, part of a worldwide movement of restless peoples – Avars, Visogoths, and the like – and this constitutes the beginning of the Dark Ages, for which

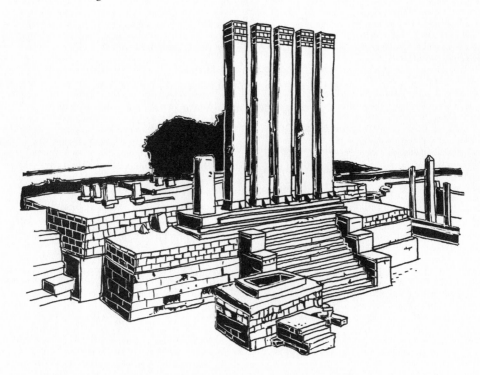

environmental degradation and traumatic climate change may well have been partly responsible.

In Yemen the foreign invaders were Ethiopians, riding on war-elephants, and then mounted Persians, who finally conquered the whole region in A.D. 575. The Persian governor was not interested in fixing the dam, and in any event, the local engineers and technicians had permanently fled to other parts of the Arabian Peninsula. The Ma'rib dam thus marks the highwater level of an indigenous, literate, innovative, and socially brilliant society, based on a pre-Islamic pagan religion, that had dominated the entire region for close to fifteen hundred years. Its lifespan was roughly equivalent to classical Greek high culture, which also began with the Iron Age and can be said to have ended fifteen hundred years later, with the last celebration of the pagan Elysian Mysteries in the fifth century A.D.

So today we were surveying a major artifact of this lost pagan world.

The stones were all constructed with male-female fittings and professionally inscribed with South Arabian characters. The odd runic notations were carved everywhere one cared to look. This dam had withstood the annual summer flood for fifteen hundred years, intact and operating. Essentially it was a huge *active mechanism* of stone, not merely an inert monument or temple like the pyramids of comparable age. This engineering marvel had been the joint effort of not one but several classes of professional engineers, draughtsmen, mechanics, master masons, and more.

The real trick here was that the Sabeans were obliged to feed the annual rainwaters into a series of interlocking sluices and aqueducts, *then* commodify and distribute the precious waters in some politically astute fashion, *and* organize repairs and maintenance over centuries, *as well as* record and find a way of *preserving* records that went back over long centuries of use (where, for example, a major renovation cropped up only every century), *while simultaneously* engaging in international trade, getting the next generation of kids married off, and fighting perpetual wars with envious neighbour city-states like Ma'in and Awsan.

How's *that* for a juggling act?

For a city the size of Niagara Falls?

Did we have anything comparable in the West?

With few precedents, it is hard to imagine what daily life was like for fifty thousand people living in this fairly compact environs, *circa* 1000 B.C., set down smack in the middle of the Arabian Peninsula desert. Ma'rib, then called Maryab, was unique in all the world. A First Millennium high-tech society, living a life of isolated grandeur and protected by its surrounding wastelands. Imagine a Pacific island filled with electrical engineers, or a Silicon Valley plunked on the moon. There was nothing beyond their immediate horizon except the donkey caravans and the vast empty tracts they traversed.

Luxor and Memphis, Jerusalem, perhaps Tyre and the other Phoenician cities beckoned from the far west; Babylon, Ugarit, and so on dominated the northeast; Oman and India held the southeast. These were the points of a Sabean world-compass whose centre was drawn on the creaking sluice gates and the eternal slush of warm, contained water. With every season, travellers brought more news and technical knowledge. Like the rains themselves, information was to be carefully hoarded and used as needed.

The land had been drying out steadily over the centuries from the end of the
Ice Age around 6000 B.C. And probably very noticeably, too, for this watchful town of tough little tablet-keepers and water-accountants kept records
and knew how to read them. They knew it was only their hard work that
kept the Big Desert out. A fatalistic determinism must have competed with
idealism and a visionary solipsism for cultural supremacy.

The Sabeans probably saw themselves as the Best People – and everyone
else beyond the horizon as something less than that. Daily life was an endlessly busy round of farming, dam work, defence, and technical instruction,
a complex balancing act that required total participation from everyone
above the age of two. An annual corvee of state labour was likely exacted,
and applied universally, not only for the vital labour it produced, but also
to confirm publicly the paramount value of an integrated community. A
religion that both celebrated and denied the essential contradictions of this
balancing act almost certainly centred on a semi-divine ruler-priest(ess).
Someone who could speak authoritatively for the haughty god that delivered the life-giving waters.

The ancient Sabean religion would have endowed the great dam itself
with a sophisticated meta-life, but then held the life-giving and ever-
threatening great wadi itself in greater fear and ritual awe. For, several times
known to history, the dam broke, and it was the flood that triumphed over
fresh corpses. So the wadi had to be placated, honoured, and propitiated as
a living thing, ultimately unknowable – while the operation of the dam
would have been bound up in magic formulas that worked on one level as
tradesmen's secrets. The essential contradiction of Ma'rib's civilization was
this opposition between the earth-shaking Water-Snake, freely coursing
through time, and its necessary arrest and dismemberment in the House of
Knowledge – or whatever careful circumlocutions they used when referring
to the sacred stone enclosure.

Snake into Meat, that's what we're talking about here.

What we know of Sabean religion is that one of the chief gods was called
Ilmuquh, a male moon god. The moon is almost universally associated with
goddesses because the cyclical nature of lunar phases parallels women's
menses, so it may not be surprising to learn that Ilmuquh was bisexual.

Archeologist Leanne Mallory, who examined the Cantex stela, interpreted the inscription as a dedication to this primary, if ambivalent, god.

When the dam ultimately broke in A.D. 570, the Sabeans left for good, and their descendants, the Sherbanis and the Shybanis (from *Sheba* and *bani*, "sons of") scattered across Yemen. So today we have Al-Shybani, the Cantex head geologist; Sherbani the restaurateur; and Dr. Yusuf Abdullah Sherbani, the director of antiquities himself. Among thousands of others.

Again, much will have to be imagined of Ma'rib's daily life, because, despite the protests of the aforementioned executive of the department of antiquities, in the 1980s most of this ancient cultural site was flooded over by a new project, a *second* dam, built by a Turkish company and financed by a Gulf sheik, Sheik Zayed bin Sultan Al-Nahyan, ruler of Abu Dhabi, whose ancestors also emigrated from the Ma'rib area. The dream of preserving the "Land of Two Gardens" as an archeological park, bowed to economic necessity. Ten thousand ancient hectares were now under modern cultivation. The recent cash crops include citrus, wheat, watermelons, and, inevitably, qat.

We stood mulling over the ruins of the dam, lost in this dream of the magical green past, when a sudden burst of gunfire made us all start. Ali and Mohammed turned as one, crouching in the rocks like feral cats. They pushed their noses up to the wind, smelling the air for the sharp bite of nitro. They nudged each other: it came from a nearby ridge. They continued to sniff. I peered at the chalky height. Could they sniff out the *intention* of the shooter as well?

"Iss okay," Ali stood up and waved his gun nonchalantly in the air.

A minute passed and another shot exploded.

We got in the truck and left.

In a few minutes we surmounted a modern asphalt ramp and ascended the summit of the new dam. I peered into the milky green waters, which appeared fishless and alkaline. The lake behind the dam stretched over several hundred acres, and it flattened and warped the horizon with the misty stew of its rapid evaporation. Except for small flycatchers buzzing the cliffs, the place was devoid of life. The silent vat of cloudy water seemed improbable, and nebulous.

Still: Water, hey?

Coming from a long trek into Ma'rib must have been near-ecstasy for the withered and burned travellers of the caravan route. On the way in to the dam I had noticed half-naked men showering at the village pumps in the wadi, stripped to their waists and laughing gleefully under the flowing gusher. This wadi had single-handedly sustained the ancestors of a large part of the present-day country, as well as the commercial sector of the Gulf. It was no wonder Sheik Zayed of Abu Dhabi had paid it homage with the expensive new dam. The wadi had washed and fed and delighted a hundred generations of his ancestors.

We had enough time for one more ruin, the so-called Temple of the Sun and the Moon. We drove down the road for fifteen minutes for a look at it. The temple precincts held only one foreign visitor. He said his name was Ben, from Beirut, but he couldn't talk to me because he was busy. He actually looked at his watch when he said this. As I strolled around the site, the lanky Lebanese student was always one step ahead of me, poking and prying at the alabaster carvings. I watched him as he promptly climbed up the central well in the courtyard and peered down, snapping off some pictures of its depths.

When it was my turn I saw nothing down there.

I sat back and enjoyed the sunshine. It was quiet and empty in every direction. No planes, just a soft breeze. A winter's day at the edge of the great desert. The palace emanated a sweet, clean atmosphere, unlike the turgid subterranean feelings invoked by doomed Knossos in Crete or, worse, the death-twisted weirdness of the Toltec ballcourt in Chichén Itzá.

Here a parapet wall encircled five raised stone pillars, with holding tanks for water and stylized alabaster carvings of cattle. The local alabaster of the Sabeans has a peculiar yellowy-green cast to it, and is rather shiny, leading one to suspect that it reflected torchlights at night in a dramatic and suggestive way. Again this made a perfect setting for a moon god, and the association of a bull with the moon obviously depends on the crescent shape of the animal's two horns. The bull would have represented zodiacal Time and the endless fertility of Time's seasons.

I rested my head against a bull-headed water-trough and watched Ahmed proudly circumnavigate the parapet wall above me. In his flowing white robes, and taking the time to pause meaningfully against the dazzling blue sky, he seemed nothing less than an actor rehearsing his lines on a high stage. Then, as if playing to a great but invisible audience he knew he had captured, he looked up, stroked his beard, and turned and walked away. A great sigh of relief seemed to greet his exit, as if the breeze hid unseen watchers, and his silent deliberations and dramatic stances were a soliloquy of the highest order, pure thought offered against the boundless afternoon. I loved watching Arabs think. They used their whole bodies to reach a conclusion.

I too had walked like that, in my study late at night, but never outside and atop a fifteen-foot stone wall. It took more than concentration; it took the firm conviction that one would reach the goal without stumbling. Travelling the inner landscape of inspiration, while perfectly attuned to the outer world. Of course he could have been thinking about the local price of qat. Who was I to judge?

I turned at the sound of an engine.

The Lebanese student was driving off, heading for the next site in a cloud of dust.

Chapter 9

Beneath the Dunes

Iqbal thought it would be a good idea if we looked in on the old ghost town of Ma'rib itself. The place had been bombed in the 1960s during a campaign of the civil war, and its inhabitants had fled. Ten minutes from the Moon Temple, we came upon a semi-deserted village of mud skyscrapers, now sinking back into the earth. An overgrown scrub, skeletons of timbers, roofs gone, the Empty Quarter looming in the distance, a hot vacuum. Abandoned, but not abandoned. Ragged children played soccer in a ruined courtyard, using a bunched rag for a ball. A head popped out of a dismal tower. A sharp whistle. The children froze.

"Who lives here?" I asked Ahmed. He shifted uneasily from one sandal to another, as if the littered ground might come alive with cobras at any moment.

"No one," he responded glumly. "Just some black people, they come here."

I didn't think he was referring to Ethiopians; he would have said so. Perhaps Somalians or *akhdam*, the lowest social class. He was happy to lead the way back to the truck. Was that the proximity of Rub al-Khali we now sensed? The incense route from Oman had skirted the edge of the great

Arabian desert for hundreds of miles, and as we drove another dozen miles or so to the Bilqish Mareb Hotel for a late lunch, I wondered again about this edge.

It was strongly demarcated, far more so than one would expect in other climes where the break from forest to plain, for example, was always subjective and conjectural. Here was more grass, there more trees. This desert was not fuzzy. It lay hard upon the land like the ocean. Here was the sand; there, was none. This desert shared one more thing with the sea: its origin. It came from the sea.

I was surprised to find this out from my geologist friends. The sand of the Empty Quarter was an enormous lost beach, blown miles from its home. That is, the sand had been swept up from the Red Sea over the course of time, falling where the dominant wind pattern tossed it, building up over eons and burying whatever landforms lay beneath it in the east of the country. Earlier, Chad had pointed out the striations visibly running northeast in these folds of sand. By happenstance (or not), these marked the direction of these prevailing winds. It was the same with the Namibia desert, he said, a geology he'd studied in great detail, because that landform had spawned a bonanza of surface diamonds.

"What you get in Namibia is a long line of mine workers, a hundred at a time, moving slowly across the desert, elbow-to-elbow, with loose bags tied to their necks by thongs. They move forward, carefully, looking for the loose gems at their feet. And the best jewels are always the surface ones, because, if they are still intact, sitting loose on the desert floor after the ancient volcanic pipes carried them up and spit them out, you can be sure that they have no occlusions or fractures in them. They're often near-flawless. Even giants."

I still could not understand why the sand would just sit there and not fritter around. Why was this demarcation so obvious and abrupt?

"It's the water again," Chad explained. "Anywhere you have landforms, you have water – rainfall. Maybe not this year or the next, but sooner or later. And whatever sand finds its way to the top of a relief, eventually it gets washed out, down to its final bed. It's estimated that the Empty Quarter may be as much as one hundred metres thick in places."

"So where there's sand, there's lots of it," I said.

"Yeah, except that the trick is to figure out the geology *beneath* the dunes."

"I thought there wasn't any?" Like most people, I had figured the great blank spaces on the globe's deserts simply marked undulating dunes, and not scientific ignorance.

Chad quickly corrected me.

"No, they are like the maps of the old days. All that pale yellow you see here? It means only 'Unknown' and not 'Only Sand.' Get it?"

So that rocky T. Rex of Yemen, that giant landform I had seen on my passenger-plane television monitor, was sleeping away on a fat bed of sand that hid diverse secrets. A whole other world, buried from view. Its mate? One could only speculate.

After a twenty-minute drive we pulled into the grounds of a luxurious hotel, The Bilqish. Its precincts were kept apart from the very sands that had occupied my thoughts by a large double-gated fence and lush plantings. Everything was green inside the fence, and I mounted the marble stair in the company of my four armed companions, through a wash of pink tree blooms and cheerful bird calls. The foyer was empty and cool and silent, except for the pad of our sandals on the immaculate marble floor. A concierge nodded to us from his little desk. I had that eerie and recurring sense of returning to yet another outpost of the international World Order. It was all here in spades: the obsequious uniformed doormen, the multilingual gift-shop operators, the spotless tile washrooms with the hand-dryers, cold drinking water served in crystal glasses. And a turquoise penumbra of a pool in which two tourists floated serenely by like white sea slugs. Fat cotton towels, frosty drinks at poolside, the infantile smell of coconut oil. ("Where'd you get *that* tan?" "Oh, the Empty Quarter.") The two men, Germans by the look of their haircuts, climbed clumsily out of the pool and exchanged their swimsuits under tiny towels for even skimpier tanning gear. Two women lay on their faces, with their tops loosened for the desert sun's full impact. Two hundred rooms and there were exactly five *farangi* tourists in the whole place, me included.

Not talking of course.

German, right?

Iqbal and Ahmed took a good eyeful before they went off to afternoon prayer. Ahmed left his AK-47 on the chair beside me for company. I noticed how their guns were always given a chair of their own at the table. The waiter came and I gave him my order. I peered over the patio wall at the women sunbathers and was disappointed to find that the two women were scary, something out of a George Grosz cartoon, or maybe Ralph Steadman. You don't see that any more. But there it was: a hard woman in her sixties, with a punk's purple hair and a black metallic bikini that exposed every ridge of her bony coccyx. This was beyond mutton dressed as lamb. This was box-horse dressed as Hello Kitty. What did the waiters and staff think, confronted every day by such apparitions? I covered my eyes when she took off her robe and belly-flopped into the pool.

Waammp!

I stared moodily at the loaded gun beside me. I contemplated my fresh lime juice and egg-salad sandwich in silence. The two German men threw robes on and sat down at a table nearby, and immediately ordered Heinekens with their lunch. I asked the nearest one, a wispy man of about fifty with the silky fingers of an accountant, why he'd come to Yemen.

"Yemen? We like za mountains. Und zi buildings. Ve go every year."

"To Yemen?" I was surprised. They all seemed so shell-shocked, so out of it. Like they'd made a clerical mistake with their air tickets, and woke up yesterday morning in the wrong country.

"No, different countries: Iran, Oman, Syria." He touched his wispy head. His hair was poofy, and bleached dry.

"I see," I said, although I didn't. "The mountains, again, you say?"

"Yes. Za mountains. Ve like za roads in zi mountains."

A new market niche: "Masoch Tours of St. Pauli presents the AK-500, a two-week self-guided tour of the world's greatest war zones. Experience earthquakes, public mutilations, and executions! Witness the birth of new Islamic republics! High-calibre jihads! Up-close and natural. Term policies included."

I sipped my drink and speculated on why all the German women tourists I'd seen in this country (there were no others but Germans) were graceless. Not just homely, either. Shrikes. From all the striking lookers parading about Frankfurt International, I would have expected to see legions of leggy creatures here, hiking about in their lederhosen.

Well, at least one, anyway.

How long were my guys going to pray? I ordered another soft drink (the beer did not entice me in these circumstances, at all) and looked on morosely as the two men slurped back into the pool like vanilla fudge. Then it was the turn of the two hard women to exercise, and they took no time beating the water into a frenzy, stroke after bloody-minded stroke. Their dogged awkwardness, even hostility, towards simple human grace and physical ease, was painful to watch.

You go travelling, after a hiatus of years, fully expecting that all these national stereotypes would have disappeared in the wake of massive pop-therapy and McCulture. And what do you find? It's worse than before.

"You have nice lunch?" Iqbal and Ahmed returned on cue from their supplications, looking far more refreshed than I felt. And Ali and Mo showed up too. The latter team had scored several pink bags of fresh qat. We were ready for the return ascent to Sana'a.

Now Ali drove. Why was it his turn? Was he working on his learner's licence? Ahmed sat in the front passenger seat, dishing out the qat buds. Ali the driver got his treat first, and soon built up a big lump of the drug in his left cheek. Now the abrupt road edge was on our right side, and to pass vehicles Ali was obliged to overtake on the blind side, pressing tight to the inside of the mountain wall. This was a total gamble. You either got free passage or an oncoming truck, as you came roaring round the bend. A surprise hand, either way.

"No thanks." I shook my head at Ahmed's offer of the herb, thinking I would preserve my focus for any upcoming photo opportunities. A heavy truck inched up the mountain ahead of us.

Ali took the plunge and aimed for the clear fifteen feet to the left, totally blind to whatever was approaching beyond the dark curve. I held my breath.

Nothing. We'd made it.

The men sat happily chewing, oblivious to these mute dramas.

Another truck. This time it was a belching oil tanker from the Hunt refinery. Ali didn't hesitate. Off we went for the long odds again. Our vehicle strained for that car-length patch of safety, a spot that might disappear in an instant. I helped him by holding my breath, thereby making our Land Cruiser lighter. It worked. Again we zipped back inside, only this time an approaching truck appeared above us, descending in low gear with a grinding blat of feeble-sounding brakes.

I quickly did the necessary mathematics: 16,000 pounds x 7% grade = Stopping Time ÷ Condition of Brakes + How Much Qat the Driver Has Consumed.

Answer: I'm back again in Vertigo Hell.

As we passed the truck driver I could see the man's left cheek glinting like a golf ball in the setting sun. It was apparent that all the drivers were chewing, and chewing big. Another truck, another clear shot at filling an inside straight. It was now clear why Yemenis didn't need to play cards. Every day was a long shot at making it home. Chew or be chewed.

"I'll have some of that now," I pointed to the pink bag. Ahmed happily handed me a selection of buds. Why should I be left alone in this crystalline-pure anxiety? Ali turned from the wheel long enough to welcome me to the fold with a greenish smile.

A few buds later and I too leaned out the window with calm curiosity at the sight of the oil tanker hanging over the mountain edge, its sixteen wheels still spinning. No blood on the smashed windshield. No open flames, either. How curious. Oh, and here was a knot of soldiers, hands behind their backs, thoughtfully investigating the scene. Now they were waving happily as we passed. Fat cheeks all to the left. Chipmunks with guns, I said to myself, mightily pleased with my wit. Yes, I told myself, this was the only way to go, when the drivers are all zonked.

Otherwise you're not on their level, and then who knows what could happen?

"So, who do you think is responsible?" Iqbal, who had taken only a few token leaves, shook them at me suggestively. He wanted to talk about work again.

"You mean Falconbridge?"

"Yes. I think, if somebody hires someone who is not fit for the job, who cannot fulfil his duties – tell me, *who* is responsible?"

The others sitting in the truck listened with unfeigned interest.

Cigarettes appeared. Rothmans Kings. With no health warnings.

"I think it is wrong to fire someone who simply makes a mistake," I said, trying to remember all those business books I'd bought and tossed. "I think it is important to say four things: I made a mistake. This was what the mistake was. This is how the mistake happened. This is what I will do next time instead."

"Yes, yes, yes," Iqbal waved his hands impatiently, as if he'd read the same books. "But what I am asking you is this: Suppose you tell someone, you must do this job *this* way, and the man *does* do the job this way, and another thing happens, and the man . . . who says to the man, that this job . . ."

He launched into his long hypothetical-but-not-really, as I looked out the window, watching the black volcanic cones flash by, waiting for the upshot of the man-story.

"... then if *this* man says to the other man, I was doing *this* all along ..."

Now I'd lost the thread, which man were we talking about now? Chuck or Iqbal? I didn't know.

And more, I didn't care. I wanted to talk about Man, not men. Man and God, and the Stars. The unforgiving Sky above and the shuddering earth below.

"Do you know?" I asked, after Iqbal had finished his circumlocutory interrogatory, "that the Americans have invented a computer machine, which they use to look for God?" I was thinking about the *Wired* article.

"No!" They chorused, shaking their heads in disbelief. But not too hard, for anything was possible with Americans.

"Yes. They think they can speak to God directly with electromagnetic waves. In the brain. *Waves.*" I made an undulating motion with my right hand. Ahmed interpreted this last as a request for more qat.

"And what did they find?" Ahmed prodded as I selected a fine bud.

"Americans. They love the machine. They fear the machine. They came to power with the machine. But who shall be Master?" I chewed thoughtfully. This qat was different than the last. I was turning into an aficionado. "Man or machine?"

"You think the machine rules them now?" someone asked.

"Even now," I whispered, "even now, satellites are passing overhead. Perhaps one is watching us at this very moment." We all looked up through the roof of the truck. "And somewhere, there are men inside the machine sitting before small televisions – perhaps even glancing at a book like the one I am writing – watching us chewing, these servants of the machine, and wishing they were here."

§§

We returned to the villa in Sana'a as the pink dust-laden sky bathed the city like an erotic bedlamp. A new shipment of sand was drifting overhead, bound for the Empty Quarter in a cloud of roses and apricots. I thought I was happy, buzzing around like a honeybee, until I heard someone in the office call Abdullah, Ahmed. If he was Ahmed, then who was Abdullah? I hovered by the fax machine, listening as they spoke together, trying to get it straight. *He* was Ahmed? If this one was Ahmed, then I had got everything wrong.

The funk took over. Everything was collapsing around me, a sinkhole appeared. The faces, the children, the lights of the town. Things began to uncouple, taking off without names.

I was last. The cloud of sand darkened and fell, heavy as night.

Chapter 10

Annals of the Epical Queen

A good sleep cures much. Today I was off to see Professor Yusuf Abdullah Sherbani, director of the Yemen department of antiquities. I was to look him up in his office after a quick tour of Sana'a's National Museum next door.

Abdullah greeted me in the narrow passageway of his temporary digs, squeezed between the jewel of the old museum, the former Imam's palace, and the dusty construction site where the future exhibit hall would go. He was bespeckled, owlishly urbane, with a few years of good lunches tucked in between the desert excavations. Charles Laughton with a tan, a man who appeared more than comfortable with middle age. The professor was accompanied by a young assistant, who looked like him but was far more massive: Maxi-me, I thought.

"So much equipment!" he exclaimed, looking at my cameras. "You are just like our Minister! Radio here. Telephone there." He clasped his hand to his chest at various points. "Equipment, here and here." He pointed between his legs. "Everywhere."

Everyone in the crowded little office laughed, including myself. This was an old politician's trick, and still a good one: Mention the Minister, your boss, poke some fun, and let everyone in on the joke. Mainly that you were well connected. After the preliminaries I asked him what he needed most for his department. There were no postcards for sale, I pointed out. The museum was dazzling but tiny, making it impossible for them to display but a wee fraction of their incredible history.

"All that will come," he assured me. "We have a budget of seven million U.S. for the new museum and the support of our president. What we really need are three things. One, continued democracy, freedom of the press. Two, security. Peace and law and order. Without security we have nothing, no protection for persons or property. Three, foreign investment."

"This book project of mine began because a Canadian company was inspired by the story of Sheba's gold," I began. "The Cantex crew found that Sabean alabaster plaque in the desert, near the gold-mine ruins and – "

"Gold! I have dug everywhere in Yemen, but I did not find any gold. *You* have the gold!" he snorted.

"Us?" I blinked, unsure where this was going.

"Your country has *one-sixth* of the world's sweet water!" His voice verged on the accusatory, and I began to feel faintly guilty watching his finger thrust upward.

"That's true," I admitted. Lake Ontario splashed outside my door, and I took it for granted.

"You see how hard we work in this country for water? You saw the new dam in Ma'rib?"

"Very impressive. What current projects are you working on now?"

"With the help of the American Foundation for the Study of Arabia, we excavated the temple of Awwam, what the people call Mahram Bilqis. Their president is Marilyn Phillips, the sister of Wendell Phillips."

"The famous archeologist?" A pinprick of recognition.

"Yes, he was a great adventurer, in 1950 and 1951. He fled Yemen after being accused of stealing artifacts and went to Oman. And, of course, he did not steal anything. A true hero."

Over lunch at Sherbani's, the same downtown restaurant we had visited before, Abdullah responded to my tight little cluster of questions about the continued and widespread force of the queen of Sheba's episodic story. Why was she so well known in world literature, and yet such a cypher for historians? Why had so many peoples made use of her, and yet no independent records existed of her reign? Why were there two divergent queen of Sheba traditions, Yemeni and Ethiopian, on top of all the variant tales from Jewish and Christian sources?

The professor had no hesitation answering.

"Of course the story of the queen is epical. I mean that it is used to confirm the authority of dynasties. You say you will be going to Axum, in Ethiopia, the site of the Ethiopian queen of Sheba. Well, Axum is a Yemeni word, and it is the name of a Yemen tribe who settled there after the fall of Saba, what you call Sheba. The coast, Eritrea, was not so advanced, and Arabs had traded there for a long time. They took the story of Sheba with them, these settlers. Even the original name 'Abyssinia' was an Arab tribal name; Ethiopia itself is Greek."

"And the language of Saba, of Sheba? The written characters? They say it came from north Arabia? What is their relationship to Arabic today?"

"Clearly ancestral. Look, you know there's a controversy over the origin of the Sabean script, whether it derives from Phoenician or not. But, the order of the South Arabian script is the same as Ugaratic, not Phoenician."

"I see." By *Ugaratic*, the professor meant the ancient Semitic port of Ugarit, modern Ras Shamra in Syria, like Tyre, a trading city and originator of its own writing system, *circa* 1000 B.C. In the early days, the invention of language was like the invention of bicycles or cars, there were lots of variations. Ugarit's had distinct features unique to it.

"Secondly, the number of letters in the South Arabian alphabet is twenty-nine." He paused and shot me a look. "That was *twenty-nine*, not twenty-seven."

"I see. Sorry, right, twenty-nine." The good professor was reading the cribbed notes I was taking from his mini-lecture – upside down and from six feet away – and proofing them while I furiously wrote. "Okay, got that. Yes, *twenty-nine* letters."

"But the Phoenician only has twenty-seven, whereas the older Ugaratic has *not less* than twenty-seven. Finally, the Greek and Phoenician alphabets are pronounced the same, but South Arabian is different. It's a stem system."

"So, the story of the queen of Sheba passed to the Ethiopians from Arab migrations. Like the story of Laertes passed from Troy to the founders of Rome? The passing of the torch, so to speak?"

"Exactly. They used the story to uphold their power. A new dynasty was created, the house of Menelik, the kings and queens of Ethiopia, which lasted for thousands of years."

৪৬

After a discussion on the merits of the local honey, we shook hands and left each other. I mulled over our conversation on the way back to the Cantex villa. The brief interview had thrown up a lot of hard questions, more questions than it had answered.

First of all, I was surprised that the professor hadn't brought up the ancient plaque the Cantex crew found in the country near Al-Jawf and delivered to his museum. Nor had he mentioned the site itself. Why not? I had started to talk about the old mines, and he had immediately gone into his thing about water being the real gold. Now this plaque was supposedly lost. Then again, if the relic had been lost by his staff, the director wasn't exactly going to trumpet the fact out loud, was he? Which meant that the plaque was truly lost. But how could they lose a twenty-five-pound alabaster plaque, unless somebody had stolen it? Was there a market for smuggled Yemeni antiquities? If there was, I'd never come across any mention of it. Most Muslims were hardly passionate about pre-Islamic things – they were considered almost taboo, in fact. I couldn't imagine an oil sheik proudly showing off his collection of pagan relics to his dinner guests. Who did that leave, since the Americans were avid mainly for pre-Columbian loot? Okay, maybe the Germans. Maybe there was an international ring operating that sold the stuff to German collectors. Germans *were* big on Assyria and Babylon, judging from the Berlin Museum's hoard.

Secondly, why this insistence that there was no gold? "I have dug everywhere in Yemen, but I did not find any gold!" Was that said to discourage looters, adventurers, collectors from poking about in the archeological sites of his country? Of course, there was disappointingly little gold on display in the museum, just the odd bit of jewellery, earrings and the like. Nothing like Egypt or even Mycenae.

When I got back to my room I took out the paper published in 2000 in *Arabian Archeology and Epigraphy* by the husband-and-wife team of Dr. John Greenough, geology professor, and Dr. Leanne Mallory, archeologist. I rubbed my eyes at the miniature size of the type – and the density of their findings – and began reading. Had I been grossly misinformed?

No, it was here all right: "Quartz veins at the ancient mine sites are typically 1–2 m across and appear vuggy [they have cm-sized holes in them]."

I paused and asked myself a question: And how are you feeling today? Vuggy.

I read on.

> Gold was readily observable in grey-stroked portions of
> veins adjacent to wall rock in a quartz vein at site ... brec-
> ciated vein samples from site 1 contain abundant visible gold
> flakes ... and samples from tailings dumps ran as high as 10
> ppm (10 g / metric ton = 0.3 Troy ounces per short ton)!

That final exclamation point seemed pretty clear. There was gold here, lots of it. What these scientists were saying is that the ancient miners had left lots of stuff still lying in the ground, and they hadn't been able to extract everything from the recovered high-grade ore with their primitive technologies. The researchers were not giving any firm dates associated with the finds, that was also clear. The interesting aspect of the report was the authors' conclusion that the gold smelting must have been done offsite (in the absence of found crucibles), with the silver content still intact, and that the whole business was somehow connected to Egypt's prodigious trade in precious goods:

> Geological similarities between the Yemeni gold camp and
> the New Kingdom Egyptian mine sites indicate that
> prospecting knowledge was widespread over the Near and
> Middle East by 1000 BCE. ... It is not known if the Yemen
> sites were populated by convicts, prisoners of war and/or
> slaves as in Egypt, but the layouts of the camps, and the size
> and paucity of the buildings and cemeteries suggest opera
> tional similarities.

But the most fascinating question of all had been baldly put by the authors:

> It is not known if the trade route existed because of the
> gold, or if the deposits were discovered as a result of
> through traffic.

They were suggesting that the impetus for the caravans might not have originated with the Omani frankincense trade after all, but – and just as consistently with the available evidence – perhaps it arose from the transport of gold bullion and its associated silver content!

Exactly what the Bible depicts in I Kings 10:

> And when the queen of Sheba heard of the fame of
> Solomon, concerning the name of the Lord, she came to
> prove him with hard questions.
>
> And she came to Jerusalem with a very great train, with
> camels that bare spices, and very much gold. . . .
>
> And she gave the king an hundred and twenty talents of
> gold, and of spices very great store. . . .

This gift equalled four and a half tons of gold, worth about US$40 million, even at today's "historically depressed prices." Yet this whole issue of local gold had been spurned by the good director with a flap of his hand. Why? Was it because, in the Quranic account, the emphasis lay on something altogether different? Was the real story about water, as he had insisted? From the Bible I turned to the Quran, the Sura of the Ant, chapter 27, with Solomon speaking to his courtiers:

> How is it that I see not the hoopoe? . . . In fact he was not
> far off, and said: I come to thee from Saba with true
> information. Verily I found a woman reigning over them to
> whom everything has been given, and she has a magnificent
> throne. I found that she and her people worship the sun. . . .

Solomon then gives the hoopoe bird a letter, addressed to the queen:

> In the name of God the merciful, very merciful. Be not
> rebellious towards me, but come to me submissively.

The queen sends Solomon a present as a test, which he rejects. Instead he commands his djinns, or desert spirits, to bring her throne to him, and it comes "in the twinkling of thine eye" while she travels to him.

When she arrived, she was asked: Is thy throne like this one?
She replied: As if it were the same! . . .

She was invited to enter the courtyard, but when she saw
it, she imagined it was water, and exposed her legs. He said:
It is but the glass paving of the courtyard.

She exclaimed: O my Lord!; verily I have wronged myself;
and make submission, with Solomon to the Lord of the
worlds.

For Muslims the main elements of Sheba's story are fabulous, mysteriously wrought. It's not about gold, but a transformative kind of magic. In fact, it's precisely about *rejecting* gold in favour of receiving a great spiritual treasure. The queen of Sheba comes with gold, seeking God. Perhaps the professor could not help but be shaped by his own traditions. As he proudly told me at lunch, he was a Sherbani too, a descendant of the ancient Sabeans. These were *his* ancestors we were talking about, and the Quranic version was *his* ancestors' tradition. Naturally, he'd stick to it.

I had already read numerous European archeological texts that attempted to decode the oblique Islamic tale, but I was far from satisfied with any of them. They seemed to favour placing the account in the context of pre-Islamic oral folktales, particularly in the absence of any dynastic records that put a woman on the throne of Saba at the relevant time. Bilqis, the traditional name for the queen of Sheba in Yemen, was a historical figure, *was* indeed a queen, but in A.D. 300, not 970 B.C. None of the archeological papers I had seen gave a good etymology for the four key elements that marked the Islamic account. Many authorities had also stumbled over the fantastic proliferation of Arabic literary texts of the eleventh and twelfth centuries A.D., which used the Quranic details to embark on romantic pastorals, adding the unsettling detail that the queen's legs were terrifically hairy and required a depilatory before Solomon would bed her.

The real problem was that no one has ever ascertained the historic (or ritual) event that *both* traditions were based on, since neither was even remotely contemporaneous with it. The Quran was dictated by the inspired Prophet Muhammed almost a thousand years after the Old Testament version, while the latter was itself compiled and edited late in the sixth century B.C. (*circa* 560 B.C.). With Solomon's reign dated to about 970 B.C., we are almost five hundred years off the mark here. And more importantly, with the compilation of the Bible we are outside the whole Wheel of the Age, since the semi-heroic Iron Age of 1000 B.C. was nothing like the classic world that succeeded it five centuries later, with its quiescent generation of Buddha, Zoroaster, Greek Stoic philosophers, and diligent Bible editors. Therefore, in the absence of any verifiably earlier accounts than these, I believed, we were obliged to see the original event *through* the key details that had survived. And these key elements were four, some unique to the Quranic version. And now I sketched them out, feeling like a detective speculating on motive and meaning, through motifs that repeated themselves.

The Hoopoe. This was the bird I had asked after in Taiz, an ubiquitous Old World crested lark, and native to Yemen. Why was it picked as the messenger-herald, and not another? It had to enjoy some special, obvious trait generally known from folklore or popular natural history. So this hoopoe was a *sign* of something. Was he like our robin, a sign of spring, of new life? Medieval Arabic tales of Sheba gave the hoopoe the job of finding water for Solomon after his djinns failed to find it, so it is likely the hoopoe was a harbinger of water, especially as it possessed a long curved beak, for digging up worms in damp soil.

A bird that could find water.

The Throne. The queen's throne was the key to the Quranic account. The hoopoe proudly informed Solomon that her throne was magnificent; and Solomon then confounded his djinns by asking them to bring it to him *before she arrived* – and "in a twinkling of an eye," it appeared. Its unexpected presence in Jerusalem compelled the queen to submit to the king. For a throne, it had three decidedly odd qualities: It was portable. It flew through time. And it was necessary for Solomon to obtain and install her throne in his palace *before the queen appeared.*

A throne that could fly.

The Glass Floor. This element of the story sounds like a classic conjuror's trick. What was the queen doing here, walking on a floor-sized mirror? Magicians like David Copperfield traditionally use large mirrors for tricking audiences when they do disappearing acts and saw people in half. But the queen thinks it's water; she doesn't know that it's a mirror. Solomon has to tell her, "It is but the glass paving of the courtyard."

What do we use mirrors for, traditionally? *To reveal what's really there.* A mirror that could see.

The Bare Legs. Note Solomon's reaction to the queen's discomfiture. She has been tricked into publicly exposing her legs. Is her host embarrassed? Is he surprised? No. Why not? Because he was *hoping* that's what he would see! His elaborate plan has worked: He's caught her. He has trapped the queen in phenomenal reality. She's been made corporeal.

A woman that was caught.

What is so striking about this Quranic account is the clear identity made between the hoopoe, the water-finding bird, and the queen the bird represents, for she is one who also "finds water." Solomon has decoyed the water-finding queen to his palace, with his shimmering glass pool. His installation of her throne in his palace before her arrival likely means that he dedicated an altar for the queen (as Solomon did for other religions for many of his foreign wives and concubines) *and that she came* – summoned forth by the great conjurer and lord of the djinns himself. Solomon was famous in the Middle East for being a great sorcerer, perhaps the greatest.

I recalled all I knew about Middle Eastern deities, the gods whose names were usually titles or circumlocutions, rather than proper names. Nameless out of a fearful respect for their taboo-power. The queen remains unnamed in both religious accounts, because she may never have been a historical personage at all but, more likely, a goddess. The Bible mentions Sheba in the Old Testament in no less than eight books, starting with Genesis, where the generations of Noah are listed (Genesis 10, Psalms 72, I Kings 10, II Chronicles 9, Isaiah 60:6, Jeremiah, Ezekiel, Joel). In the New Testament, too, in Luke 11 and Matthew 12. The Bible, which is so concerned with recording genealogy and true affinity in its lengthy lists of *begats* and family expulsions, is wholly silent on the name of the queen. So too is the Quran. Attempts to find a historical queen to match the event from Sabean dynastic records have also proved fruitless to date. There are no named queens in the Sabean account. Since there are more than six thousand stone and other written Sabean records preserved – far more records than Israelite, Phoenician, or Sumerian finds combined – it is certainly not from lack of hard data. The reticence comes from the fact that our nameless queen is likely *The Queen*, she who must always be referred to obliquely, like "The Lord," through roundabout metaphors. "The hoopoe's *friend*," or some such term, if ever. Her power is such that to invoke her directly, by name, is very bad manners, to say the least. Only a great magus like Solomon knows how to invoke her, and yet in the Quran even Solomon never calls her anything, either. Just *you*.

That's the negative evidence. What's the positive? How does the above scenario work in the historical context of the Sabean kingdom, with its rise as a warrior state around the time of Troy, 1000 B.C., and its ultimate downfall in 575 B.C.? Let's return to that thrilling question poised by the archeologist-geologist team of Mallory and Greenough: "It is not known if the trade route existed because of the gold, or if the deposits were discovered as a result of through traffic."

This is the ultimate question, always. It really asks, What starts history off, anyway? Is history accretive, happenstance, contingent? Does it simply collect itself around random events – say, a convoy of a few donkeys carrying firewood that eventually and naturally grows into a transworld trade route? Through *traffic*? The sheer mechanics of the ordinary business of moving commodities?

Or is history fundamentally *inner*-directed, the product of a shared vision? An *ideal* that communicates itself to its adherents (adherents in the widest sense of the word) through various material strategies it always transcends, turning its successes into additional symbols of that common vision? History as a creative yield, history *because of* the gold *thoughts*. Surely this was the view of people like the Incas and Aztecs, who couldn't comprehend the Spaniards' lust for raw bullion, when their sacred gold was already transubstantive and luminary.

For the Sabeans, history proved a source of raw intelligence, one that they encountered in its many guises, immediately. Some of the oldest Arabic words illuminated their world view better than the stone artifacts themselves. First the *wadi*, the seasonal river. Then there was the *sayl*, the flash flood that provided the only significant amount of rainwater the ancients would get in the year. How to contain the wadi's force, store it, and divvy it up? The *Arab*, in its original sense of nomadic herder, as opposed to the townsman farmer-warrior; not always someone to be opposed militarily, but certainly, from an ecological and ideological standpoint, someone to be resisted and denied. The *mukarrib*, the Sabean king, who was not a true king but rather a "federator," who must rally all the people for war, yet consult with his council. How to vest military authority and life-and-death power in one individual, while preserving the commonweal over generations? These words are a few of the transformative relationships that dictate and inform Sabean history.

In the reign of the great Mukarrib, Karrib il Watar (undated but possibly mid-seventh century B.C., judging from the script used in the war monuments he dedicated), the Sabeans marched out of their capital of Maryab eight times. They smashed their rivals south of Taiz, killed sixteen thousand at Awsan and razed its capital, took five thousand slaves from their conquests near Aden, laid seige in the land of Al-Jawf to the north (was the Cantex alabaster plaque torn from its original temple during one of these original depredations?), and then destroyed the rival dam works at Nashshan. According to French historian Jean-François Breton, the Sabeans spared only that part of Yemen lying in the highlands to the west, lands inaccessible to military devastation. Karrib il Watar also sent Sabean colonists across the Red Sea to Ethiopia.

What did they want with Ethiopia? What impelled them to leave a land they had just conquered? To seek a new home a thousand kilometres away, and a trip full of every conceivable danger?

The Sabeans brought with them to Ethiopia the South Arabian script, their religion of the moon and the sun, and the story of the queen of Sheba. I decided I would have to fly there, and find out what they were saying about her, some twenty-seven centuries later.

Chapter 11

The Genius of the Place

I staggered into the villa under the influence of yet another out-of-control Yemeni lunch. Sea bass, whole lamb shanks, forty-pound loaf of fresh bread, the works. Telling myself, as I looked for a couch in the sun to nap on, it was okay. Stuffing my face could be construed as a pre-emptive strike against future privation. After all, I was headed off to Ethiopia the morning after next, and who knows what they had to eat over there? If anything.

I had spent the day taking photos in the Sana'a National Museum with the kind permission of its saturnine and robust director. The recurrent images of those chubby enthroned goddesses, and especially a peculiar crescent-moon-and-solar-disk symbol carved on incense burners, done in a variety of local materials (alabaster, wood, limestone, and copper, but no gold), were now all busily reprogramming my brain into obscure, but painfully novel, neural pathways. I could feel it, a general electric hum emanating from my medulla oblongata.

Or maybe it was the altitude thing again. I was kind of dizzy.

"Where are you going now?" I had spotted Chad Ulansky stuffing cassettes into his pack. "You just got back here."

He turned his lean, field-burnt face towards me.

"Leaving for the field again. Ten days in, two off. That's the drill."

"So, do you get any training in, out there? Or do you just collapse in the tent after humping samples all day?"

"I stuff my pockets with rocks and go until they run out." He sighed.

"What do you mean? You use them like breadcrumbs? Like Hansel and Gretel, to find your way back?"

"Nah, for the village dogs. Rocks are the only language they understand."

"Who do you listen to?" I noticed his tapes were home-recorded.

"Van Halen, Rush. Anything loud. It's just so I can get some peace and quiet when I'm working. Otherwise I always have a whole herd of villagers crowding around me, watching my every move with total concentration and picking up every rock I hit like it's alive."

"At least you don't get lonely."

"*You* try going off to do your business in the bushes with a dozen villagers in your face, stepping on your heels! They watch me do *everything*!"

"That's not how I pictured your job, somehow."

He waved his earphones at me.

"These are a geologist's best friend!" They went into the sack too.

꙰

The next morning the office staff flew into a frenzy. Maps were rolled and unrolled; men appeared whom I'd never seen before, scribbling notes and checking the blazing-red landforms on the computer screens; a fellow paraded about with a thick yellow GPS antenna sticking out of his backpack like a lost Martian; Iqbal cracked out orders in an increasingly hoarse voice; the accountant carefully parcelled out thick wads of grey two-hundred-rial banknotes; armed drivers jumped from roof to roof of the Land Cruisers, securing old-fashioned Turkish mattresses with nylon cords; and the phone rang and rang. The blue-uniformed security man opened the steel gates, and with a roar the engines came to life and they were all gone.

The crew were headed back to the new area, Wadi Qataba, which Chuck had surveyed the week before. The one with the weird gossan in it, and the hushed intimations that it contained the delicious new Cantex grail, platinum and palladium. Now we could only wait, and see what they brought back this time.

I took the opportunity to sort out my flight plans and visa for Ethiopia. I had to see for myself why these ancient Sabean colonists had crossed the Red Sea about 650 B.C., traversing a thousand kilometres of the most violently disrupted terrain imaginable, to set up a little kingdom in the middle of the great Ethiopian plateau. My theory was that their original impulse was cognitive, not material. Although how this could be proved was beyond me. Ahmed Mossen – the Ethiopian-born driver who looked like Joe Louis, except paler – went with me to the embassy.

It was filled with beautiful Ethiopian women waiting for their transit documentation, and it was hard not to stare at their bare faces, the only female ones I had seen in Yemen for the past month. Their faces were luminous and unmannered, and if they were wearing makeup it was applied too skilfully to detect. On the way out, with my visa triumphantly in hand, I asked Ahmed about the country. He told me something interesting:

"You hear the news? Yesterday they announce big find in Ethiopia. Platinum and cobalt. Close to where you go in Axum. They sign agreement for big mine."

The epical lady, I thought immediately. It looks like she's in Ethiopia.

And Chuck? He telephoned the villa that night from his hotel, somewhere on the Indian Ocean, looking for Chad. His voice was faint, edgy with static. I asked him where he was, exactly, but he didn't seem to hear me.

"Chad sent me a fax saying they were going to change the plans, hey? You know what plans?"

"I'm sorry, Chuck, I'm alone here. They're all out in the field."

"I see, okay."

"About the plaque, Chuck? I met with the museum director, and he never mentioned it."

"That's because they never got it."

"I'm sorry? What?"

"We gave it to another geologist to give to them, and we just found out he's still got it."

"Oh, I see."

There were long pauses between us. I couldn't tell if it was the Maldives telephone system or if Chuck was distracted. I hung up without finding out where he was exactly, but if it was on a tropical beach, I wanted to be there too. I had discussed future trips with Chad before he left for the field, trips that were all on the water. By the water. Through the water. Not like here, with water sputtering through the taps at odd hours and that dizzying, cloistered feeling of the ex-pats, always dreaming of somewhere else. Or there either, that tragic land across the Red Sea.

Was Chuck crazy, trying to get investors to come out here to this dry barrenlands with their money? A country where foreigners had stopped coming in droves since 1998, when four kidnapped tourists were killed in a shootout with police? Chuck was betting the company store on making a deal in Yemen. Had he lost it? Or did he know something nobody else knew? The entire staff, down to the drivers and guards, knew the whole situation was risky. They knew you not only had to find the gold, you had to be a superb diplomat to get it out. Chuck was playing long odds, the long-odds search for Sheba's gold.

Ahmed told me how it was. It was like this:

"Okay, the poor people in the village. It takes more than two men to carry the heavy copper wire for the geophysical up to the mountain. The mountain is steep. Even a donkey won't go up. So the local people, they want to work. Even five hundred rials a day is good. It is their land. And Falconbridge say, 'No, we no give you money.' Even though it is little money, five hundred rials for twenty people for one, two months. That's all. You have to know how to deal with the people, otherwise you get nothing."

I could understand his criticism of Falconbridge, for somewhere in the office I'd seen a copy of an official handout the company had prepared for distribution to the local villages, a long, carefully worded manifesto that contained numerous rhetorical questions like, *Do you understand that you will not be paid money for jobs that do not exist?* And instructions, such as *Do not encourage the villagers to talk. They must listen and understand!* It had a harsh, peremptory tone. The authors had come here from South Africa. Was this South African business culture talking? Was it only a coincidence that the sole heavy-metal mining company successfully operating here in Yemen was ZincOxy, a U.K. company with three hundred years of British diplomatic experience behind its business practices?

I was somewhat confirmed in this suspicion when Iqbal called me down that afternoon.

"Lah-ree! Film people to see you!"

Descending the marble staircase, I found a young gentleman in immaculate cream slacks and a fresh navy shirt, as if he had just stepped off the plane from a shopping trip in Abu Dhabi. He appeared to be Indian. Plummy voice, confident air.

"How do you do?" He shook my hand. "I understand you're writing a book about the queen of Sheba."

Ben Hirsi was a documentary filmmaker with Felix Films, a native-born Yemeni based in London, who had been interviewed by the *Yemen Times* the same week their journalists had talked to me about poetry and the story of Bilqis, in Taiz. Hirsi had just returned from a shoot on the jungle island of Suqutra, far off the Yemen coast.

"We just finished up the job, actually. What a place! Unbelievably primitive! Pristine. Huge insects, fantastic birdlife, the trees. It was totally alive. We saw this thing crawling, and my researcher says, 'Oh, look, it's a flesh-eating millipede!' and the villagers went crazy when they saw it, smashing it with sticks, telling us its bite was worse than ten thousand scorpions. They bite you, then they eat you! And the people. We went to these caves. People were living there with the skulls of their ancestors. And they still make fire by rubbing sticks together.

"We went around the coastline in a small boat, not a dhow, a dugout you know, and the waves were huge, so we had to pull into shore for three days, running out of food, and the local people had never seen white people before. You should have seen them when we got the generator working."

I nodded benignly. But inside I was deeply envious. It didn't matter a whit that my friends back home would think I had been on a grand adventure. The Maldives, Suqutra. The truth was, there was always a greater adventure out there, wasn't there? More hot action waiting around the next bend, more banzai joy out there somewhere, beckoning you onwards, *more life*. A new beginning . . . to behold, to become. To beget.

The Epical Queen, as irresistible and insatiable as the transitive verb, *to be* . . .

৩৫

The night was warm and the villa courtyard sweet with flowers and I was thinking about Chuck Fipke's brain.

I had sent the guard out to buy mango juice. Now I sat alone on the stone steps of the compound and reviewed my impressions of Chuck, derived both from direct observations and from his impact on his staff.

"He's got some deep plan for me, but I don't know what it is," Chad had said to me on more than one occasion. *Deep plan.*

What I realized (and this was not true of many people I'd encountered) was that, inside the skirt-chasing, party-loving, and clever hard-working businessman, there was this fathomless *intelligence* at the controls, a force to which these other attributes had attached themselves like loyal but mischievous crew members. It had hatched out of a farm kid from Alberta, this thing. And it seemed nigh unstoppable. The Arabs sensed it too.

The Greeks called this enabling force *genius*, the tutelary spirit. In Chuck's case it seemed to operate on the order of fifth-dimensional thinking, a force plotting out his next moves in chesslike hyperspace. It was this hyper-intelligence that his multicultural staff – Western, Ethiopian, Arab, Indian, South African – sensed, respected, even feared. Not the man, mind you, he was human enough. This other entity was beyond quotidian experience. That it dwelled within the hyperkinetic body of a cowboy rock-troll only added to the mystery.

It confounded even a man of Iqbal Jailani's keen intelligence. Before he left for the Indian Ocean, Chuck had looked up at a mountain and publicly announced, "Do the grid-sampling this way, two hundred yards apart, southwest lines top to bottom."

Then he was gone, his words left ringing in the air.

Now, after more investigation, the operations manager had found compelling reasons to amend the pattern to south-southwest. Logic had spoken. Yet they didn't know what to do, except follow Chuck's earlier directive. Blindly. They could do nothing else. For they knew in their hearts, they had not seen what he had seen.

I was also thinking about Arabs, and their long chronicle on this huge peninsula. They resolutely claimed, many of them, to be able trace their origins back fifteen hundred years and more, beyond that dim time-line where even the Windsors got into serious trouble. Certainly the commonest villager knew his ancestors' names and history, to six generations or better.

The Arabs also travelled enormous distances. A current newspaper identified two Yemeni Bedouin tribes tenting atop the ruins at the tourist site of Luxor in Egypt. Drought hit the highlands unpredictably, and masses of men moved out for new pastures in organized concert. The ancestors of the present emir of Abu Dhabi had descended on an oasis on the Gulf coast, two hundred years ago. Now they were successful shopping-mall merchants and hoteliers. And as for the roadside vendors outside Sana'a, waiting for scarce custom under their filthy tarps, the Winter of Compunction exacted its terrible toll, yes. But something told me they would endure, hanging on to their lands with a supernatural tenacity. Their relationship with "ancient history" was immediate, and intact.

As for us in the West, we respected only the future. Our past was mere mummery, a show suitable for parody, an attic trunk opened for costume parties: See how far we've come from all that nonsense? Oh, certainly we'll dig here and there, for quick lessons, for useful household hints. But basically we agree with Henry Ford, it's bunk. And as for ancient history, it's an expression of disdain. Double bunk. That's ancient history, my dear. *We're* already packing, getting ready to leave the house and all its mouldy contents for the auctioneers to hammer down.

I was thinking about Yemen too. This spiritual place, the life of this land. Much of it was invisible, to be found neither in the ancient ground nor in the black, zodiacal sky overhead. A contemporary poem I discovered in a massive tome on Yemen in the Cantex office happily explored this unseen expanse:

Now I've done with silence
And with those private outpourings
I'll go out
Stick myself on the gum trees
in the ground
Stick myself to the long noses
and the salty leaves
I'll go in ...
I'll go out.
... Then I'll draw on it the circle of light
with a piece of black coal.

– Abd al-Rahman Fakhr, *Yemen: 3000 Years of Art and
Civilization in Arabia Felix*

Maybe Yemen wasn't meant for the twentieth century, or the century
after that.

Maybe it was a place for the twenty-fifth, when man had finally conquered the machine.

Interregnum

I telephoned my brother in Canada from the villa, to tell him I was leaving for Ethiopia in the morning.

"That's cool . . . Guess where I'm headed for this summer?"

"Where?"

"Outer Mongolia," Vernon said crisply. "For a month, by myself. Endless plains, clear rivers, sexy women. I'm going to do a book about our ancestors."

"Our ancestors?"

"You know, our grandmother Mary? Mom always said she had the Mongolian eyes. Those Tartar rapes and all."

"I see. What's the book going to be called?

"In Search of Genghis Khan."

"And the theme?"

"Oh, you know, it's one of those search-for-the-Father journeys."

Ahmed Mossen drove me out at four in the morning. The Sana'a airport emerged slowly from the bleak dawn, a thin scattering of buildings in the hollow of a four-hundred-million-year-old moonscape. Black volcanoes rose behind the searchlights, indifferent and aloof. A cold breeze blew steadily. Were the past and future the same thing? Was the present merely an odd dream flitting brightly over the rocks?

In a country of believers like Yemen, it was impossible not to believe in God. Travelling into the West, it was impossible not to believe in the machine. As for the machine, it only believed in itself.

Suddenly I got it. He *was searching for the Father.*
That meant I *was searching for the Mother.*
But then, where better than in Africa?

PART TWO

Axum

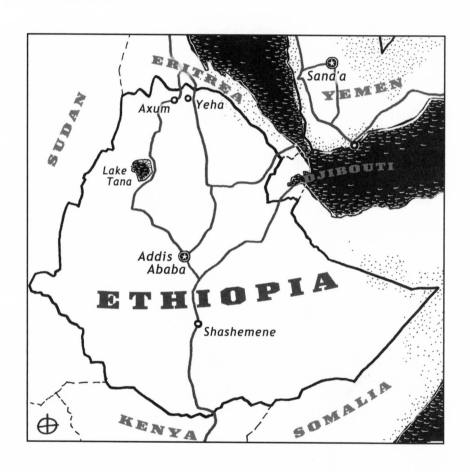

Chapter 12

Kurtz, He Not So Dead

Before the flight to Addis Ababa, Ethiopia's capital, Yemen security frisked all the European and American travellers thoroughly, patting them down, checking under their tams and baseball caps, even looking pointedly into their beards. The soldiers removed the usual assortment of Swiss army knives, letter openers, laptop peripherals, and other oddments that appeared suspect under their two-camera X-ray machine. They confiscated a dinner fork from the bag of the man behind me.

"They think I'm going to hijack the spaghetti?" He commented sourly. One camera monitor showed a black-and-white image of our luggage contents, the other a colourized picture that measured density or temperature, and rendered it accordingly in hot pinks and greens. My film rolls were pink, I noted sadly.

Meanwhile, the bearded and wild-eyed nationals on the same flight got warm handshakes and the happy grins of welcome aboard. The men, that is. The guards were not so lax with the local women. Many of the black-robed female travellers were ordered to open their purses so the soldiers could rummage through them at will, and I could not help wondering if this was the authorities' not-so-subtle way of registering disapproval at the mere fact of their departure. These passengers were already draped out of social existence in their voluminous folds of black cotton, including tappy patent death-shoes and piratical eye-screens, covered in black to the point where many also wore long black gloves, the kind once favoured by Surrealist models. How Man Ray would have loved this scene!

As I sat brooding on the perennial question of national culture, a fiftyish businessman with a barrel chest and a sunburnt nose approached me. Blinking hard, he asked me to read his ticket for him. He had the pale, colourless eyes of someone who had seen much but knew he was going to heaven anyways, as long as he just kept on going and didn't dally. I shot a glance at his beard. Gingery, slightly unkempt, but hardly the beard of an illiterate. A Mennonite missionary maybe, going slowly blind in Africa?

"Excuse me, but unfortunately I lost my glasses," he explained, blinking again at the proffered ticket with red-rimmed eyes. "A few days ago, and I cannot read a thing."

We were on the same flight. I took him for a German, a Bavarian southerner maybe, hale and schnappsy. But Marek, as he introduced himself, was a Pole from Gdansk. We were obliged to sit together when, just before take-off, the Ethiopian crew of the Fokker aircraft instructed us all to move up.

"Please all passengers move forward to the front of the plane, for balance."

We jumped up to comply, unwilling to be left behind in the now-treacherous rear of the aircraft. Marek told me he was the local representative for a steel company based in London. He had started out in the Polish merchant marine, one of the few ways to leave the then-communist country with ease, and came to Africa with his first wife in the early 1980s, to the Sudan.

"I stayed in Khartoum six years, and Djibouti four. Now I travel between Addis, Sana'a, and Cairo. We get our steel from Russia and Ukraine, and ship it through the Black Sea. Last month we had a real disaster, a ship with fifteen thousand tons of good steel is late getting into Aden. Six days later, the ship that was supposedly carrying our cargo sinks near Cyprus. The crew has all their luggage, personal papers, all ready for rescue when the British navy arrives."

"So the crew hijacked your steel."

"Yes, only we can't prove anything. We're insured, thank God, but investigators from the insurance company cannot find anything suspicious, except that the log book is not saved from the 'disaster' – 'too busy saving themselves!'"

"So they can't say where they were for six days."

"That's right. Unaccounted for."

"And the steel?"

"Sold to a nearby country. Syria, I think."

"And how much does the captain get? For the steel?"

"Who knows?" Marek calculated. "One million five hundred thousand dollars – less discount. One million plus the value of the boat. Good business."

"So it's hard to make money out here?"

"No. You have to find out what you like to do. For two years, for example, I was a shark fisherman. I had two boats, we went out to the Red Sea. We used long lines with big hooks. I poured the cow's blood into the water. The hooks were bare except for a couple. We attached them to empty plastic barrels and we would come back the next day. The sharks would always be dead already, twisted. They would break their necks trying to get away from the hook."

"They were what, small sand sharks?"

"No, huge ones. Tiger sharks, hammerheads. For the liver, you know. We would get up to seven thousand dollars for a barrel of the oil from the livers."

"For health products?"

"No, mainly for jet planes – for lubricant. Shark oil is the best lubricant there is for high-heat machinery. But my wife made me quit this business."

"She was worried about you getting eaten?"

"The smell. You have to cook the livers very slowly, in a pot. It doesn't smell great."

We talked about Poland, the fact that the winters were ameliorating in the northern hemisphere over the last few years and whether this was a good thing. I mentioned Joseph Conrad. I told him I thought *Heart of Darkness* was about the almost inhuman driving-force behind history. That there was growth, energy – and decay, moral and economic collapse – and the "colonial experience" was but a commentary on this question from the centre line. Nations rise and fall, but no man can say which and when.

"Conrad, yes," Marek nodded. "It's funny that you should mention that book, because I have a friend, Kurzen, almost the same name, and it's because of him that I lost my glasses."

He paused, glanced at me, concluded (I supposed) that I would be receptive to his story, and allowed himself a little shudder of recollected hysteria before he continued. We were flying twenty thousand feet above the Red Sea now, and I briefly wondered how many giant sharks were still cruising the limpid waters below.

"It's like this. I don't suppose you know Djibouti, but it was a French protectorate, and the only thing it had to sell was salt, from the salt pans – you have seen them from the air – and the port facilities itself. In the old days, before the war between Ethiopia and Eritrea, it was quiet to the point of extinction. But with the closing of the port of Massawa in Eritrea, the Ethiopians had to get supplies through the south, and now Djibouti gets six or seven ships a week. And also the foreign-aid programs. That's how my friend Kurzen came, to work on a project. You know, Bob Geldof and all that?"

"Yes, there was much publicity."

"Well, the brand-new trucks arrive in the height of the rainy season, to take food inland to the hungry people, but they get stuck in six feet of mud, and so they leave the trucks: 'Last one to leave please switch off the engines!' The food, marked *Not for Commercial Sale*, ends up in the shops, of course. A research paper estimates that only 7 per cent of the shipment goes to the people, the rest gets grabbed up by operators on the take and everybody gets a cut. Then the aid people go somewhere else politically exciting and profitable. But Kurzen stays."

"In Djibouti?"

"Yes, in Djibouti."

"Why?"

"The usual reason. A girl."

"Of course."

Marek sipped at his plastic tumbler of Sprite before continuing. I watched the sparkle of bubbles giggling in the intense morning sunlight at thirty-five thousand feet. Distant chasms below. The rifts of the Ethiopian massif.

"A girl. The girl is of course very beautiful, a half-caste, beautiful as only a half-caste can be. There are many different types here. The girls from the south with their fine little wrists and thin ankles, you could snap them like matchwood, with one finger."

"You mean the tall ones, like the Masai?"

"No, the Masai are well-proportioned," he smacked his lips appreciatively, "but this girl was really something. Her father was a French soldier and her mother, from the local people but a respectable trading family . . . So he tells me, after the wedding, in so many words but not directly – we still do some business – that he is not happy. But he does not say why."

Marek paused, looked down at the coast shimmering in the littoral light.

"She wants him to take her to America? She runs off with a lieutenant from the Foreign Legion?" I tried to guess at the outcome.

"No, the Foreign Legion, they're a bunch of crazy guys, not normal. My friend is *too* normal, but some women *like* that. So finally, I have business in Djibouti, I go out for a beer with my friend. He has another and another, and let me tell you, in Djibouti the beer is six dollars a bottle, so if you are getting drunk you must be very serious about something."

"And he told you?"

"That her shit stinks."

He looked at me appraisingly.

"I'm sorry?"

"That he could not bear the smell of her in the bathroom."

I shook my head, trying to imagine their living quarters in Djibouti, the heat, the primitive plumbing. Nothing came, really.

"That was it?" I mumbled.

"Yes, I didn't know what to say either. I began to think of my friend, his past. Was he always this crazy? Did he know anything of women before he married? Was he developing some obsession, a mental disorder?"

"Did he want you to go and, uh, *verify* his complaint? To justify leaving her?"

"I don't think so. He only wanted to talk. Anyways, I was not drinking too much, and it's lucky for us. Because after we left the café, he is walking on the pavement, and suddenly for no reason he jumps out on the road to cross, without looking either way, and a car comes and hits him. It doesn't run over him, but it knocks him down hard. And I have to carry him myself to the hospital. He is completely unconscious, and blood is coming from his ears and mouth."

At this turn in the story, Marek's face grew stricken. Plainly the shock of the event was still with him, deeply etched into his features. That, and the physical strain, the stupendous effort, carrying the victim all the way to the hospital, had cost him, and left their mark. I could imagine the silent crowds watching them go by. One bleeding, limp, the other staggering wild-eyed through the streets. White men in Africa.

"After an hour or so, he wakes up. And of course he has no memory of anything, not the bar, not the walking. But the story only, of meeting me and the bottle of whisky I brought him."

"So he was okay?"

"I don't know. The hospital, well, you know how it is. Dust, thieves, old medicines. I stayed with him, and he complains to me. He insists, 'I can't taste this food!' He is almost angry, although I think he is lucky to be alive."

"So he lost his sense of taste from the accident? Permanently?"

"No, his sense of smell. Can you believe that? The doctors, of course, don't know anything. That's how I lost my glasses."

"In the accident."

"In the hospital. Looking after him, playing doctor." He snorted, then shook his head.

"So, your friend Kurzen. He'll be happy now. Now that he's lost his sense of smell."

"No," he smiled thinly. "I don't think so."

"It's maybe a big strain to be married to the most beautiful girl in Djibouti," I ventured.

Marek shrugged and pulled on his beard. He stared out the window at the approaching coastline. Now he appeared as a professor of postcolonial studies, a man who had finished his lecture and was returning to his little study, preoccupied with his thoughts.

Below us we could make out the isosceles of Ethiopia's brown-and-green fields. They grew more variegated and piecemeal as they climbed the burgeoning highlands and aimed for the highest peaks, in disregard of gravity and all good sense.

Chapter 13

Lucy in the Sky with Suitors

An aquarium of pure air. Purple frangipani glowing like LSD trails in the sky. I have stepped into a Jimi Hendrix cover. Addis. Luminescent faces, taxis flowing molten yellow over the roundabout. In the outdoor café by the airport parking lot, the drivers sit quietly, delicately eating chocolate cake with shared forks, sipping *makiatos*, short lattes in china cups. I buy a bottle of Ambos, a carbonated spring water, for the fire of its yellow-green label.

The bottle glows too. My fingers are brilliant. In the intense light of the high plateau up here everything glows, blooms like a fever. I walk to the taxi like a man who has learned to see the fire at the heart of all living things. Who sees all things are alive. The cab is a lumpen Mercedes that might once have ferried Willy Brandt around; it wheezes out of gas at the bottom of the first hill, but I don't mind. The driver pours in another quart from the emergency Pepsi bottle in his trunk, and we're on our way again. When I pay him, he'll buy enough gas to get him back to the airport again. It's that close here; I can see it myself without the statistics, thank you very much.

But then everything glows, turns like a wheel, on fire. I order fresh orange juice the minute I check into my hotel. In the courtyard I am surrounded

by birds and coral trumpet flowers. The girls folding laundry are beautiful.
I am happy.

Organized religion bores me. Almost as much as *Wired*'s vision of high-
tech heaven. But it's Sunday afternoon in Addis, the first day of Lent, and
the shops are closed and Addis Ababa is nothing if not churches. The north
of Ethiopia where this sprawling capital of five million people lies, spreading itself over the lower slopes of the Entoto Mountains, is Christian, and
the south, Muslim and pagan-animist. Somehow the queen of Sheba, who
began her camel journey in the Old Testament, then walked in her bare,
pretty feet through the pages of the Quran, has made it to this land of
devout Orthodox monks and beheaded martyrs. With a baby. And a name.

For here she appears in the *Kebra Negast*, the Glory of Kings, the
national epic written in the fourteenth century A.D. in the ritual Ge'ez language. Ge'ez is the Semetic linguistic predecessor to Amharic, the modern
language spoken by the late Emperor Haile Selassie and his people. Stories
of the queen's life abound, a potent mix of political savvy and religious
insight, and the main thrust of them is that the queen of Sheba was in fact
a native Ethiopian princess called Makeda, who travelled to the court of
Solomon from the ancient capital of Axum, and had a baby son with the
king, to be named Menelik. Menelik grew up to manhood, visited his father
Solomon, and with some disaffected adventurers from the Jerusalem court
stole the Ark of the Covenant and brought it back home to Axum, a town
five hundred kilometres north of Addis. It is with Menelik that the dynastic line ending with Haile Selassie began. Again, as with Bilqis in Yemen, the
dates make no sense; the historical Makeda arrived on the scene hundreds
of years too late for a big date with Solomon.

Addis was quiet on this Sunday afternoon. I walked by a Greek
Orthodox church; it was empty, but the gate was open and the caretaker let
me in, and it was exactly like the Greek Orthodox churches at home: the
blue vaulted ceiling with the gold stars, the Last Judgement in red and blue,
the heavy velvet drapes with holy chalices hand-stitched in gold thread. The
last time I was in one of these places they were burying my father.

In the St. George Cathedral down the street, I was the only person to go
through the ticket booth to see the adjoining museum. A little elf with large

ears led me through the dark passages, flipping light switches and directing my attention to the crowns of Haile Selassie and those of his numerous and august-looking relatives. Selassie had been crowned in the cathedral. The royal family loved their crowns and parasols, it was obvious. Parasols made of that same blue and purple church velvet with the heavily embroidered gold thread. A Victorian-era relic? Much of the display had to do with the last Italian-Ethiopian War of 1935, blunderbusses and bayonets, a battle that seemed of great consequence to the Ethiopians. The British had retaken the country from the invading Fascist Italians with the help of local fighters in 1941, after five years of occupation and some plundering, and Selassie entered Addis in triumph on camelback. But of thirty more recent calamities, there was nothing. Where was the loss of Eritrea? The loss of Somalia? The loss of Djibouti? The losses of the great famine of 1984? The loss of the emperor, smothered to death by a pillow in the night by agents of the Derg, and losses of the civil war against the Derg, the militaristic socialists, in 1989? Where was the display about the new battle against Eritrea in June 2000, which caused thousands of land mines to be scattered on the borders?

Marek, the Polish steel-broker, had told me of seeing mummified Ethiopian bodies strewn like sausage casings on both sides of the Djibouti highway after the last war, desiccated by weeks lying out in the equatorial sun.

"Which war was that?" I had asked him, and he'd shrugged. What was so special about the 1930s Italian war?

Selassie's body was not in the St. George's Cathedral grounds. It had been moved to private grounds at the request of his family, but the relics of his long reign, chief of which was an enormous carved throne, at least twelve feet high, and which he of all people would have needed a ladder to mount, occupied the central place of honour in the adjacent museum.

The cult of Haile Selassie, the Lion of Judah, had become prominent in the same era that spawned the Big Brother dictators, the hot radio-screamers of the black-and-red 1930s, and I like most people vaguely knew that Selassie's cult had continued to thrive in the millenarianism of the Rastafarians of Jamaica to this day. This bearded little gnome with his fancy blue-velvet umbrellas had survived Mussolini and the rest of the bad guys, apparently with the help of rusty muskets and sabres, judging from the

Imperial Guards standard issue on display; and more, he had gone on to a glory few politicians dream of (or maybe they do). Deified by a cult that claimed him as a kind of black Jesus, only martial. This St. George's Museum was like a large and dusty curiosity shop, and I wouldn't have been at all surprised to see a stuffed Italian soldier in the next cabinet, with mouldy straw spilling out of a hole in his gut, representing the spaghetti of his last meal before a glorious patriot used one of these spears as intended.

Intrigued by this weird largesse of artifacts, that afternoon I hired a young driver, Johannis Aychew, to take me up to Entoto Maryam, St. Mary's Church, in the suburbs above Addis. The Ethiopians were famous since classical Greek times for their piety, and I wanted to witness an Orthodox ceremony, and to study the famous exterior of mural paintings depicting the lives of the national saints. I wanted to see a real living religion in action. Johannis drove well, considering the number of potholes.

The church was perched atop a twelve-hundred-metre mountain that had been replanted with thick groves of eucalyptus trees from Australia, giving it a sylvan, festive air. Johannis's car, a Russian Lada bought in the great used-export-car market in Amsterdam, chugged up the steep hill and shuddered uncontrollably over the Entoto road washouts, but Johannis was confident we'd make it to the summit. In the golden light of the late afternoon, the women descended past us in pairs and threesomes, loaded down with their forage. Some carried great jars of water, others the bundles of broken firewood that they were officially allowed to pick only from deadfalls. There was a sweetness to the light and an open warmth to the people – or was it the same thing? For the millionth time I wondered if the natural environment shapes us, as surely as plastic-injector moulds shape milk jugs.

St. Mary's Ekido was a pentagon of wood surmounted with odd gold finials, surrounded on the outside grounds by groups of white-robed penitents, both men and women, who prostrated themselves and reverently kissed the stone entrance gates, circling the building to perform their acts of silent devotion. No one seemed to be venturing inside the building, if indeed the doors were open. Strange wailing music issued from the speakers. A hypnotic blend of pagan African tribal melodies and Orthodox devotional chorale echoed across the hillsides.

The effect was fantastic. The golden cake of the church, the recumbent, sloe-eyed pilgrims, arrested in poses taken from Doré's *Purgatorio*, the serial music that kept building to an unrealized climax, the clouds of incense, burnt cinnamon and violets, heaving in great blue masses towards the cupola of dying day. The intensity of belief charged the air with sharp electricity.

"You want to go up?" Johannis asked me.

"Up?" I gazed back at him with alarm. The sky was hot pink overhead.

"The road, it keeps going." He noticed my doubt. "Not too far."

The summit was green with grass and fresh with alpine forest mist. Children skipped in the sunshine. I hadn't seen a full blade of grass in many months, and I had forgotten the pleasure of walking freely on soft turf. We were up about 2,800 metres, with Addis below us at 2,400 and the panorama of Ethiopia stretching away into an unbroken series of purple ranges and brooding, still volcanoes. A drumbeat sounded from a nylon backpacker's tent. Intense, unmusical *boomps*.

Haihuh hoho! Haihuh hoho!

"Come. See the American!" The children cried, beckoning us onwards. "Take pictures!"

Here's a bit of Last Days, I told myself. Cautiously, I approached the tent, camera at the ready. The drumming came from a set of bongo-style drums, only bigger. The children opened the flap of the tent wider. A white guy sat inside, his back to us, hammering away with all his might.

Haihuh hoho!

He wore a white shirt-gown and the big white-cotton dread-thing on his head, and he ignored my photo flashes while he chanted and banged away as if his life depended on it. Before him sat a framed colour portrait of the Late Emperor Himself. Candles burned in the tent.

"He has been here for two days," the children told us in remarkably good English. The country is starving, but everybody's bilingual, I said to myself. I snapped off another picture. The Rasta took no notice of me, just kept chanting. *Haihuh hoho!* "He drinks only mineral water and orange juice. No food."

"What does he say?" I whispered.

"It is not in our language," the children shrugged.

Around us the edges of the vast volcanic dish of Addis began to twinkle in the closing light like a trembling flower filling itself with new dew. The city had spread itself like brilliant pollen on the slopes of the Entoto Mountains; now the flower was closing up. This was the sister of the Sabean kingdom, all right. The place to which all earthly treasures had come to rest, in the fullness of an epoch.

⚭

The next day I wandered over to the national museum to examine Don Johansen's spectacular 1974 palaeontological finds. Johansen was the anthropologist who had chosen to dig in Ethiopia rather than in Louis Leakey's bailiwick in Kenya, and in due course found "Lucy," the presumed ancestor to humankind with rather complete-if-diminutive bones, dating to *circa* 3.5 million B.C. The little hands were especially compelling evidence of our biological connection, for these were complete and seemed fully functional, like ours. Piano-player hands.

Lucy's tiny skeleton, a plaster cast of her bones actually, was laid out in the final sanctuary of the museum after a series of exhibits arguing for the cause of adaptive evolution. The local curators had used elephants and warthogs for this purpose, although the more common Darwinian icons, horses and gypsy moths, were also displayed on the walls. The usual credo appeared on the walls in captions: A species of wild African pig with omnivorous habits fails to survive, while its cousin the warthog, apparently a fulltime herbivore, does prevail. Why? Because its teeth are adapted to grass-chewing in an increasingly dry environment of savannah Africa. Ditto the antelope family.

What *survives*, of course, is egregious hindsight. The logic is spurious. We're in another church here, a church that claims not to be one. Real science predicts, it does not deliver tautologies. How did the Beast get that way? Because he *survived?* Nothing in these exhibits explains why (for example) there was a sudden radial development of at least eight species of elephants. The exhibit minimizes this procreative outpouring by claiming *three* species. This point would be of theoretical interest only to biologists, except that it concerns our own evolution, and our fate.

Lucy, for two decades considered to be our direct ancestor, has been recently shunted aside in favour of a 1992 discovery in Chad, a sub-Saharan country fifteen hundred miles west of the African Great Rift Valley and a place no one thought human evolution could take place. So Lucy's an aunt at best, not our grandmother. The likely candidate was yet another Homo, this Man from Chad, one of a dozen men-species. This unexpected proliferation has mystified scientists who have hitherto focused on the supposed end-game, the Last of the first Survivors, and not on the opening rounds, the explosive genetic Free-for-All. The vast outpouring of human species – human *species*, the plural – makes for a distinctly severe chanciness, and is no proof whatsoever of the power of the opposable thumb or some other "exclusive" attribute catalogued by Darwinian supremacists. These multiple versions, *Homo erectus*, *Afarensis*, *habilis*, and *Neantherthalis*, and their southern African cousins, all had fire and big thumbs and walked upright and enjoyed sexual dimorphism. Big guys, and sexy smaller women. It's the old story of Snow White and the Seven Dwarfs. Who shall survive the

terrible witch of extinction? Humpy, Grumpy, or Doc. When you're down
to one dwarf (as we are today), you want to believe the witch is dead . . .

To illustrate how speciation works, the Addis museum staff (and who
were *they*? Postcolonial administrators working with foreign grant money?
Led by certain agendas, like the Christian and Muslim missionaries before
them?), these curators, whoever they were, have set up a large placard
showing Haile Selassie's lineage beside that of an animal family tree. In this
display, Selassie's immediate ancestors split off the line that ran for hundreds of years and led first to Emperor Menelik (d. 1913), a descendant of
the queen of Sheba's son, and then turned right to culminate in the Lion
of Judah himself, Selassie.

Thus Darwin has been used to buttress the authority of the Ethiopian
state, and the problem with the theory, both in its wider implications and in
the narrow uses of political exigency, was how it ignored history for the
nineteenth-century determinism that produced not only Darwin, but a vast
outpouring of other social determinists such as Freud and Marx. These
nineteenth-century men refused to consider the possibility that history was
a product not of natural laws but of *will*: they believed in the "naturalness"
of history, its inevitability. Mechanisms or laws that operated unconsciously.

Collective will, individual will: how could brute animals exercise such
will, if men themselves were always suspect? Calling the study of man
beyond the time-line of state literacy, *pre*history, was the heavy weapon in
the armoury of militant scientism. It implies that nothing consciously
creates, it blindly obeys. To *create* is to invent, improvise. To discover, and
devise stratagems.

Humpy, Grumpy, Chicken-Chest, and the rest of these species of early
men likely lived and died from the endless round of politics we call war and
peace, like the murdered Selassie himself and his cousins. And the fact that
we don't know what their stories were is no reason to consign them to evolution's doorstep. I found this whole museum if anything was proof to the
contrary of the assertions pasted on its walls. If proof of anything. The cre-
ation and maintenance of the Ethiopian nation against all odds was itself
evidence of an overwhelming procreative urge. What force was so hellbent
on using the flotsam from all these historical ebbtides to fashion itself a state,

in a land where no such state ought to exist? Who made this country up from a semi-desert plateau with its dubious rain patterns? Here was Haile, the lion king of tribal fable, over here was Haile, the celebrity of the Radio Age, there was Haile, the evolved man of Darwinian destiny. But the metaphor was never the means. Yes, each new layer of culture superimposed itself on the previous layer, but it always submitted to the utility of a manifestly *political* will. Wherever *that* came from. There may have been kings and queens aplenty in the animal kingdom, but how Snow White chose her prince was a mystery the scientists were not even close to fathoming.

Or were they? Oh, the grail of our election! The age-old dream of joining the gods! Back at the hotel over a frothy cup of *makiato*, I reviewed a research paper from the December 2000 issue of *Nature*. The authors, geneticists M. Higashi, G. Takioto, and N. Yamamura, found evidence in fish populations to show that reproductive isolation occurs without physical isolation:

> Specifically, we show that variation in male secondary
> sexual character with two conspicuous extremes and the
> corresponding variance in female mating preference around
> no preference may jointly evolve into bimodal distributions
> with increasing modal divergence of male and female traits,
> pulling a population apart into two prezygotically isolated
> populations. This mode of speciation, driven by two
> runaway processes in different directions, is promoted by an
> increase in the efficiency of females in discriminating
> among males or a decrease in the cost of male conspicuous-
> ness, indicating that sympatric speciation may occur more
> readily if barrier-free or predator-free conditions arise.

What the Japanese biologists were saying, is that the female fish were entirely capable of withdrawing their future lineage from the general gene pool by breeding only with those males *they saw* as fit, and the trend was accelerated by these females' ability *to discriminate*. They consciously *chose* the characteristics of their new lineage. If a group of female fish only mated with males with reddish noses, then pretty soon there would arise a new red-nosed fish species. *Females* chose the new king, if you will, the heir to the throne. And this new, intentional speciation could be incredibly rapid, too, in a process that could be observed not only in African fish populations, but in antelopes and monkeys. Why not human populations? It was a case of Lucy in the sky with her suitors – and the one *she* picked as her consort would go from bachelor dwarf to lucky prince in a single kiss. So perhaps the founder of a lineage was a female, not male; and in the case at hand, it was Solomon that was chosen by the queen of Sheba, not the other way around.

I sat back an ordered another coffee. Around me, the beautiful women of the Hotel Baro laughed and chatted.

Chapter 14

The Biggest Stella in the World

Axum is a hot and dusty town swarming with batteries of aggressive African horseflies. There are few vehicles. Clouds of choking grit chase one another without restriction down the main road, a broken track that divides one row of jerry-built shacks from another, the whole interspersed with few solid stone buildings erected in an earlier and prouder age. The sun presses down hard too, an unforgiving African sun that barely stirs the heavy coat of dust lying everywhere, as grey and thick as an old elephant hide.

I have stumbled out of the Air Ethiopia two-engine Cessna sharp at midday, after flying since early dawn on the northern milk run serving the little prehistoric towns along the Rift Valley, Gonder, and Lalibela. Although we are now only five hundred kilometres from Addis, it feels like five thousand. Primitive horse-carts ply the road before me, heavily packed camels disappear off into sidestreets, their owners crying, "*Chooft chooft!*" and "*Wheetah!*" respectively. Pilgrims in white robes walk barefoot and with eyes downcast towards a distant church. And everywhere I go it's in the company of these dogged bluebottle flies and horseflies.

What distinguishes Axum from the other fly-towns of the world are two things: the Ark of the Covenant of ancient Israel, allegedly stolen from King Solomon by the queen of Sheba's own son, Prince Menelik (and now supposedly cached in a small church at the end of town); and the megaliths of the Axumite Dynasty. I can see them myself, these megaliths, without need of a guidebook. They are everywhere, huge stone plinths, carved from solid granite and weighing up to 520 tons each, and they lie *thunked* face down on Axum's open farm fields like bowling pins scattered by the pre-Christian gods. Quite a game someone once played here. Research teams from all over the world are working on these ruins, for Axum's strange history has provided intense fieldwork for generations of archaeologists, and to date the experts have barely scratched the surface with their trowels.

I have come to Axum because it was the capital of a Semitic-speaking kingdom as early as the eighth century B.C., and local tradition holds that Makeda, the Ethiopian queen of Sheba, kept her palace either here or in Yeha, a tiny village two hours east from Axum, which was originally settled by Sabean colonists from Yemen. How and why they came to this remote place in the middle of the vast Ethiopian plateau is a mystery. Many of the local ruins are called Sheba's Palace and so on, and the queen's tradition has figured prominently in the annals of historical Axumite kings in local popular accounts.

But I'm confused, and it isn't just the heat and altitude. This hot little town is close to the disputed border with Eritrea, and there are still leftover soldiers in camouflage uniforms hanging around the tiny bars. I've arrived here only a year or so after yet another major Ethiopian conflagration, and when people I meet talk about *the war*, I don't know which one they mean. A fellow on the plane, returning home, spoke bitterly of the war that caused him to flee to America; in retrospect, I guessed he meant the 1989 civil war, not the 2000 border war. I am confused and disoriented by nearly everything I see, and hear – and *read*, trying to understand what it is I've seen and heard. What's the *point* of these incessant local wars? Or is it simply one war with endless phases?

And the accounts I have read, of the history of the Axumite kingdoms, don't make any sense either, especially this daft proliferation of the queens

of Sheba and, more, the mindless multiplication of her so-called palaces and temples. There is a large water reservoir here in Axum town, quarried out of living bedrock, named the Queen of Sheba's Bath, or Swimming Pool. A *swimming pool*? From the eighth century B.C.? Where did this nonstop production line of historical narrative come from, something that clashes with and contradicts all logic and good sense? Even the local use of familiar words confused me, above all the word *stela*. Plural, *stelae*.

Based on everything I have read, I thought a stela was a smallish plaque or inscribed tablet, for it was such a portable artifact that Chuck Fipke's mining company found in the Arabian desert and then subsequently lost to an unnamed geologist somehow, and the only proof of it was the photo I still carried in my pack, in which the Cantex geologists hold it up in their hands (albeit upside down). It is an alabaster tablet the size of a breadbox.

But here stela refers to these giant granite columns that soared 110 feet high and weigh as much as iron-horse steam locomotives or, more tellingly, the giant stone heads of Easter Island. They are *not* portable, not unless you count the fact that the Italians managed to ship one of the biggest stela back with them to Rome in their war of 1935-41. If a technical term of art like stela was capable of such distortion, what about the more common words

like *kingdom, palace,* and *queen*? Was Axum's weird history now obliging me
to reset my thinking and recalibrate all my prior conceptions?

For my fieldwork, I decided to stay at the Africa Hotel on the main street
across from the one bank, where, according to my information, all the big
archaeologists stay. It was built like a motel from the 1960s on the outside –
car park, fountain, flowering shrubs, balconies, a pub room. Inside, it was a
different story. The green walls of the cool, terrazzo-floored dining room
were covered with garish cartoon murals, illustrating highlights from the
lives of martyred Orthodox warrior-saints and their redoubtable kings.
Chopping saints into precise cuts of meat was a big part of the Christian
epic to date. Lopped-off heads looked back at their cleaved bodies with
amazement. In the west wall of the dining room, the queen of Sheba
herself made an appearance at the court of Solomon, the latter a dusky and
sinister blackbeard surrounded by stacks of elephant tusks and gaping,
wide-eyed courtiers, who stared at him with the same expression as the
decapitated heads of the saints stared at the butchered meat their bodies
had become.

It was a pleasant place to sit, in the cool shadows and out of the direct
down-beat of the sun, listening to cheerful lilting echoes from the kitchen
and drinking my fresh orange juice. Easy to imagine myself digging away
out there in those ancient trenched fields, surrounded by stacks of artifacts
and gaping, wide-eyed graduate students. Ready to storm the world with
my grand new theory, perhaps lugging the recovered loot back to my air-
conditioned room for a gin-and-tonic, before a collegial five-course dinner.

What really excited me was the idea that, even as I sat here, drinking my
third orange juice and smashing the flies off my table, stupendous discov-
eries were being made. Yes, right here, outside the creaking front door of the
motel. Right now, there in the dusty hills immediately beyond the town
limits. This was where I could have ended, had I only pursued my anthro-
pology degree to its logical conclusion. Of course, I did end up here. Only
now I was going to talk about the archaeologists and their exciting fieldwork, not walk the clay trenches with them.

That was okay, though. Aklilu Berhane, the hotel-owners' son, was
pleased to tell me that the German team from Hamburg was presently

digging up the Kaleb Palace, a site two kilometres beyond the Ark of the Covenant church at the west end of town. The Italians were due in May; they were working at Betesioergis, a site named after a local saint and dated to 1250 B.C. Catherine D'Andrea, of Simon Fraser University, led the Canadian team that was also working that site. The Americans, from Boston University, had shown up in Axum faithfully all throughout the troubles of the 1980s and 1990s, every terrible season without fail. The French, naturally, had their own exclusive dig at Yeha, the Sabean site a two-hour drive east of Axum, a place I certainly intended to visit. The U.K. team had finished their program.

It was evident a high civilization once prospered here through farming and the sea-trade between Africa and Asia, lasting from 800 B.C. to its final decline in the twelfth century A.D. The economy was based in part on the engineering possibilities of elephant-power and the export value of the great beasts' ivory tusks. These elephants were a species similar to the tractable race of pachyderms Hannibal used to invade Italy from Carthage; Axum had an exotic war-elephant culture, something out of *Tarzan and the Jewels of Opar*. Today the ancient loot still threw itself out of the dirt everywhere. More than enough for everybody to pick over. It was Christmas morning for all these archaeologists, tons of stuff waiting under a eucalyptus tree. And if you think your brother got a better present, well then, try this next lot!

Frankly, I found it overwhelming, this surfeit of carved and inscribed runic death-poles imposing their magnificence everywhere one cared to look. Massive stelae were heaped like logs under the gnarly eucalyptus trees, even littering the grounds of a nearby outdoor café, at the entrance of a commemorative park set in the centre of town.

The Axumite stelae are columnar tombstones. Giant ones, and there are hundreds of them all over Axum, some dating far beyond the time-line of the Solomonic era, *circa* 1000 B.C. These pillars mark the presence of underground tombs lined with three-foot-thick blocks of the same grey granite, room-sized hollows in which the nobles were buried along with an assortment of grave goods, trade beads, and food offerings. The tall stelae marched relentlessly across the skyline. They demanded my study whenever I went outside, shrilling for attention when all I wanted was another *makiato* and some lively pop music to go with it. Worse, the ruins nauseated me. An ill wind seemed to blow across the town. It was a vast mausoleum, like camping in a giant graveyard.

Eventually, however, I dragged myself out of the cool recesses of the hotel and forced myself to take a tour of the most immediate tombgrounds, the classic-Axumite Northern Stelae Field, a fenced hillock a kilometre or so west of the hotel. There were few tourists around, so I had to wait for the tour to collect. My sole companion on the tour proved to be a long-faced Austrian named Gerhard. Gerhard was about thirty, with a glum Teutonic air that bespoke some personal misfortune, a combination perhaps of recent hair loss and a religio-maniacal bitterness towards Disco and All They Who Dance. The mannerisms of a guy one minute away from taking the monk's cowl out of sheer spite. The pale sweats, in other words.

As he and I ambled our way through the first small stelae field in the café park, I tried to grasp the secret source of Gerhard's sorrow. A broken engagement? The marriage of a beloved sister to a rash Latin adventurer? The death of his mother and the loss of his safe inner being? None of these: he refused to respond to my suggestions. Whatever it was, he was keeping a tight lid on it. It was a very private thing, so I was of course even more determined to find him out. Now I followed at a respectful distance while he prodded at buried rocks and poked at dusty inscriptions, pondering why he had bothered to make this journey, five hundred kilometres from the full-services capital of Addis, with its bath houses and willing attendants of every persuasion. He wasn't really looking at the old stuff, either. Now done with his preliminary survey, Gerhard turned, sighed, and, with an air of resolution, headed for the nearby museum, a small building inside a compound. I followed. I had lost my Lebanese wayfarer back in Ma'rib's temple precinct; I was doubly determined to find out what had prompted this one to come all the way out here by himself to kick at rocks. Earlier, I had asked Aklilu Berhane about the sort of people who came to stay at his hotel.

"All of the archaeologists except the British, who stayed at the Kaleb, come to us. Of the tourists, we get French and British mainly, then Germans,

Italians, and then everyone else. Except Americans. No Americans tourists come here. I don't know why."

He seemed perplexed by this, and awaited my answer.

"I really couldn't say either." I thought hard. "Maybe the famine? From the 1980s? There was a lot of media coverage; maybe it was overkill."

"Overkill?"

"I mean, maybe . . ." What *did* I mean? That Bob Geldof and all the rest had done such a good job, the country was permanently etched in the world's mind as a big-belly war orphan? I didn't know, but the Western PR guys surely did. Right down to a market-share base point of plus or minus, point two.

"How many tourists do you get in a year?" I eased away from the delicate topic.

"About two thousand."

"In a year?"

"Yes."

"I see."

Forty a week? That figure seemed ridiculously low, given that there were fifty or more souvenir shops on the main drag and a dozen hotels, including the Remhai, a smart new establishment of sixty rooms that had opened its doors that very week. But then again, I was the only tourist beside Gerhard out at the ruins today, and this was prime season. There were a few others staying at the hotel: Jenny, a pretty black woman from the United Kingdom, and Howard, her sullen brother, and a couple of complacent dot-comers from Switzerland, who had devoted their holiday week to collecting really bad souvenirs. And three exhausted-looking old Germans. Jenny was a former World Health Organization nurse, returning for sentimental reasons, and her brother plainly didn't want to come here. So the label *tourists* was a bit of a misnomer; these were bare-knuckle *travellers*, and more. Gerhard himself was obviously some kind of *pilgrim*, a species not previously encountered on my journey. I had asked Aklilu about this third category, but he assured me there were none such. But pilgrims did not arrive with nametags pinned to their chests, nor did they pray to conventional powers. They all bore signs of their devotion, certainly, but subtle ones.

After a few minutes' march, I sat down on a fallen basalt column in the little museum by the Northern Stelae Field and watched the gloomy Austrian determinedly tramp up and down the narrow defiles around the tombs, pausing dramatically at the biggest one. The Sorrows of Young Gerhard, contemplating the Great Stela. So determined to *see it all*. Forget the heat and the flies, ja? I was picking up lots of cues from Gerhard, but nothing at all from the carved rocks themselves. They stayed mute, unreachable. Was it their great age? Their obscure purpose? Or were they, too, faking it in some way?

There *was* something off-putting about the ruins, self-consciously ennobling. The artful display was all too clever by half, a department-store display window. I didn't quite believe in either of them.

I gave up on Gerhard for the moment and thought about my conversation that morning with Jenny instead. She and her brother were U.K. nationals whose parents had emigrated to Britain from Jamaica in the 1960s. Jenny told me that on this African trip she had already managed to visit Shashemene (to Howard's evident surprise, for he declared he had no knowledge his sister had left him last week, for this purpose). Shashemene was the Rastafarian community of Jamaicans and American blacks established in the 1960s, some 220 kilometres south of Addis Ababa, in veldt Africa.

"I'm purple," she announced to us both. "Levite."

Meaning, she explained, that her birthday was in June and her "tribe" in the Rastafarian community was fixed like astrological signs by the calendar. Not to be outdone by his freewheeling sister, Howard responded, "Well, *I'm* silver. Ashok, December."

"So what made you go to the Rasta community there?" I asked Jenny.

"Just wanted to see what they were up to. When I told them I was Jamaican, they let me in. It was interesting," she replied coolly.

"How did you convince them you were Jamaican, with that English accent of yours?"

"They believed me," she said with an English laugh. The English laugh better than Americans, I thought to myself.

I wanted to know how these two black English people related to the back-to-Africa movement and the lifestyle goals of the Rastafarian movement, with its focus on the divinity of Ras Tafari, the original name of Haile Selassie before he was crowned in 1930. How did the politics of race fare, with the onslaught of recent DNA evidence that linked and divided the world's peoples in far more subtle ways than the old colour codes? Howard, for one, refused to believe that blacks could come from whites.

"You take two people like you, light, and say they had a kid. He'd be light too. Black's the recessive gene. No way the kid's going to be darker than his parents." He crossed his arms.

"What do you think about these Ethiopians, then? These local people, they're kind of *brown*. Where'd they come from?" I asked.

"Well, it's obvious, ain't it? They're a mixture. I think *everyone* came from West Africa, and they evolved depending on their environment. These blokes went halfway, if you know what I mean."

"Well, the latest genetic testing shows that West African blacks were the most recent to evolve."

Intense scepticism greeted this remark on his part.

"You mean whites are *older* than blacks?" Howard clarified my point. I nodded.

"Apparently Europeans split off from the ancestral pool earlier."

"I don't believe that. The way it had to happen was, the original population was dark, had to be, being hot and all in tropical Africa, so there's no way blacks could come from whites."

"You don't think it just goes back and forth then, depending on the environment at the time?"

"What do you mean? Black to white and *then* vice versa? I don't think *that's* bloody likely."

I looked at Jenny, and she looked at me. She was cool, Jenny was. And she knew it. Her brother was like any number of Scots-Irish working-class blokes of my acquaintance. A pint, the football, not much for books, thinking about that new truck and whether he could make the payments if he ordered the Special Edition. A good friend in a punch-up, but then you had to ask yourself, Why was there a punch-up in the first place? Howard had more in common with these guys than being black would allow him to believe. There were no separate categories, just black and white with various dilutions thrown in between. A palpable tension hovered between the siblings; Howard needed a trip "to relax." His sister needed someone to accompany her on this remote excursion. He was angry at her; plainly what he'd needed was a beach holiday, not this town with one track called Denver Street and a dead dog in the ditch. And nothing to read.

He'd already finished his Harold Robbins.

"I *told* you to bring more than one book," she interjected primly. His eyes flashed, but he kept them focused on his unfinished plate of vegetarian spaghetti. This was no holiday. It was Lent now, and you couldn't even get meat around here. The tourists were obliged by management to be observant as well. Bloody hell!

I sighed. Despite the heat out here in the stelae field, and my grudging sympathy for Howard's position, I was obliged to be observant too. Actually look at this stuff. Now I got up off my basalt column and decided to play the mad Englishman to Gerhard's young Werther. The Teuton had already made it up to the big ruins at the top of the mound, and now he was inside the iron fence. When I caught up to him, he was patiently listening to a long dissertation from the official ruins guide, an ex-schoolteacher named Haile Selassie. He was a little man with a quick nervous energy and a long brown forefinger he waved about like a baton. Haile quickly took my growing inattention as the sure sign of an obstreperous student. He flapped his arms as he recited, a brown sparrow discharging flashes of nervous excess energy.

"This column is thirty-three metres long, the biggest stela in the world – "

"*Stel-la!*" I yelled. A joke.

No response. The two men stared at me.

Then the Sparrow spoke:

"Are you listening? There is much to talk about and you have already missed a lot!"

"Sure. That's fine. I'm just taking a few pictures. Good light right now." I hid behind my camera.

Click.

"I see." The guide recollected his thoughts. "Yes, as I was saying, there are one hundred and forty smooth stelae, and six decorated ones. This is where they sacrificed men to the gods."

"Sacrificed? Men?" I came back to life. Our guide was pointing to a concavity chiselled out of an eight-ton rock slab. It was designed to be level with the ground, a platform with little runoffs perfect for cultic butchery of one kind or another.

"*As* I was saying," he fixed me with a sidelong look, the bright-eyed sparrow-man with the bird's quick, furious temper. "The inscription might read, in the pre-Christian times, 'I defeat my enemy, by my Lord God Aris's help, for sacrifice I gave him one hundred men.'"

"Aris? You mean Ares, the god of war?" I was dubious. "How did the *Greeks* get here all of a sudden?"

"So the point *is*," Gerhard smoothed the sparrow's feathers, "that they performed human sacrifice here."

"Yes," the guide beamed at hearing this. Gerhard the good student. "But afterwards with the Christian Axumite kings, they say only 'I made sacrifice.' No mention of killing men . . . Now, this way."

I knew that the Christian kings had replaced the original pagan dynasties after A.D. 500, when the Great Stela snapped in two and collapsed sometime in the fourth century A.D.; that is, around the same time that the Ma'rib dam itself burst for the last time in Yemen in A.D. 575, scattering its inhabitants across Arabia. In other words, both of these great kingdoms, Yemenite and Axumite, were dependent on technology and they *crashed*, literally. But why?

Now our guide turned and led us down a short flight of stairs, deep into a slab-covered tomb.

It was cool and quiet down there. No pestering flies. Above us, a single slab of hewn granite served as a roof. No chance it would suddenly snap in two, I told myself.

"Here, look." The guide leaped over the step with the delicacy of a chorus member from *Swan Lake*. "Listen to these sounds."

He tapped on the walls.

Chunk, chunk.

"Hear that? *Now* listen!"

He tapped on a large, mummy-shaped white stone lying upright in the gloom behind him.

Choong, chooong!

"See, it's hollow!"

"Hit it again," I said. "Up and down."

The guide complied.

Choong, choong! Chooong!

It was a regular Xylophone of Death. Then: "*No one knows* what's inside," the Sparrow intoned ominously.

"No one? Not even the archaeologists?" Gerhard stared at the fantastic stone apparatus. Maybe *this* was the Mystery he had travelled thousands of miles to see!

"*No* one," our guide confirmed solemnly, "has ever opened the Tomb of the False Door."

We nodded, and duly stared at the dark blank wall for what seemed like several long and portentous moments. If this was a koan, nothing came to mind. Eventually we emerged into the light, no wiser for our subterranean jaunt.

Outside the tomb I dutifully snapped off more pictures of fake granite doors, false granite windows, trick granite monkhead-style support beams, and sham porticos, all hewn by their cunning artisans from exactly the same granite we use for our own cemetery monuments back at home, the smooth, grey stuff with little black specks in it. Apart from the script and the huge scale, we could be in the middle of Park Lawn cemetery, wondering how to get out again after an annual visit with grandmother Mary.

Brown long-tailed flycatchers and pink doves settled in the flower-laden trees beyond the stelae field. Through the groves I could see the Abatu Enessa church, a pentagon topped with Hindu-like lightning rods. It was one of four other-worldly churches in the immediate vicinity, and I was drawn to its bright colours. A mural, much like the one in the hotel dining room, had been painted on its exterior walls, a carousel of New Testament characters inviting the penitent to make the rounds and be instructed. There were two churches called St. Mary's. Looking south the other way, I could make out the crown-topped basilica of the brash new St. Mary's Church

rising above a gathering stream of white-robed pilgrims, who hugged its marble-clad walls for solace.

"Where's the Ark of the Covenant?" I asked.

"Come. I show you now."

Gerhard deliberately overpaid the entrance fee to the grounds of the old St. Mary's Church, by a factor of three. The churchmen, wrapped in yellow and white bolts of cloth, emerged from the dark stone cubicle under the wall and quickly took his money without a word. Guide Haile Selassie was talking about the kings and the stone thrones, seats of honour for the judges who officiated over the centuries. Many kings of the Ethiopian dynasties had been crowned in Axum, he told us, including his namesake, the Emperor Haile Selassie himself in 1930. How many times was he crowned, I asked myself. The granite platforms that had been used to raise these thrones above the dust were scattered about the yard.

"And then there are four girls, virgins, each one wearing a cross of gold and silver, and a long gold chain around them all, making a square, and inside the square is the coronation ceremony. Haile Selassie came here, he was the last king to take part in the ceremony."

Now we were back in the present, somehow. He went on.

"And these were the guns we captured in the Sudan from the Mahadists."

Sudan? Mahadists? Now he was talking about a war in 1888 against a Dervish army from the south that had attacked the nearby town of Gonder. As we walked around, we saw brass cannons pointing south in the church grounds, and carvings of spears, and pots of holy ashes that disappeared by sunset, and iron urns with red-and-pink crown-of-thorns bushes growing out of them, and more relics from the glorious war against the Italians in the campaign of 1885, or maybe it was the battle of 1896, or perhaps the war of 1935.

"I showed you that hole? Where the Italians stole our stela? This is where Haile Selassie came for prayer, before he was crowned king and defeated them."

"They used spears and stones," I whispered to Gerhard encouragingly. "Shows you what faith can do."

"No, they lost," he whispered back. "The Italians were here for five whole years, from 1935 to 1940. They had all the time in the world to take back whatever they liked."

"Oh."

The Good Student knew more than his teacher, but he wasn't going to let on.

"And now for the Ark of the Covenant." The guide led us around to a red iron railing set before a black stone church. Our fourth and penultimate church, the least impressive of the four but the one with the highest associations, the chapel that housed the Ark was a snug and prim little stuccoed box. The chapel did not look more than a few hundred years old, if that. Since scholars claimed the Ark disappeared with the fall of the Temple in Jerusalem, I wondered what was in there.

"*Ende Selate.*" Sparrow looked right through us to a different plane. The

Church of the Ark.

"This is where they keep the jewels," Gerhard nodded, peering through the railing. "That's the collection box," he added with a short laugh. I didn't know it, but he was making a joke.

A yellowed sheet-metal box the size of a commercial air conditioner stood a few feet away, inside the railing. It was locked with a padlock. We waited as the flies found us again. A young fellow in yellow drapes strolled over and chatted with our guide a bit.

Then he opened the box. A half-dozen battered gilt crowns sat inside, together with an illustrated manuscript he claimed was four hundred years old, but could have been made in the fall of 1994. The colours were as bright as yesterday's cinema posters

"Where's the Ark?" I said, my mouth open at this absurd theatrical production.

"Inside the old church. Only one man can see it." Our guide pointed to another yellow-robed churchman, sticking his head out of the red velvet curtain of the doorway. This one was older than our companion. "No one else."

"Yes, the duty is passed on," Gerhard nodded sagely.

I looked at him, about to say something, when a fly flew into my mouth.

Not just into my mouth, but actually down into my throat.

Deep down. I stood there speechless.

I began to spit. Right there. On the church grounds in front of the Ark of the Covenant. Absurdly, the fly wouldn't budge. He clung there to my gullet like his life depended on it.

"What's wrong?" Gerhard inquired solicitously.

"Fly, *accch*, in my, *ekk*, throat," I gasped.

I spit and spit, and spit again. They stood and watched me as I careened around the yard, trying to gargle the fly out of my throat.

Beelzebub, I kept thinking. Beelzebub is trying to get me!

The fly stayed there, lodged tight in my throat, not moving. I spit until my throat was dry.

There was nothing to do but swallow it.

Swallow the pestilent fly, and hope that my stomach juices would dissolve it.

Big mistake.

I began to retch, violently and with increasing passion.

"*Achieew*! *ACHEWAAAHA*!"

I wheeled about, flailing my arms and bent double, racked by uncontrollable spasms.

"*Achieew*! *ACHEWAAAH*!"

At a great psychological distance from the unfolding drama, Gerhard and the Sparrow watched silently, and, even in the throes of my passion, I could tell what they were thinking: The Bad Student Gets It.

This was it, I was going to die here. Right before the Ark of the Covenant. Choking to death on a bluebottle fly before two credible witnesses to my uncanny end.

Finally, a mighty last effort:

ECHUCHHHH!

And the fly, slimed with enough spit to drown him a thousand times over, came sailing out of my throat. Up, up . . .

And plopped down into the green grass of home.

"Am I going to die?" I asked Gerhard, thinking of all the pestilence I'd just swallowed.

"Probably," he nodded solemnly.

"What from? Leprosy, hepatitis, cholera?"

"Maybe all of them."

"You're very pious," I said to him.

"'Pious?' What means that?"

"It means you pretend not to enjoy the sufferings of others," I said.

"Maybe it was a sign," he smirked.

"I – "

Another fly danced over my cheeks.

Or maybe it was the same one again. I shut my mouth all the way back to the hotel and kept it shut. That night I could still taste the evil violation in my throat. I came out to the courtyard balcony for relief. A star-filled sky.

Below me a ragged chorus of hacking and gut-coughs rose from the guest rooms all evening long.

Ack, ack . . . Hacoom!

They sounded bad, like they had swallowed flies too. All of them. And now they too sought the elusive power to eject the filthy pests, in the dim light of their lonely abodes.

Chapter 15

We Have Ways of Not Dealing with You

I met Peter Boehm the morning the German archaeologists refused to talk to me.

"Pleez. I ask for a knife, something. How can I spread this butter without a knife!"

Typical German, I thought, yelling at the rain-skinny waiter. Peter saw me watching his drama and nodded. I picked up my curdled, blanched coffee and some cutlery and joined him, lurching between the tables because I was still woozy from the invasion of the pestilent spawn the day before. Was it psychosomatic, or was I on the last legs of *farangi*-dom?

"I brought you a knife." I set it down carefully by his toast.

"You know, it's not so bad. It's just that the water was off this morning and I really wanted to take a shower."

He looked pretty clean to me. He was lodged in the room next to mine, and I had heard his shower running for an hour last night.

"Bad night?"

"I got in late on the bus from Aswan. You been there?"

173

"No. Aswan, huh?" The names were beginning to confuse me, they all sounded like somewhere else. Aswan the dam in Egypt? Goondar, from the Tarzan novel? A million churches called St. Mary's, and no guidebook available. I hadn't seen a single bookshop since entering the country. Maybe he'd said Adwa, a town fifty miles away and the site of a major Italian offensive.

"Chust look at this butter." Boehm used the knife as a pointer. "It's green!"

"Think it's from a cow?" I sighed in sympathy.

Somewhere down the road were the real travellers, the ones lounging around the pool of the fantastic hotel, the real trekkers who had done all their homework, had made the right contacts, and were right now breakfasting on luridly fresh fruit by a crystalline waterfall after a night's romp through local sex-voodoo ceremonies. While I was too lazy to make the effort and exit the Africa Hotel with its intermittent water and Lenten-Fast menus.

Peter looked as if he felt the same way. I took to him immediately.

"I'm a journalist," he sighed. "I'm writing a story on my trip through Africa. East to West at the Widest Point."

He said this last somewhat tentatively, like it was a working concept, and waited for my reaction.

"What's that, Mauritania?"

"Senegal."

"And east?"

"Somalia."

"ss," I said, shaking my head.

"Fuck it," he said. "I had a shitty day yesterday, so far. Those crazy Germans wouldn't talk to me."

"Crazy Germans?"

"The archaeologists." He pointed behind me.

"Where are they?" There was nobody there.

"They just left."

"You mean the three old people? I thought they were unhappy schnapps-meisters from Dusseldorf who took the wrong bus!" I was amazed. Those three dour grumps who stared at their plates in cell-nine silence were *scientists*?

"Yes, they won't talk to me. Maybe because I'm German. You should try. Do."

"What happened to Fritz the Jolly Bavarian, with the red beard and bad graduate-student jokes?" I could not believe this. Those three old stiffs! I got up from the table and went into the parking lot as he directed. I approached the sandalled woman in the shapeless Tilley-style gear. She was packing chrome cases into a Toyota truck. I told the dread in my heart to lighten up, and politely introduced myself.

"It is not possible," she said curtly, barely looking at me as she continued to load her things.

"I beg your pardon?" Her blatant rudeness was fascinating. I stood there, rivetted.

"If we let everyone come and look, we could say no to no one."

She threw another box in, with unnecessary force.

"I just wanted to ask you about your job as architects," I said, flustering out a bit. "What's it like, the experience? How many flies you swallowed yesterday, that kind of thing."

"Someone comes, once, and writes an article, and we don't know what they are saying, so it's completely out of the question! No, never."

I stood there, thinking about my grand-uncle, General Mikhail Zalenko, First Red Army Division, 1945, at the gates of Berlin. BOOM BOOM BOOM go the big guns.

Down down down go all the rude ones.

"What do you expect," Peter told me, picking at his lump of unleavened Lenten-Fast bread. "They are old-style Germans, like the bad guys in *Raiders of the Lost Ark*."

"It's not like I *care* what little secrets they're getting ready to spring on the academic world," I said. "It's just, 'How's it going?' *Click, click*."

"Yes, in my experience most of them welcome journalists. They need the publicity for their grants."

"So, east to west across Africa, yes?" I looked at his uneaten breakfast. The toast was a little dark. "And this is your second country so far. How many more to go?"

"I don't know," he replied. Like he was rethinking the whole thing. Fast and hard.

෯෯

By mid-morning, the last of my flyish stomach shudders had passed and I began to believe there would be no gastric earthquake, so I hired a donkey cart for 25 birr to fetch me to the top of the Kaleb Hill, where the tombs of two kings had been excavated in the early part of this century. The first was King Kaleb, whose elephant armies had conquered the Sabean kingdom back across the Red Sea, in battles that coincided with the final collapse of the Ma'rib dam in A.D. 575. Tradition claimed that five thousand elephants had been used to build this tomb, and original reports from Greek travellers in the sixth century A.D. indicated that four brass or gilded rhinos kept guard at the four cardinal points of the conqueror's tomb. The logistics of the ancient campaign defied all understanding. How do you ship brigades of war-elephants across the sea in the sixth century? What did the world look like then, that you could feed and water the great beasts while mobilizing?

Where, in this burnt toast of a land, did they get elephants and rhinos in the first place?

It was pleasant to sit beside the driver, a boy with the face of an angel, and go clip-clopping down Denver Street and up the dirt road hard right by the Queen of Sheba Pool. The story was that the queen had bathed in these depths, and the power of the ritual waters caught and drowned at least one boy a year.

"*Chugh! Chugh!*" The boy urged his donkey on, and the animal smartly picked its way through the iron-hard cobble that littered the landscape. We drove through street processions of older women in their Lenten white robes, strolling with magnificent carriage, and svelte young girls in gauzy floral dresses and patterned umbrellas. In fifteen minutes we had passed as many potential supermodels, barefoot and radiantly smiling, as Milan might consume in a month.

"You! You!" The children called out.

"*You! You!*" I answered and they screamed in appreciation, bowled over by their own laughter.

We reached a red-dirt rise and the driver jumped off, and the donkey picked her way up the heady incline, through fields of imported sisal cacti and yellow patches of *dendere*, a scratchy flower that gave up its sap for an ointment for insect bites and rashes. Shattered plinths everywhere. Distant volcanoes gnawed dully at the low clouds on the horizon. Below us a tiny family group plodded on through the vast land, heading east along a roadless tract. There were no Germans to be seen. Only the clip-clop of the donkey, the hushed, unguent urgings of the boy-driver, the smell of fresh donkey sweat, and a breeze full of sweet grasses. I was happy again. Glad to be out of the town and in the open fields.

Down in the royal tombs of the Kaleb brothers, it was cold and dark, and I tripped over an unseen threshold in my eagerness to see the carved elephant on the wall. About two feet long, the elephant proved to be more naturalistic than stylized, so I studied its ears carefully with the flashlight. The ears appeared to be more like the Asian species than the African, smaller, and rounder, not ragged. Its behaviour patterns were certainly Asian, if the

Axumites could get the animal to roll rocks and carry troops into battle. What a different world that must have been! A society built on elephant power! I was almost comfortable down there, where it was cool like a rathskeller, examining the faint carvings until the thought struck me: What did these kings die of, exactly?

Up top, the land was bleaching away like an overdeveloped film. Scene after scene from the New Testament continued to run silently, robed patriarchs leading donkey trains off into the hills, little clusters of families losing their way across the enormous sky, farmers tirelessly hoeing stony plots. Jesus' home movies without sound. And here was the best part: By the time the donkey cart brought me back to the town, all the white-shawled women began to look like witnesses returning from the crucifixion. Then one woman turned her radiant face to us, and I swear, I thought it was Mary herself.

⚘

There are different kinds of pilgrims and the most interesting is the modern, seeker-type pilgrim. Sayaka Ota, age twenty-three, was a social worker from Tokyo, travelling alone. Back at the Africa Hotel, over weak milkless coffee in the big cartoon-decorated dining room, I remarked to her how I had seen large groups of Japanese touring here as everywhere, older people. Bifocals and half-walkers. She replied earnestly.

"These are rich people, who made their money when times were good in Japan. Now there is a need for adjustments, for new methods, and so it is very difficult for young people."

To illustrate her thesis, Sayaka gave me a list of present-day social problems in Japan. *Hikiko mori*, children who "stay in, don't go out." This phenomenon I had already heard about, the masses of adolescents who suddenly became recluses, shutting themselves in from outside contamination and refusing to have any social existence whatsoever. A form of autistic rebellion, I supposed, akin to anorexia because it centred on the denial of selfhood.

But there was also the growing problem of *shounen hikou*, juvenile delinquency, with its two subclasses.

Gakkyu houkai was "class collapse," in which the teachers lost control of their students. Sayaka's social-work speciality was dealing with *sensi goroshi*, teacher killings; and more specifically, students who attacked their teachers with small penknives, intent on stabbing them to death.

"Things are changing so fast, workers get cut off from jobs, students see no hope, no future. The economy depends on America, and it is *transitional* now."

By degrees, Sayaka told me over the balance of the afternoon where she'd been travelling previously: Iran (by bus, dressed in a chador, the traditional black robe), Syria, Lebanon, and Jordan. And Turkey, two years ago, twice. Once to help the victims of the earthquake of 1998. She had also organized food drives for the victims of an Indian flood. By this time, Peter Boehm had joined us at the hotel café and sat listening to her account in utter silence. His mouth was open in awe. I could tell what he was thinking.

I studied her calm face once again. Seeing my own inadequacies clearly in the light of her deep commitment.

"Why are you so *good*, Sayaka? I'm such a terrible person, lazy and indifferent." I meant it too, although I was hoping to get a rise out of Peter as well. He didn't bite, though.

"*Me*? No, I am very selfish," she insisted firmly. "Besides, my friend? She was helping remove the, *what* do you call it, the bombs in the ground by the border?"

"The land mines?" I knew the Eritrean border was loaded with vicious explosives.

"Yes, with the Dutch . . . *she* went across the Sudan by herself, hitchhiking, and bus also . . . She is brave!"

"You could write a book: *Travelling Tips for Girls*," Peter offered.

"How about *Planet of Single Women*? With a picture of you in a chador on the back cover!" I looked to Peter for his reaction, and he nodded glumly. This was a far better idea than anything he or I could come up with, on our own.

"Hey," I said to him later, by way of compensation. "I found a sleazy little bar with a girl who bleaches her hair totally platinum. Want to go?"

"Sounds perfect," he said.

·❧·

The International Bar was distinguished from a dozen other holes-in-the-wall by its grim, hand-painted mural of a large green serpent. Peter and I were joined by Jason Langford, a Welshman travelling Africa north to south, to Peter's east to west. Here we were, at the very crossroads of it all, we three, at the International Bar, where the beer was two bucks and the snake was free. Jason told us he'd quit his multinational employer as a logistics manager to begin a whole new career as a sports psychologist. But the Grand Tour first.

The two African hands had a lot to say to each other.

Peter: "Well, shit, one week out of my trip the Somali soldiers are pointing their guns at me in the desert and someone steals my cable from my computer, and I get sick, really bad. I've been in Nairobi for three years without getting sick once, and I think, 'Could this be *psychological?*'"

Jason: "Well, I'm going through the Simien mountains last week, three thousand metres up, with the most inept mule driver in the world. All my stuff is loaded in the pack, passport, everything, and the driver twice almost lost the animal down a cliff!"

Peter: "So, I've got eight thousand more kilometres and sixteen countries to go. Somalia, Ethiopia [here he lists them all]. I'll be finished in six months."

Jason: "Me too. After I reach Cape Town I'm flying to Auckland and then Laos and Cambodia."

Me: Guys, guys. Let me ask you one question, about *saturation?* I mean, *travel* saturation. How much can you *absorb*, going from place to place like this, month after month? I mean, I was going through Scotland once, and even there, in boring old Edinburgh with not a hell of a lot going for it, I got really saturated, travelling fast. What about *you?*"

Peter: I am lucky as a journalist, I guess. I write up a biweekly story, and that helps me to remember."

Me: "But doesn't that just replace the actual memory, the way photos often do?"

Peter: "Yes, but you have to have something. A *point* to what you are doing."

After a few more beers we headed out into the Axumite night. Peter said he wanted to see the stelae by starlight. I looked sharply at him to see if he was being cute, but he marched on into the gloom without a trace of self-consciousness. Children whistled tuneful dirges at us from rag-covered doorways. The streets periodically filled themselves with crowds of men and women, then emptied out again, as the students, mostly, made their way to the technical school that usually stayed open until 10 p.m. for three or more shifts. Electrical repair, truck maintenance, nursing, and welding. They were learning the basic trades for what would hopefully become a postwar recovery.

Bands of junior hustlers popped out of the darkness to offer us, the happy trio of *farangis*, our choice from open packs of cigarettes, peanuts, and chewing gum. I bought a stick of mango gum for 1 birr, grossly over-paying a pretty little charmer who could turn on her hundred-watt smile at will. She snatched the bill out of my hand and skipped off gaily into the night. Leaving me to wonder how it worked, this system. Did their parents set them up in these micro-businesses? Or did they take their kids to whole-saler Fagans who controlled the various submarkets?

After twenty minutes' walk we arrived at the museum grounds by the Northern Stelae Field. The grounds were pitch black. Peter was ready to wriggle through the guard fence when a low hiss shot from the bushes.

"Watch out! Iss closed for night. Go home, misters!"

We returned to the International Bar, where the charms of our plat-inum-blonde hostess grew with each round of Meta, the stubby local brew, dark with malt and delusion. We gloomily studied the HIV poster above her head. We already knew the statistics, 15 per cent of the country, one out of every six. How many people in this bar? One, two . . .

We left.

On the street outside Peter took umbrage at some slight fellow in mechanic's overalls who was dogging our steps, keeping pace in Peter's blind spot.

"Is there any reason *exactly* why you must do that?"

"Hello? Hello?"

"I mean, really. Can I just walk in the night for one minute without somebody at my elbow all the time?"

"Peter, relax. He's harmless," Jason interjected.

"I just can't stand it."

"Well, you're going to have to get used to it." Jason offered him a smoke.

"I know. Eight thousand kilometres to go, with someone always bugging me every step of the way. Human mosquitoes."

The Reluctant Pilgrim, I dubbed him that night, adding another category to my list of pilgrims that already included Sayaka with a question mark. We passed another boîte, the red-lit Happy Bar, where a tall soldier in camouflage fatigues was doing the boogaloo in the front doorway to a Joe Tex tune. The bar girl seemed impressed by his thrusts.

"Don't go in there," Jason warned as Peter started moving towards the red light.

"Why not?"

"It's kind of crowded," I suggested.

"What? One soldier?"

"He's kind of busy. See? Let's just go to another place." The soldier was now popping his hips at the girl like a piston on *full*.

Peter told us about his problems in the next canteen. One of his three newspaper contracts had fallen through, two weeks into the trip.

"I got them two weeks of test copy first, and they paid me, but then they said, 'No thanks, it's not for us.' So I've got two-thirds of what I thought I would have. Still, it's not the end of the world, is it?"

I looked at Jason. He tugged at his close-cropped beard.

"It *could* be," he said.

But he had to be thinking of his own journey, eight thousand kilometres to the south.

That night I dreamed – a vivid dream, in Technicolor. I was teaching Ethiopians about photography. We were in a classroom.

"Repeat after me: The Significant Moment!"

"The Significant Moment!" The students yelled back.

"What is this picture of?"

I flashed a slide on the wall, a photo of a happy person biting into an ice-cream cone.

"A Significant Moment!" they yelled.

"No, this is the product, the easy shot!" I yelled. "Not the Significant Moment!"

"Not the Significant Moment!" they chorused enthusiastically.

I showed them a second picture, an advertising crew of three who had taken the first photo and were now studying its effects as a billboard, on passersby.

"Is this the Significant Moment?" I yelled at the class. "Three people backstage of the performance?"

"Yes! No! Maybe!"

Weak voices, my class was unsure.

"No!" I yelled. "For *look upon this!*"

I showed a third slide. It showed a fat soldierlike bureaucrat, lying on a couch and paying the advertising crew with a bag of gold.

"Is this the Significant Moment?" I screamed, my voice hoarse with frustration and rage.

"No! No! No!" They waited happily for the next slide.

"You are a good class." My voice cracked as I showed them the fourth slide.

This was another man, a stranger, who had the money for which the three small figures had prostrated themselves. These latter three had somehow become the fat soldier's wife and their two children. You could see that these three were tied to the unknown man's wrist by cords around their necks. The man's face was blank.

We all studied the man's blank face for a moment.

"See?" I cried. "See?"

"*This* is the significant moment!" they hurrahed, and the clicking of their student cameras sounded like a whole field of crickets outside my bedroom window.

In the morning Jason told me he'd slept badly too.

"I don't know what it was. I was reading from that book I told you about, a passage about these judeo-pagans who had special robes and made animal sacrifices down in the south."

"South of here?"

"Yeah, in Ethiopia. And they were all muddy and greasy, from the animal fat I guess, and they kept coming at me with their sacrificial knives, not threatening me so much as exhausting me, and I couldn't get rid of them, and I went round in circles, round and round, without letting up."

"How long have you been out here?" I asked.

"Two weeks." His face ran to different shades of red, from a crimson lip-crack to a strawberry cheek-burn, with a mysterious fuchsia stain spreading around his burning eyes. I wondered what film would best capture it. His significant moment, I mean. Jason went on.

"I wonder if my body is breaking down first, so as to save my mind. Know what I mean?"

"Yeah. I bet you that for two weeks or so, your mind can effectively block out all the weirdness and risks of travelling, but then eventually the Ubangi get in."

"The Ubangi?"

"Yeah, the natives who were always trying to rip Tarzan apart, between the two bent trees. In *The Jewels of Opar*."

"Oh, right."

"Just collapse and get it over with."

"Thanks . . . So how did *you* sleep?"

"Like a baby," I lied.

Chapter 16

The Virtual Ethiopian

I was hanging around the town waiting for a four-wheel drive to take us to Yeha, a sixth-century B.C. site and the original kingdom of the Sabean colonists, which today still boasted a nearly intact Sabean palace and an adjacent Orthodox monastery. A cheerfully chunky fellow in an Izod T-shirt and a heap of heavy-duty camera equipment showed up and introduced himself.

Baheleb (Bob) was from St. Louis, Missouri, a boiler engineer who had returned home to Axum after twenty years abroad. Over lukewarm bottles of Pepsi in a tiny street bar called the Black Cat, he told me his story.

"I was twenty-three when I had to get out of Ethiopia, with my wife. The Derg. We lived in Sudan and then in Cairo, working odd jobs, before coming to the States. Our first son was born in the Sudan, the other two in the States."

"That must have been quite an adventure."

"It's only an adventure when you choose it as your undertaking. When you're forced to, it's a different story."

"And what's it like, living in America?"

"Well, of course the whites don't really accept you, and they don't like it at all if you try and live in their neighbourhood, not in St. Louis. And the blacks, they don't like it either. So you live in the mixed area, in the middle; then you're okay."

"St. Louis has a mixed area?"

"All the cities in the States do. Washington, Raleigh, my friends there tell us the same thing."

"So America is divided into thirds?"

"Exactly. I am working as a boiler engineer, making okay money, but I'm not rich, you know? And my relatives here, they all expect me to come back here and throw it around. I told them, Look, in America you have to work very hard. I do the best for my kids, extra computer courses, sports after school, but it costs, right?"

"And are they into the hip-hop thing, the baggy pants and all?"

"No way, man. I'm paying the bills, they have to be normal, intelligent. Not idiots. But my family here, I told them, I'll bring you a nice tie, something that says 'Made in America' but don't expect me to throw buckets, I don't have it."

"But you still gave them money," I nodded.

"Of course." He shrugged and looked around the dusty little bar and out into the desolate afternoon road outside. A couple of camels ambled by, lugging firewood. He shook his head. "I prepared myself for the worst, coming here."

"And?"

"It was pretty bad. No improvements to the town. Bad politicians. And everybody says to me, we don't know you. You're not one of us. They charge me like they charge you." He pointed at me. "Charge *him*, he's a *farangi*, not me. I'm one of you. Look, I speak your language!"

"It doesn't work," I said flatly.

"No, they still charge me double, like a foreigner. I don't like it." He shook his head and looked at his companion, a younger man who had said nothing so far.

"Where's home then?"

"Here. But then it's where your family is."

"What about the music, it's pretty good, huh?" It was actually better than good; the music was wild and haunting.

"Ethiopian music?" He brightened at this. "You buy any of the tapes they sell?"

"Yeah. I just go and grab what I like. It's pretty cool, some of that stuff."

"Don't bother. This is what you do: I have a collection of about five hundred Ethiopian albums I got for free. I'll show you how to do it too."

He excitedly told the man I thought was his driver to go get him a pen and paper.

The young man returned with the items.

"This is my brother," he nodded as he bent over the table and began scribbling.

I nodded hello, and received a shy smile in return. His brother sat stiffly, careful not to crease the pastel-blue leisure suit Bob had obviously just bought him in Addis.

"You need a burner. You got one? Or, you download a player from the Internet. Okay?"

"Right." I was taking notes as he directed. Donkeys brayed outside the doorway.

A high-tech lecture in a low-tech land.

"Then you use a search engine to find listings of North Ethiopian Music. Then you . . ."

A lengthy technical discussion followed, for Bob was a collector with a collector's passion for the best, the brightest, the most original.

"Some versions? They're secondary. Not primary recordings. Balti Music, their MP3 files? They're crystal clear, like Day One in the studio."

"So you really get off on the Internet, huh?"

"Listen. In America they treat you okay, but they don't really accept you there, and in Ethiopia it's the same thing. But at home, on my computer – I just got a new Gateway – it's a different story. Nobody cares who you are. You like Ethiopian music? Fine. Welcome to the club!"

We got up to take a picture. Bob's brother hastened to unpack the camera, and pulled out a Canon with a large telephoto lens.

"He seems to know how to use that thing," I said as I edged over to Bob's shoulder as instructed.

"He should. I trained him how to use it last week," Bob said, smiling for the camera.

"Could it *be*, that . . . it's *actually* true about the Ark?"

We are finally on our way to Yeha, the mountain stronghold of the Sabean dynasty, sixty extremely rough kilometres southeast of Axum, and Jason Langford needed to talk about mysticism. The kind of mysticism that his well-thumbed copy of Graham Hancock's *The Sign and the Seal* retailed to the masses, a book that had kept him tossing feverishly the night before. Planetary alignments, alternate sciences, incredible coincidences, legends of the Pharaohs' curse. The British author Hancock had written a pop-bestseller about the Ark's magical powers, loaded with innuendos.

Could-it-be-true speculations, in other words.

"He doesn't actually *say* that the Ark of the Covenant was a technical device, and not a religious one. He says, 'Could it *be* that the Ark was used to give Moses' sister leprosy, like a radioactive tool-belt,' and so on."

"A radioactive tool-belt? That's what he calls it? I see," I countered. "You've heard of the mythical Welsh tree, half green leaves, half flaming fire?"

"Of course. It's an old Welsh story."

"Well, Robert Graves wrote a book, *The White Goddess*? About the levels of complexity in art and religion. The tree stands for a letter, the letter stands for a name, the name is part of a magical poem, everything is interlocked. So you just can't read this stuff left to right and expect to get it right, like a puzzle on the back of a cereal box."

"Well, it is odd the way the temples and so on do line up. You take the three pyramids in Egypt. They form almost a perfect line, and point directly to Orion's belt. The same thing with Ankar Wat; all three sites are aligned in very specific ways."

Outside the windows of our truck the mountains showed no inclination to straight lines. Instead of the usual pointy cones and round domes, we saw a dancing parade of twisted humpbacks and forsaken behemoths, some split down the middle by unimaginably titanic forces. Looking through the cleft in one cracked monster, I could see a succession of tiny green tableaus receding into the distance, miniature people following miniature donkeys carrying tiny perfect loads of wood, and beyond them, yet more perfect little scenes, tinier and even more exact, the work of a Dutch Master God who loved optical tricks and every precious detail, for here was the same scene exactly, repeated as before, except reversed and reduced again by a factor of two.

"It's like those medieval paintings in the *Book of the Hours*," I shook my head. "The clear hyper-air makes the smallest details stand out in sharp relief."

The completely dry air indeed acted like a perfect lens.

"This is where the big battle was fought," Jason said, consulting his guidebook about the Adwa battle in 1896. "The Italians came in through that valley and Menelik's men were positioned all around those hills."

"Yes, yes," Tsehaye, our driver, spoke up for the first time. "Air force come over and drop bombs."

"Air force?" Jason and I looked at each other.

"You mean the Eritrean army?"

"Yes, yes, they bomb city."

We were now driving through the outskirts of Adwa itself, and on our left we could see the large refugee tent-camp with the blue UN insignia. Twenty-five-thousand refugees from Eritrea had come through at this point. The border, peppered everywhere with live land mines, was only forty kilometres away. Menelik, Mussolini, Mengistu, all the players merged seamlessly into a red blur. The layers of recent history were as dense and complicated as the layers of archeology, but far more dangerous. Rude academics eventually left the country after their research grants expired, but not the land mines. Now we passed hundreds of soldiers marching along the road in their bright-green jungle fatigues. The country was demobilizing, but slowly.

"For God's sake, don't take their picture!" Jason pleaded.

"I wouldn't dream of it," I replied. The bright-green uniforms, fetching as they were, seemed wildly inappropriate as camouflage given the washed-out terrain. I wondered how many men had been lost to this fashion statement so far. Still, the people looked cheerful; for all their recent woes no one scowled or gestured rudely at us. A river of happy people, I told myself. For maybe this day, this month, this year, there was food and peace in the land. At long last.

Once again I was struck by the oddly familiar attitudes of a country coming to terms with the styles of peace. There was the desk clerk in the new Remai hotel in Axum who kept half-turning to catch sight of himself in his new uniform, surprised and delighted by his smart image in the lobby mirror. There were the local women in storebought dresses and wobbly high heels at the restaurant, the ones who kept darting their eyes at various details of our clothes and habits, straining to listen to our conversation. And especially, a serene beauty waiting for her date in a battered white Lada outside the café back in Addis, a girl-woman who still haunted me.

Who was she, that regal teenager in the sleeveless white dress? And where was she going at midday, with her hair done up in a high bouffant, enigmatic half-smile on her lips? Another Audrey Hepburn at the beginning of her career? Was every peacetime a love affair after a long war – like our 1950s? How I envied them, these postwar victors, these sharply dressed mods, these inheritors of everything we'd lost to the digital darkness; I envied their new polyester ties and their carefully ironed shirts and their shiny patent shoes and their innocent thralldom to fashion. How lucky to walk in the spring sun of victory!

There was one last patch of eroded paving east of Adwa, and then we were out in the rough countryside again, following the banks of a long river that snaked its way through the flattened grass. On either side of the nameless river stood happy groves of columnar trees. Poplars, perhaps.

"Look, a patch of England down there!" Jason enthused. "Wonder how that got there!"

There were flocks of Egyptian geese, bright red-and-white finches, hunting kestrels, a flourishing parkland, all benefit of the serpentine creek rolling sluggishly by like molten bronze. We ascended the shoulder of another irregular mountain and the patch of sceptred isle was lost in a choking cloud of red dust.

"There's the lion!" The driver exclaimed to Jason, sticking his head out the window as if he'd never seen it before.

"Would you please keep your eyes on the road, Tseh!" Jason shook his head in exasperation as we lurched towards the boulders.

I tried to look over their bobbing heads. Rural terraced countryside, stone farmhouses. Nothing.

"Up there," Tseh pointed.

A huge boulder the size of an outlet box store resolved itself into a library lion, only this lion was the natural product of erosion and incredible coincidence, as far as I could tell.

"That's not the lion I meant," Jason muttered crossly.

I turned to look at him.

"There's supposed to be an ancient *line* drawing of a lion around here," he explained.

Line drawing of a *lion* only confused our driver; Tseh gave up scanning the horizon, and we all settled back to watch a succession of camels, scimitar-horned Ethiopian cattle, donkeys, and indolent brown-rumped sheep compete for living space on the bestiary-busy highway.

"I don't know why I did this," Jason admitted.

"You mean come to Ethiopia?"

"I mean this whole trip. Africa."

"How long have you been out here now?"

"Two weeks. But it isn't just the athlete's foot, or this red patchy thing I got in the mountains, last week." He showed me a scaly wrist. "It's Mary Jones. Have you heard of her? She was Irish. Walked the whole of the Ethiopian plateau in the 1930s. By the end, her feet were ribbons of torn flesh. The royal family took her in, then she set off again, in the opposite direction, across the countryside. No one knows why."

"No. Sounds like a martyr."

"Yeah, well this is what you do now: You're obliged to make up your own route, your own pilgrimage, and do it alone."

"Right, secular pilgrimage ... Don't they still have those deals where you go in a big truck with a bunch of other people, Cairo to Cape Town, cheap and cheerful?"

"Overlanders. Sure, they're swarms of them in Kenya. I'm going to go on one in Uganda. It's the only way to see that country."

He brightened up at the thought; it seemed he was just lonely.

"So why did you come?"

"I suppose my friends. They all have two mortgages, their houses, their investments, working up to a £80,000-a-year job. At least I'll be able to say, I went here, I did that. I did *something*."

"Are you having a good time, travelling by yourself?" I decided to be blunt.

"Last week? I was invited to this Ethiopian wedding. They slapped a one-birr note on my forehead as an honoured guest, there was dancing, the groom slaughtered a sheep in the doorway of the bride's father's house. That would never have happened if I were travelling with someone else."

"She would have to be near-perfect for *this* trip," I commented. "Anything less, and you'd be screaming at each other in no time."

"There was one. Sweet, wonderful. She lived on the moors with her parents; they were wonderful too. They'd go for walks every day, in the rain, laughing. Warm, loving family."

"So of course you broke up with *her*."

"Of course."

"Did you have a serious girlfriend back home?"

"The love of my life, but we broke off a couple of years ago. I phoned her up once, to get the number of a mutual friend, and her mother answers: 'Caroline's not here. She *is* seeing someone else, you know, Jason!'"

"The old stab-from-the-girlfriend's-mother routine, eh?"

"Exactly. But the worst was, the day before I left I got this e-mail from her, Caroline. She found some old cassettes and she played them, and the memories of our time together really made her happy. She said."

"What did you do?"

"I e-mailed her back. It was a rather long e-mail, I'm afraid."

"So it's starting to happen all over again?"

"That's just it. She calls out of the blue *just* before I'm leaving for a year. I just can't believe it!" He sounded exasperated, frustrated. At a loss for words.

"You think it was just coincidence?"

He gazed out the window and thought about it, about Caroline's motives. The next pair of mountains we passed looked like two tawny breasts to me, but I sensed he was looking right through them.

"*Could it be* that she really likes you?" I offered, mustering a sage expression. "*Is it possible* that she'll be waiting for you in Cape Town?"

"All right, enough already," he nodded and grinned contentedly when he thought I wasn't looking.

Yeha was on the high point of a small rubble-strewn hill some kilometres off the main highway. Over two and a half millennia ago, when Rome was a smelly village, Arab settlers from Ma'rib had come here with their pagan religion, their written language, their Iron Age technology, their epic story of the queen of Sheba – and, most importantly, a profound sense of destiny and entitlement. What was the relationship of these five strands to each other? And why had they come here? All I could think was that this landscape had been a vastly different place twenty-five hundred years ago, wetter and incredibly lush with animal life, and that the indigenous people they found were not organized at a political level that could resist the Sabean colonization. Indeed, the Yemenis were like the Greeks in Anatolia, or Asia Minor, who at roughly the same time founded numerous fortified colonies in those fertile lands, far from their original homes.

The actual palace, said to have been built by Sabeans as early as 1000 B.C. (but probably closer to 600 B.C.), was surrounded by a stone church wall a dozen feet high. The usual assortment of pilgrims, beggars, and itinerant monks pressed themselves flat against the grey walls, or squatted motionless in attitudes of other-worldly contemplation. Some were handless – from leprosy, I supposed. Many had squinty, pustulant eyes from cataracts, or worse. The gatekeeper strode to greet us, holding up a small, bronze Ethiopian cross in one hand. The faithful shook themselves alive and limped over to kiss it, and our passage was slowed by the shaky ancients, who hobbled with all their might for a quick benediction as we entered the main compound within the ruins.

"First Vermeer, now Breughel," I commented as we crossed a graveyard, stepping over rough chunks of hewn granite. Primitive stick-houses and rough bric-a-brac were heaped over the plots. Did they bury their dead or did they just throw dirt over them?

"Careful where you walk," Jason warned. The earth we trod was freshly dug, and I realized that the feeble throng at the gates was waiting to get in, literally. Is religion about life or is it about death? I thought fiercely.

A toothless oldster in a white robe eyed us with a double squint, and showed us a tiny leather book with curious script, and Jesus and God in red letters.

"He want it you buy," the driver explained.

"Sorry, but I can't read Amharic," Jason apologized. The senior grinned delightedly.

"You're so polite," I told him.

The church was built immediately next to the palace; apparently its physical proximity had kept the ancient monument reasonably intact from pillagers for hundreds of years. The palace's high, tottery walls of pink sandstone were still standing, and you could see where the well water was kept and the scullery kitchen maintained at the back, and, like any monster home built today, it overdominated its immediate parcel of land. It gave me the uncanny sense that it had been squeezed into a narrow lot, so there must have been a vast number of lesser habitations pressing in around it, ancillary outbuildings that had failed to survive. I looked through the chinks in the walls out into the countryside, trying to see what a Sabean nobleman or guard would have seen; the palace commanded a view over dozens of kilometres. I could even make out the army barracks we'd passed earlier. There were probably similar barracks standing out there, twenty-five centuries ago. And trees, and someone teaching them how to domesticate the elephants that they would use a thousand years later to reinvade their ancient homeland of Yemen. (Did not the English and the Germans have a similar relationship?)

An old monk came into the ruins and sat himself in a sunny corner by a rickety homemade ladder. What feelings did these pagan ruins arouse in these Orthodox hearts? They had lovingly preserved the ancient carvings too, as I soon discovered; the prelate who had greeted us at the gate now led us up a creaky wooden staircase in the church rectory into an attic of hand-hewn timbers and nail-less joints, a building at least a few centuries old itself.

In the gloom of the garret we could make out a strange Dickensian jumble of fusty objects. This was a storehouse of sorts. Wooden cups and reliquaries, faded black-and-white portraits of fat African queens and mustachioed Mediterranean generals, brilliant heaps of processional robes, blackened silver chalices, velvet umbrellas caked with dust, a giant ceramic crock, function unknown but highly suspect. Jason and I looked at each other in mute astonishment. In the centre of the clutter, by a small open window, stood a huge, varnished wooden cabinet with glass doors. The sharp smell of fresh beer assaulted our nostrils. It appeared they were fermenting strong drink in the double gloom of the windowless floor below.

"Please sit down," the driver translated the priest's odd gesture. The prelate's hands were long and expressive, and we watched them closely now for further cues.

I immediately discerned that the alabaster capitals plunked on the floor by our feet were Sabean. So were the sacrificial urns with the crescent-moon-and-solar-disk symbol carved on them. These, and the alabaster vessels with the bulls' heads, were as distinctive as a complete set of fingerprints weighing sixty pounds each. They were identical in every respect to the artifacts I had studied in the Sana'a museum, twelve hundred kilometres away. Where had the Yeha rulers procured the same yellowy alabaster? Had they dragged these ritual objects all the way from Yemen to Ethiopia, by camel and dhow over mountains and sea? Or had they secured local sources of material and simply imported the artisans? Or was this stuff just loot from the Axumite reinvasions of Yemen, a thousand years after the Sabean colony was founded? This last had to be ruled out, for by A.D. 600, old Yeha itself had been long eclipsed in favour of the "classic" Axumite sites hundreds of kilometres away, so why would any victorious generals bother to favour Yeha with their triumphant plunder from abroad? No, the only thing that made sense was a parallel industry, a parallel cult of Sheba.

The varnished cabinet itself was bursting with old leather Bibles, and dozens of pinealated crowns, belonging to Christian rulers, each with its own curious history. The priest pulled out a volume at random. He flipped through the pages, stopping at the odd, dreamlike illustrations. It was William Blake in Africa. Here was Solomon and there was the Ark.

"Is this the palace of Sheba?" I asked, looking at the picture but not understanding its meaning.

"Sheba, yes, yes." The prelate nodded agreeably and slowly turned the pages, offering us rapturous visions the way others might offer tea.

"Oh, look." Jason's attention had been caught by two live red-and-black birds with bright-orange beaks that had landed on the ancient window frame and were now inspecting us with their beady eyes.

I had the uncanny feeling that the fluttering pair meant to convey some important news, and so did Jason, for we both froze and watched them wordlessly as they took it in their minds to hop a little closer to us, the strangers, interrogating us silently with their bright-eyed bobs. Then, apparently satisfied with their examination, they slipped off chirplessly into the midday ether.

Jason turned to me with a question forming on his lips.

"Don't say it," I said. The hoopoe?

"Would you like to take picture?" Tseh asked. Our priest was already striding purposefully towards a bundle of ritual gowns stacked high in the corner like so much brilliant laundry.

Facing us with a demure expression, the priest pulled a glamorous purple-and-yellow confection down over his head and smiled sultrily, preening as he smoothed out the wrinkles in his habit with long sensual strokes.

Click, zap! Click, zap!

Our cameras flashed, and he turned a bit, to give us a better angle.

Click, zap!

He arched his eyebrows and fixed us with his best runway gaze.

Click, zap!

"You know who he reminds me of?" I said to Jason, who was trying hard just to take the picture.

"Who?" he muttered, refusing to look my way.

"Little Richard," I nodded encouragements to our model. "Or maybe Screaming Jay Hawkins."

"Well, he *certainly* likes dressing up." Jason bit his lip, and we exited the church without further incident.

"Could it be," I postulated as we sat in the army canteen drinking warm Pepsi and closely following the evidently warmer bare belly of our statuesque hostess, she with the dour, unapologetic eyes, "*could it be* that that's all there is at the bottom of religion? A screamer in a tutu?"

Now the bar-girl cleverly turned and stretched, so that we could see her bare navel. Our server had an impressive navel, indeed.

"Have you ever smelt the money?" Jason suddenly thrust a stinky one-birr note right in my face.

"Please, not while I'm dreaming."

"It's got a peculiar smell; oddly familiar and yet curiously ghastly."

"That could be my next book: *Smelling the World's Currencies: The Definitive Guidebook*."

We got back in the Toyota truck and barricaded ourselves behind our personal thoughts.

Finally Jason spoke out.

"So what's the answer then?"

I knew, of course, he was referring to our original conversation about the traveller's dilemma. Whether to go alone, or with somebody. And this, a metaphor for a whole life:

Which to bet? Black or red?

"Are we alone?" Jason said, fixing me with one opalescent eye.

"Perhaps there are no answers, only questions?" I volunteered after a moment.

"You mean everything?" he nodded.

"The whole nine yards. Maybe the answer is a question?"

"The world is a big question mark?"

"There's a religion for you: Asking yourself big, hard questions, bigger and harder all the time."

"You think God might be a question, then?"

"The biggest," I replied.

"Could It Be?" He tugged his beard.

It was easy to talk like that. The brown mountains dwarfed the green hills and the blue Ethiopian sky dwarfed everything. All of us were motes, passengers and drivers, all lost somewhere in the clouds of road dust dancing around us, coating us, coating everything, blinding us with the dust of centuries.

Chapter 17

Left of Yesterday

"**S**o what do you think about the queen of Sheba now?" Jason asked me as I packed up that night, making ready to leave Axum in the morning. "You know Haile Selassie? The ruins guide with the famous same name? He told me that they proved conclusively, a few months ago, she was Ethiopian."

"Really?" I had my medications spread out around the table but, mysteriously, nowhere to put them now, in my bag. "I didn't know that."

"By the granite quarry, on the outskirts of town? They found her *actual* palace, a new discovery. The *third* Sheba."

"The quarry, huh. Not the one they *call* her palace, Dongar, that rock heap west of the town, and not the Yeha place, which is about the right age, 800 B.C. or older. But a *third* Sheba's palace?"

"Could this be the one?" He picked at a scab.

"You know how that Hancock guy says in your book that the Ark was actually a supercivilization's technology?" I gave it my best shot. "Well, I think that religion itself is a technology, a specific kind of brain-active technology, and I think that this technology *did* come from 'somewhere else,'

199

since it only had to be invented once, and then if it's any good, it gets passed around. Like fire, and the bow-and-arrow."

"You think the Sheba story is a technological device?" Jason pulled at what was left of his sparse reddish beard. It seemed to shrivel by nightfall.

"It stands to reason," I went on. "Think: There's the Sabeans, on the trade route, way out in the Empty Quarter in the Arabian Peninsula. Now from there it's overland across the Haraz Mountains, the steepest, scariest mountain range this side of the Himalayas, and down into a hot coastal plain, then across a dead-flat, shark-infested Red Sea in a dinky dhow, across the furnace-hot salt pans of Djibouti, and then up into the boulder-strewn Ethiopian highlands, with crevasses deep enough to swallow the entire moon, all before reaching a few farmable plateaus. Or you go the other way. Whichever."

"Okay, then what?" He fixed me with a sun-creased pair of blue eyes.

"Something *made them* come out here. And I'm betting that thing was a dream."

"A dream?" He pondered the word.

"For want of a better word, yes. A vision, a *calling*."

"And that moon-thing we found? The altar-piece in the Yeha church? Same as in Yemen?"

"It looked like it was carved by the same guy! 'Sabean.' Whatever *that* means."

"They came out here then, as colonists?"

"It's not just the months of fearsome travel. It's the certainty of the goal, the quest. It worked! The technology reproduced itself, like fire."

"On both sides of the sea." Jason nodded. "What do you think it *meant*, then? Their religious symbolism?"

"You're the lovesick Welshman mystic, you tell me."

He was staring out the window of the hotel room, examining a black immensity loaded with desert stars. I had a thought to share. "I can tell you this much: *Saba* means 'morning.'"

"Well, the moon goddess. In Wales, she's called Buana; in Greek, Artemis. That's her sign, the crescent moon. It's extremely old, that."

"And the round ball above the crescent?"

"Potential, maybe. The Fullness of Time."

"All things come to pass?" Now I was pulling at *my* nascent beard.

"Yeah, the crescent is Time, the cycle of the seasons. The disk is Eternity. They're ... married."

"The Marriage of Time and Eternity, *hmm* ... You know what?"

"What?"

"I think you're right," I nodded slowly.

"And the queen?" He threw back his head.

Had a comet just gone by?

"A goddess. Maybe *the* goddess. On one of the incense burners, I noticed they carved the crescent like a pair of arms, reaching up to encompass the solar disk, and the body below it was a triangle, for a dress. So it's *her* symbol. And whoever the Sabeans were, they were like the Vikings. Creating dynasties as they went along, as the Vikings did in Kiev and Normandy."

"They created one here?"

"Ethiopia was practically the only state in the whole of Africa to resist colonization, after the Sabeans came and built Yeha. If that isn't proof of the power of this Sabean technology, then I don't know what is. It's not like the Ethiopians otherwise have defensible borders, or a homogenous population, is it? There's thirty different ethnic groups living here, and yet they've made a nation out of it, against all odds, for hundreds of years."

"How do you think it works? This religious 'technology,' if that's what you call it? You think this myth, the story of Sheba, actually had an effect on their history?"

"I don't know," I admitted. "There's nothing on it in current theories of history, which is all microeconomics and statistical materialism, not idealist ... Maybe it – the myth – creates a template or catalyst, something that gets stamped on the collective mind. These palaces and so forth weren't *big*, but they were powerful. And why they came here, chose Axum in the middle of nowhere, as their new capital, I don't know ... Something about the area, a high plateau like Ma'rib. Irrigation. Gold. Trade, maybe."

We talked on the balcony, about ancient history, about our history, our luck with women or lack of it. I didn't tell him that long ago, before he was born, there was a girl, a Celtic girl, and if the baby had lived he would be exactly Jason's age now.

And what better name than Jason, he who sought the golden fleece?

§§

Before I left Axum I had to buy some Ethiopian crosses from the boys who had waited patiently outside the hotel for days on end with their wares. Waiting for me to buy from them, and them alone, Johnny, David, Joseph, Michael, at a friend's best price, so they could buy dictionaries and note-books for school.

"So many dictionaries!" I joked, and they laughed.

The fact was, I was the only game in town. There were no other tourists worth the candle. They had stopped coming two years ago, after the war with Eritrea. Before that even Yemenis would ship their cars to Djibouti and then drive along the winding highway to Axum. But not any more.

Michael was tall for his age, fourteen, and in school. His father was a guard at the town water pump. Like his friends he would keep his eyes peeled for tourists from behind his schoolyard fence, noting their movements and anticipating their daily routines. Calculating their likely trajectories through the main sites of the small town. A few days ago, when I took a donkey cart several kilometres out of town to see the Sheba Palace number one, a heap of rocks in a wheat field called the Dongar site, there Michael was, a few minutes later, patiently waiting for me outside the official gate.

On one side of the fence was the confederation of tribal stones, silent plinths spelling out *prehistoric* in their haphazard crudity. On the other side stood this lone boy in his red Levi's vest, an outfit smuggled in no doubt on the freight train from Djibouti with great cunning and effort. Every time I cast my eyes in his direction, he held up his stock-in-trade: A couple of silver Ethiopian crosses. A set of brass necklace pieces. An alabaster carving of the queen of Sheba, in miniature.

On the one side, a furrowed farmer's field with cryptic rocks, inviolate graves.

On the other, the living.

I tell myself Michael could easily be a descendant of the queen of Sheba, if any there were. People don't get out of this country much, they either survive or they die. Tonight I ask him to write out his name and address for me. He speaks good English, street English accented by the urgent need to close a deal.

"Now what about the stone Sheba?" he said, tucking my payment away. "Good price. Look, it's got a seal at the bottom. See?"

I looked down at what he had written on my notebook, and saw immediately he had misspelled his country. *Ethoipia.*

⚵

"Johannis, please tell me a ghost story. Something good."

I have returned to Addis Ababa tonight with pleasure and anticipation; I like this sprawling, disjointed city, although I can't say why. It's not just the excellent coffee and exquisite girls, or the unearthly music. Maybe I like Johannis Aychew; he's a good driver and companion, and we laugh at the same things, although he is only twenty-eight. Still, he's lost his father to the Eritrean high command, so he's older than he looks, with his shaved head, wraparound shades, and cool skate gear. He's Amharic, Christian, and educated, driving a taxi because that's basically all you can do in a country with vast underemployment and constant wars. Tonight we drive fast through the empty streets of Addis, going nowhere in particular, sightseeing, with shadows falling heavily around us, purple daubs cast by a loathsome nocturnal god. Evening in a city with murderous walls at every turn.

I wanted to hear a good story. I have been without books or magazines apart from the *Wired*s and an old *Herald Tribune* ("BUCHAREST MAYOR DECLARES WAR ON STRAY DOGS") for weeks now. The Ethiopians were renowned storytellers; the oral tradition emphasizes lessons of survival, in which magic, the power of the imagination, plays a huge part.

Johannis nodded.

"It seems there was a man, and he looked like most men do. He wore a *gibala*, the robe, like the Arabs do, and a hat, out of respect, so you would not know that he was a wizard, a *tanqua*. But his real name was Graz

Tlantena, Left of Yesterday, which of course is not a Bible name like John or Peter. And also, he chewed the chat and smoked the hashish, and felt his power getting stronger.

"And the *tanqua* was out walking in the market when he saw a young beautiful woman, a tourist, yes? She was getting out of a Land Cruiser and taking pictures of the boys selling peanuts and such things. Her husband must be very rich, he thought. So he decided to test his powers.

"Because of his powers, for he was a young and strong *tanqua*, he was able to make the lady think he was a beautiful young boy with bright eyes like grapes after the rain. He knew she was hungry, and this was the best way. He knew how to do this, because the woman, he could see now, was vain. She tossed her head and laughed when the other boys smiled. He would smile too, but with reason.

"Soon she came to his eyes. 'Come look at my raisins,' he cried softly. He swayed his hips a little. She was curious; she came forward, and her mouth was open a little.

"It is a bad thing to open your mouth when a *tanqua* is present. This is how they steal your soul.

"'So would you like to take a picture of me?' he asked, his mouth smiling like a boy's and his eyes shining like dark plums.

"'Do you want money?' she said. He could see she was hesitating. The other boys could not understand why she was talking to this man. The *tanqua* only made the magic for her, not them.

"No, no. No money. Look." He held up his box of raisins. She looked into her big camera, through the long telephoto lens. Then she saw that his eyes were not alive. They were like raisins, squinting and dried out.

"But it was too late. Now she was his! A sudden blow descended on her, the worst headache in the world. . . . When she awoke she was still in the market, holding tight to a box of raisins, with a boy's hands, and the truck was gone with her life."

Johannis turned to me, to see if I was still with him, satisfied. I thought a bit.

"So he was in her body, the wizard?"

"Yes. He went to Paris. He walked into her house. He knew everything. Where her house was, her car, money – *everything*! Except for her husband. Because the power of the living is different from the power of things. He knew her things but not her life. Even her body, it was like a horse that refused to be ridden. He had many bruises and bad scrapes on it, getting to Paris, and when he walked it was like a drunk person, sometimes falling against a doorway for no reason, especially in the evening when he was tired. For it was the living body, not wanting to go where the *tanqua* wanted it to go. Bad places, of which I will say no more.

"So finally he comes to the house where her husband lives, and he walks into the main room. Furniture, paintings, carpets, many fine things.

" 'Adena!' The husband calls out, and opens his mouth and his arms, and his heart is beating fast, a bird in a cage that must get free or die.

"Left of Yesterday is a very powerful now, for he has fed and done many bad things, and he knew it would be easy to kill the *farangi*. He has a wooden rod for pounding the coffee beans. He would not even need his magic to kill the *farangi*. He strikes him down. Then he decides to freeze his heart instead, so he ties him up with the dried gut of a cat, which is stronger than rope and only partly magic.

"Then Left of Yesterday goes out of the house. He is careful, for one eye appears normal, but the other one shows what he is. And it is this eye that he must keep to the wall, otherwise he will be found out."

"And the girl, back in the market?" I interjected. "What about her?"

"She remembers everything. Her life before the *tanqua*, and after. And the body the *tanqua* gave her was a young body, a good body. Otherwise it would not keep her soul wrapped tight. So she gets a job, in a hotel, and because she is smart she makes enough money to pay the *nightmen*, the body smugglers, to take her to France.

"So after many adventures and the help of God and all his saints she comes to her own house. She sees through the window. Her husband is tied to the ceiling and hangs there like a dried salami. The *tanqua* is saving him for a special occasion. He is still alive though, for his eyes flutter like winter flies.

"And the *tanqua* is making ready for his *petit-dejeuner*. He has stolen the afterbirth from a woman in the hospital, lying and saying he is a doctor, and smiling with his one liar-eye at her.

"Adena makes a sound, creeping into the house. But the *tanqua* does not hear, because he gets more and more hungry every day, and he must eat these strange and terrible things to satisfy his blood-cries.

"Adena knows what to do, for she has covered her ears with white linen-cloth, so that when he SHOUTS his terrible SHOUT she will not fall down. She has covered her mouth with the white cloth so that the *tanqua* cannot fill it with poison of one kind or another.

"In her hand she has the quill of the African porcupine, the only thing that will kill the hyaena. Twelve quills, one for each of the apostles.

"Now the *tanqua* sees her and rises from his table, the bloody froth of the dead baby covering his mouth and breast, now he turns his terrible eye towards her, and besets her. She almost faints, for she sees that the bad eye is not an eye, no, it is but a black hole where she herself is kept prisoner, as in a black cell or cave, and crying to get out.

"'Now you will die!' he shouts and begins to shut his terrible eye, to bring the final darkness down on her.

"Seeing her fate, she almost falls in fright. But the porcupine quills leave her hand, flying off one by one of their own power given by the saints. They fly right at the hyaena man.

"And kill him.

"She cuts her husband down and together they wash the blood of the house away. All that remained was a scrap of dirty hide.

"'Adena' means *saved*, and this is a story of how she was saved by the power of God and His Twelve Holy Saints."

Chapter 18

The Rasta with the Documents

The Rastafarian community in Shashemene lies 220 kilometres south of Addis Ababa, off the main railway line to Djibouti and in the middle of Omoro country. The Omoro are cattle-herders, a proud, aggressive people who insist on using their own language and have resisted the government-favoured Amharic for decades. They bear some resemblance to the Masai farther to the south in Kenya. I asked Johannis if the Omoro believe all cattle are theirs, and therefore have no compunction against stealing others'.

"No, they don't take others' cows. Unless they want to die soon."

About four hundred Rastafarians were presently living in Shashemene, I was told, and I was curious to learn what uses this new religion, now only sixty years old, had made of the Solomon-and-Sheba story. It was Shashemene that Jenny, the British traveller, had visited on her own after giving the slip to her brother for a day, and it seemed that the community served an important symbolic purpose for black travellers. I had seen rich American blacks cashing wads of traveller's cheques in the big bank in Addis, and Johannis informed me that Shashemene was their typical destination.

The Rasta community had originally been created by a land grant from Haile Selassie for Jamaicans and others who arrived in Ethiopia after his coronation, seeking the sanction of a black king, the Lion of Judah.

The highway south was good, straight and wide, and there was little truck traffic, this being a Sunday – but then, it also served as the main thoroughfare for herds of long-horned cattle, camels, goats, and the ubiquitous horse-carts. It took us more than three hours to reach our destination, hurtling through the little towns, scarcely slowing from the 140 km/h we made on the open stretches, then braking constantly for sudden obstructions, and then accelerating again to make up for the lost minutes. Johannis kept a sharp lookout for the subtle cues that meant an animal was about to bolt. Me, I couldn't tell, and neither could other drivers.

We passed a squashed sheep, a freshly killed dog, and the carcass of a huge black bull that must have totalled anything less than a semi-truck a few hours earlier. At night, this Noah-like traffic would become a nightmare of floating yellow eyes and screeching tires once again, so I kept my attention on the tropical sun as it made its rounds over the horizon.

We halted at Lake Langano for lunch and entered a huge gated compound, with extensive bungalow cottages set out in the Englishman-Abroad style. The lake was a murky pink. The muddy shoreline was iron-rich and the daily-rental jetcraft buzzed about noisily, stewing up the roseate chuff even more. This was a kind of tourist resort, close enough to the capital for a day's outing for diplomats, foreign-aid workers, and their families. Extremely pale people walked about in frumpy, old-fashioned beachwear, exposing themselves unmercifully to the fierce African sun and splashing in the turbid wake of the buzzing craft. We had entered a 1950s time warp, where the dangers of skin cancer and *bilharzia*, or gut parasites, were unknown. Either that, or these people were profoundly stupid. A strange group of young men had the dining-room table next to ours; they sported the shaved heads of punks, most of them, and complicated tattoos, yet they spent more time calculating their respective shares of the lunch bill than actually eating. Biker accountants? The waiter tried to overcharge us by a preposterous amount, and given that Johannis and I each had only a simple dish of cheese macaroni and an orange pop, he played his part as the dumbfounded waiter magnificently, going over the figures again and again with a pencil and still getting it wrong, as if the operation of adding five birr and five birr was far beyond his calling. I was almost fooled.

"They always do this," Johannis tightened his lips. "In the big hotels especially. See how he makes the addition on a separate piece of paper? That's his money, the difference, if we don't catch it. Don't leave a tip."

Outside the restaurant we approached one of the punks from the group, who said his name was Martin. He had stripped his shirt off, and he was already reaching a nice fried pink. He told us he had just arrived from Sweden and was working for the international aid organization, Youth with a Mission.

"I hope to be here for two years. We figure on working with the RCs, as they have some organization. Then we branch out, youth clubs, discussion groups. I hope it works out."

The RCs? He must be one of those country-bumpkin, life-hating Calvinists out of *Babette's Feast*. Where did these people come from, with their outmoded denominational categories and their insistence on failed conversion programs? Where did they get off even *coming* here? After all the long centuries of colonial nonsense?

"We're strapped for money, but my job is to set up a printing press, and get the Word out."

And no cash either. Just endless Bible tracts on cheap paper.

Martin had taken his jeans and cut the legs off, badly. What other accommodations would he be making soon, to the hard realities of the country? I was about to ask him about punk-church doctrine when he spotted a likely prospect strolling ahead of us, a black youth with the Jamaican toque and the tricolour Bob Marley T-shirt. As if to impress us with his missionary zeal, Martin loped on ahead, and the youth turned sharply at the sound of footsteps crunching on the gravel. From his blood-red eyes, it looked as if he had been smoking powerful herb for breakfast.

"So have *you* read the Book of Revelation?" Martin asked him, heavy on the meaningful timbre.

"*Whaah*?" the youth replied, his eyes widening in alarm. "Me?"

We got back into the hot oven of the car, and watched the ensuing encounter without sound. The local youth appeared hypnotized by the prominent blue triangle-tattoo on the punk-missionary's shoulder. He was probably wondering what it *meant*, this alien delta-symbol, that and maybe this whole encounter. Jammin' down the beach groovin' on the breeze, and then this white dude comes outta nowhere, starts talking bout rev'lations at him ...

When we had driven through the village of Meki earlier, the temperature had soared to over a hundred; it held me breathless for a spell. Now it happened again, a bludgeoning heat descended from nowhere, and fifteen minutes away from the lake I was once more completely whacked out, suffocating. I didn't know how Johannis could keep driving in this heat. These variations in climate came fast and severe. Suddenly we found ourselves in a baking acacia plain. The lakeside greenery had completely disappeared. Hundreds of tall white mounds now dotted the bereft fields, punctuated by hand-painted gravestones. Those comical Ethiopian cartoons again: kingly riders on black steeds for the deceased men, and sweetly drawn grey elephants for the women. Johannis said elephants were female symbols, older than the Christian uses to which they were now put. And the bleached-white mounds?

"*Yemist bait*," Johannis commented. "Ant houses."

There were thousands of them, termite mounds. The farmers simply planted around them, wherever they could. I thought of the recent anthropological theory that our big advantage in the Palaeolithic came from our ability to fashion termite probes from sticks, using them to secure a lifetime supply of fat- and protein-rich insects at little risk. Something no other animal could do, except the chimpanzee, who in any case couldn't stand the heat of this savannah. Termites were obviously a huge and unexploited source of food otherwise, and this ability would have conferred enormous selective advantages on our species. Maybe as global warming continued and the grasslands spread, we could go back to eating them.

The good road ended at Shashemene. Now it was pockmarked and riven with washouts. We spotted some Rastas, then a small concrete building with a black lion painted on it, beside a fruit stand. The lion sported a crown, with a banner. *Museum*, it said.

We walked to the gate, paid our *farangi* entrance fee of twenty birr, and found a messy yard filled with kitchen refuse and a couple of tin-roofed buildings inside. Vultures checked on us from overhead. I didn't know what to expect, but I certainly didn't expect an older light-skinned man in grey dreads and a checkered workshirt greeting us with a New York accent.

"Robinson," he said and stuck out his hand. "How ya doin'?"

"You're American," I said unnecessarily. *Robinson*, what a perfect name!

"And you? Canadian? That's cool, man. Come on in."

Gladstone Robinson was seventy-one, but he could have passed for fifty. A naked baby crawled in from the next room, and Robinson held Haile Mikal up for a look.

"I had ten children, so Haile here makes eleven. My wife is pregnant with my twelfth and that's *it*, man! Twelve, like the twelve tribes of Judah. I'm quitting right then and there!"

Gladstone told us he was born in New York City, son of a Pentecostal minister mother, a woman who believed in education. He graduated in pharmacy. His father was from Barbados, and his mother, part Cherokee. As he rolled a big spliff, he put Marley on the cassette player. The anteroom of the tiny house was bursting with papers, photocopies, and pictures.

"No thanks," I said to his offer of herb. "I got an insurance medical coming up, and I don't want to blow it!"

"Man, in the lab where I worked everybody was smoking – so nobody got failed on the urine. But now? You get what you call Rasta-Paranoia, man, that's when you look out your window, and you see your neighbours talking to someone you don't know. Could be the police, man. They want to bust us, take away our land that Haile Selassie – HAIL HAILE SELASSI! – gave us."

Here he rose from his rickety chair and offered the portrait an energetic fist-salute. "And looking to find your bush with the help of some *so-called* Rastas. Know what I mean?"

"Do you always listen to Bob Marley"? I wondered how many songs the late artist had recorded, that you could keep on playing them into your seventies.

"No, I got jazz records too. Charlie Parker, Dizzy Gillespie. I was up on stage with Dizzy, you know."

"How did you get into the Rasta-thing then?"

"I was introduced to Rasta Doctrine in 1963." He proudly showed me a picture of himself as a young, horn-rimmed guy, with more than a passing resemblance to Malcolm X. "It was part of the Back-to-Africa Movement. I sent a delegate to Ethiopia to meet the Emperor in 1963, later I came myself. The Emperor, he gave me five gashes of land."

"Gashes?"

"That's two hundred hectares, my friend, or five hundred acres. Prime land and worth millions now that the highway is coming through, but the local people, the government, man, is corrupt, and you can quote me on that!"

I was writing all this down, on a sturdy notebook with a good pen he had provided.

"See, the local people, the Omoro, it's the bribe, you know. How things are done. I see all these people in judgment, there's too many people here for me to fight, you take my refrigerator right there."

I nodded. It was covered with stickers from the United States: *100% Pure Florida Orange Juice*, that kind of thing.

"They took my *refrigerator*, man. It was loaded with fruits, fish, everything. They were pulling it over the guard wall with ropes. They were going to feast that night, and laugh at me. I began to bang my cutlass, and they dropped my refrigerator off the wall. I came here with a clean heart, and they steal from you, man, and they think that's okay."

"So this is the land that the Emperor gave you?"

"Me and nine others, but you see the Derg [the Mengistu socialists, who assassinated Selassie in 1975] took my land, left me with only six hundred metres. I'm fighting it in court, man! I'm known here as the 'Rasta with the Documents'!" He showed me more wads of paper. "Thing is, you got to write in English, then translate it to Amharic, then to the local language of the accusers. Omorian, whatever, and each time it's sixty birr, man, for a piece of paper!"

"So the local people are giving you trouble?"

"Some call us foreigners. These Omoro, it's all in the *tribalism*, to take our land from us. We're supposed to be free here. We know the next thing is reparations, the terms we say, for the U.S. slavery. We stand to get three trillion dollars! We open up a bank account here in Shashemene, a Reparations Bank – you want some of this?" He held out his spliff.

"No," I was still writing furiously.

"See? You don't need this. You're getting high from my story!"

"You're right." I looked up at him, and his mocha-light eyes crinkled in pleasure. "You *are* getting me high. So what's the story of Solomon and Sheba? Is there a Rasta take on that?"

"King Solomon was the wisest king. You know why? They found herb on his grave! She went to visit him, she said, and he said, 'You're so beautiful.' Both. They complimented each other. For royalty to have *relations*, you know, it's a big thing.

"She, being the queen of Sheba, she told Solomon that you can't take me by force, and he said, as long as you don't steal anything that's valuable from the palace, I will not touch you.

"Then he spiced the food extra hot, and during the night she had to drink, and when she drank the water from the jug placed near his head, he grabbed up her arm.

"'Don't take me!' she cried.

"'What is the most valuable thing a man has when he is thirsty? It's *water*, and I told you not to take something valuable!' . . . That's the story."

This was more or less the version given in the *Kebra Negast*, the Ethiopian epic composed in the fourteenth century A.D. I wanted to know the relationship of the ancient Ethiopian cult to the contemporary Rastafarian agenda.

"How does this story relate to the Emperor Haile Selassie?"

"Well, Marcus Garvey, he – you know who that is? – he prophesied in the States that a king would come from the East to save the black people. All the Caribbean island people were looking, and when they heard of the coronation of the emperor – ZODKAN! – of the king of kings, the triumphant lion of the tribe of Judah, the Emperor was a triumphant lion, *not* a lamb to be slaughtered, well, every Rasta wanted to be in Ethiopia with him."

Of course, I thought.

The black lion is the complement of the white lamb. One for slaughter, the other for salvation. Garvey was a radio preacher in the 1930s, and the Rasta myth of Haile Selassie's divinity began when the rain fell in drought-ridden Jamaica the very minute he emerged from the airplane at Kingston Airport.

"You know," Robinson said, musing on his fat, smouldering spliff, "I was the last international president of the Ethiopian World Federation, before we split with the new divisions. We were infiltrated! The Boboshanti, the Niabiasi. The Twelve Tribes? *That* local is integrated, the big chief is a white Jew. Suddenly we have Oriental Rasti, a Japanese Rasti, Belgians. I had thirty people here, in from Norway, a while back . . . Come on, let me show you the place."

Robinson led us through the kitchen. I could hardly see a thing in the windowless gloom, and I wasn't sure that he had electricity. His young wife of twenty (maybe) was African, the daughter of a friend, he said, who had died a few years earlier. We went back into the yard and he showed us a concrete washhouse.

"See? See this?" He cranked the tap and water sputtered out. "My daughter, she's coming out from New York, next month, and I want to be ready for her. She works for the police, her husband's a cop."

"She wouldn't try and bust her own dad, would she?" I joked.

"She's been here before . . . anyways, that's the cookhouse."

Another small concrete building, but this one had a blackened open window.

"We just got to teach the people about sanitation," he said as I stepped around some excrement.

"So what about the fork in the road, Gladstone? You happy with the choices you made?" It was a fair question for a seventy-one-year-old, I figured.

"You know what?" He fixed me with a clear gaze, as if he hadn't been smoking dope for fifty-odd years. "You're right here, and I'm right here, and we're together in the same place at the same time. *That* says *something*, don't it."

"You're right," I nodded sagely. It did. Karma, coincidence, the trajectories of our common pursuits led me to ask the questions, him to answer them. A 1950s jazz musician, and a pharmacist, into politics. Where would he have been if he'd stayed in New York?

Robinson called his wife outside for a photo. In the sunlight I could see she was more beautiful and much younger than I thought.

"I'm like the man in Revelation!" he was jubilant. "The woman had a male child and the man ran into the wilderness and there was war in Africa. But I'm okay. I get $522 U.S. a month, social security, that's 4,000 birr. The whole thing is to get the Ark back, for whoever possessed the Ark would be victorious in battle. Therefore the West is going to fail!" He declared, now playing the part of the Old Testament prophet. "The Ark will bring victory to the righteous!"

His beautiful wife smiled. He spoke to her in a language that neither I nor Johannis recognized, so it was likely she understood nothing of his English orations apart from their repetition and pattern.

"And because they don't have justice, Matthew 24, the Last Days, it will all come very soon."

"Thanks for showing us your house."

" 'Give my regards to Broadway,' " he said as he led us back through the front gate. "Just don't tell them where I'm at."

I was uncertain if this was the line from the song or his own sentiment, and I never had a chance to ask him, because we were suddenly beset on all sides by a gang of aggressive street youths who demanded money for watching our car. There were eight or nine, Omoro boys, and I gave then each a one-birr note, but suddenly they were snatching at my hands, pushing me back, and snarling in my face.

Robinson yelled at me, "Step back!" I did so, and stepped behind him. Then he led us to the car and we drove slowly off, mindful of the press of bodies closing in from all sides.

Our host gave us the hopeful v-sign, but his unhappy face did not go with it. We kept our windows rolled up against the flurry of yelled insults and fender kicks, and arrived in Addis at nightfall.

Interregnum

Packing up before my flight to Turkey, I decided to ditch the frankincense or myrrh or whatever it was, a cello bag of glittery crystals I had bought in the merkato *in Addis for a dollar. It resembled crack cocaine, and I did not want to end my trip as the author of a sequel to* Midnight Express. *Turkey had its own agreeable tradition of* Saba Sultana, *the queen of Sheba, the third culture to promulgate the story, but it was ferociously strict about such things. Into the garbage it went.*

The thing I could not jettison so easily was that image of the elephant from the Axumite tomb. It disturbed me, and as I packed it came to me why. The African elephant we knew had giant ears, used for fanning itself cool. The extinct war-elephant of Axum had small ears, which could only mean only one thing: the climate around the Red Sea had sharply deteriorated since 600 B.C. It had heated up.

I finished packing, and went downstairs to wait for Johannis in the hotel café. I talked to an Israeli ex-soldier about the prospects of peace in the Middle East. The conversation was short, for he thought there were none. I kept watching out for a young woman who was staying at the hotel, a white Rasta. She was no more than twenty-four. Her boyfriend had telephoned, Reiko from Berlin, and I had taken his call, because I was in her former room, and he had asked the operator for her only by room number. His voice sounded edgy, anxious.

"Please tell Griet to call me, when she comes back. I'll be waiting!"

217

Pleading with the stranger to deliver his message. He had good reason, for eventually she came into the café. A young, good-looking Ethiopian guy with dreads came in with her; they were laughing. They talked away the afternoon over cigarettes and tiny cups of coffee, at a corner table. She laughed and laughed, crossing her legs and uncrossing them. She seemed in no hurry to make that call.

PART THREE

Ephesus

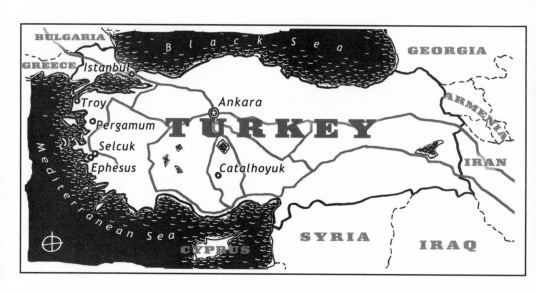

Chapter 19

Culture Matters

The plane dives between a curious corkscrew medley of clouds into the steely claws of rain. A sharp arc of indigo water rolls, straightens out. The Bosporus in March. Below, red-tiled roofs, encircled by swoopy lines of red-tailed traffic. "Stambool! Stambool!" The children in the front rows cry out, thrilled by the sudden appearance of home after the long, dull passage from Frankfurt.

The taxi ploughs through great sheets of water spilling over the Kennedy Cad, the seaside thoroughfare, and we pass the Bokocyp, the fish market with its soaking canopies, rolling by slowly enough for us to count the silvery offerings left out under the dazzling arc-lights. Bullets of rain continue to fall hard in the growing gloom. Water, water everywhere. I go for a walk to the Cagaloglu Hamam, the old Turkish bath. It has been twenty years since I was last in Istanbul, and I remember nothing except the smell of its waters.

Did the Turks come out of the drylands of Central Asia, drawn by this free water? Did they conquer Constantinople to secure themselves a piece of the European rainfall? The thunder cracks over the city in deep staccato groans, almost drowning out the insistent radio-whine of the muezzins. How they must have laughed and sung, splashing jubilantly about, when they finally conquered the fabled city in 1354, after sixty years of trying.

Why *am I* in Turkey, I ask myself peevishly, sitting in a canopied café as the cold rain seeps through my hood and into my neck. I down a hot bullet of thick black coffee and stare moodily at the gushing streets.

Later, the rain beats in gusts against the window of my hotel room, continues to thunder and rattle the panes until morning. It takes a good breakfast of oranges and eggs and apricot jam to help me recognize that persistent feeling: I am spoiled by all this water, after the aridity of Ethiopia and Yemen. This glut is overgenerous, profligate. Everyone is rich here; the sweet rain falls and falls without surcease, and disappears into the gutters and pours out into the sea, and nobody cares a whit. On the TV, various Afghani imams are mortaring each other silly in the name of Allah, then sitting primly in white robes, holding press conferences and facing the shaky camera with impassive but slightly doleful eyes, and I think, No water.

The Israeli ex-soldier back in Addis told me about the settlers and their deep wells and their Palestinians neighbours and how the Israeli government could not afford to give in to the settlers, and could not afford to force them out of any agreed-upon borderline, and that the only security his country had was the atomic bomb ("America's?" I asked, and he shook his head sadly, looking into my face with his burning blue eyes.)

And I think, Is this fight about land or about *water*?

Also in Addis, Johannis, my driver, suddenly got serious in the coffee shop, telling me how the end of Ethiopia's childhood was near, how for too long now his country has stood by and watched its people endure famine, while the Egyptians have taken all the water of the Mother River for themselves, without allowing the people at its source a single drop for their own poor fields. Now he said, the day of reckoning had arrived. Ethiopia was strong now, and would not be stopped from taking its birthright, the long and powerful Blue Nile.

Then I recall an article in the German-published text on Yemen, about the ancient religion of the Sabeans, which centred around the cult-worship of a powerful Serpent and which archaeologists have found depicted everywhere, in cast-bronze snakes and carved symbols. One such bronze snake, found in Timman, a port on the Red Sea, had a gold head. This was the numinous power of the wadi – the seasonal river, made manifest – and it explained to me why the serpent in the Bible was the keeper of the fruit from the Tree of Life. Because he was the very spirit of the winding river that gave Life. *Water*.

Even Chuck Fipke and his men, hunting for gold in northern Yemen, were obliged to follow the course of the wadi to seek the fabulous secret of its head, buried somewhere in its winding path. And the secret of the queen of Sheba? Dr. Abdullah was right, I was convinced. Her secret treasure *was* water. It was plain to me that water was the subtext of the Ethiopian tale, the *Kebra Nagast*, just as it was in the Quranic account.

In the Ethiopian national epic, Makeda grows up a princess, survives a venomous serpent that is threatening the palace, and visits Solomon, who roughly seduces her over a simple drink of water. She is revenged by Menelik, her son from the brief union. The prince returns to Israel, and along with a few other first-born sons of the Hebrew elders, hatches a plot. Fuelled by the rage of the misbegotten son, Menelik snatches the Ark of the Covenant from Jerusalem, and takes it up into the highland capital of Axum forever. But who exactly were these Ark-rustling Axumites, these renegade Hebrews led by the celebrated love child? One authority, Giovanni Garbini, has this to say about the linguistic composition of that land in the first millennium B.C.:

> Around 500 B.C. southern Arabian groups from Hadramawt settled in Ethiopia. A few decades later they were followed by the Sabeans. As a result of these tribal migrations there emerged ... the last Semitic language group, Ethiopic, which can be described as a form of southern Arabic transplanted to Africa. Where the Sabean influence was strongest there emerged the northern Ethiopian languages (Ge'ez, later Tirinya and Tigre) while the older immigrations produced ... Amharic.
>
> – "Semitic and Indo-European Languages," *Yemen: 3000 Years of Art and Civilization in Arabia Felix*

What is arresting about this passage (and the whole of Professor Garbini's thesis) is its implication that language itself can be *wholly* fluid – water, not stone. Here, a language emerges from a migration; like water it *emerges freely* from the sudden nexus of different peoples. The migrants mixed here in Ethiopia, and two new languages developed.

This was not how earlier generations saw language developing; rather, traditional linguists like German philologist Franz Bopp distinguished between a series of fatherless daughter-languages, all born of an unknown ancient Mother (Indo-Europa, or "Wiro"), all of pure birth and provenance, except perhaps for those impudent loan words, vulgarisms, etc., such as the ones the French Academy so stoutly resists to the present day. That language structure itself could be borrowed, or created relatively quickly *and spontaneously*, was anathema. Surely the basic *structure* remained intact, self-evolving, isolate? This was the Good Daughter Theory of culture.

Yet the Garbini school argued compellingly for fluidity and permeability at every level, including structural, and even described the relationship of Semitic and Indo-European as permeable and open, both to each other and, moreover, to the raw material environment of the pre–Iron Age. He continues:

> The languages we historically term "Semitic" probably
> evolved in the 4th millennium B.C. in the area between the
> Tigris and the Mediterranean, and their formation was
> directly linked with the establishments of the first human
> settlements. . . . [T]he chief characteristics of the Indo-
> European languages developed in the 3rd millennium . . .
> north of the Semitic region and north of Anatolia, but *still*
> *close enough to Semitic in order to be able to develop with it*
> *an inflection system.*

No other language groups developed an inflection system, just these two, apparently in tandem, and only because of their sheer proximity. So here we have two superlanguage *groups* influencing *each other*, Semitic and Indo-European, and each in turn being creatively advanced by the technical strides of their novel neolithic and chalcolithic (pre–Iron Age) communities.

Here then, is the Tuning Fork Theory of Culture: Contiguous culture systems excite and resonate with each other, spontaneously generating wholesale transformations within their walls. Ge'ez and Amharic were not "Arab" daughter-languages, but something new. Axum was an admixture of the new technology (war-elephants) and the old traditions (the queen of Sheba myth, etc.) that collectively advanced through history in a tight dialectic with its immediate neighbours (the centuries-long battle-flow with Yemen, the religious tensions with Israel and Christianity).

So on one plane, perhaps Menelik, the illicit son of Queen Makeda and King Solomon, is more than just the founding ancestor of an Ethiopian dynasty in desperate need of legitimacy. He is also the very symbol of the heterogenous nature of Ethiopian society itself, of its mixed and mysterious roots; and his theft of Israel's Ark is a telling recognition of Ethiopia's essentially self-created pedigree. For this great and notorious thief asserts the independence of the *not*-son, the freebooter, the bastard prince who will not be recognized, and who therefore must assert and recognize *himself*. The national languages, Ge'ez-Tigre and Amharic, are Semitic-Cushite hybrids, like the prince. The progeny of a Semitic father and an indigenous mother, Menelik seems blessed with ontological knowledge of God. Culture matters, in other words; it irresistibly transmits itself whole through the ancestral bloodline.

This is the real secret of the Ethiopian epic: *Water flows.*

It will move, this life-giving element, this creative sparkle, this impulse to destiny, and it will only be contained and appropriated by those who are worthy, who are privy to its mysteries and adept in its ways. The Israelites lost the Ark for good reason, according to the national legend, because Solomon proved ultimately the callous deceiver, tricking the queen over a simple glass of water. That is why the great conjuror must always be shown in profile in all Ethiopian Orthodox artwork: Solomon is the base manipulator. While Makeda looks out to the world in full face, innocent and wholesome, the guileless Mother of her people.

But why did she, this princess of a desert royal house, go to Jerusalem in the first place? When in ancient history did monarchs leave their kingdoms, except to conquer? So the mystery remains, why the queen of Sheba left her well-watered oasis – whether it was from that desert abode by the Empty Quarter, or from somewhere high in the lofty plateaus of Ethiopia – to travel the many dusty miles to Jerusalem? Quran, Bible, *Kebra Negast*, all the accounts agree on the answer: to meet Solomon.

Looking over the brooding, rain-dark metropolis of Istanbul from my fifth-storey hotel window, I try to imagine what the world looked like, at the dawn of the Iron Age that gave birth to the present world order.

It is around 950 B.C. (now we go into History, a different place). Saba, with almost fifty thousand inhabitants under its dominion, is one of the few dozen cities in a dark world. Memphis in Egypt. Babylon, Harappa, Ur, Nineveh, two or three others in China. Word of Solomon and his city comes from the many caravans passing through Saba. The Sabeans will have detailed knowledge of all matters on their route – politics, resources, currency, markets, terrain. The queen is able to deliver messages and preliminary gifts to Solomon. He likewise. He has already married innumerable women for dynastic purposes, the daughter of the Pharaoh by some accounts. A queen from a desert kingdom? He will marry her, even if her God has not favoured her with any charms but the royal blood.

So.

She decides to leave her kingdom. But how can she do this, at a time when the person of the monarch and the body of the city are joined as one? When the ruler is descended from the ancestor-founder of the city, and is the very child of the divine house? What will the people do in her absence? Does she appoint a viceroy? She goes – and the people must have come to understand this, because they let her go – she goes because she is making a pilgrimage on a sacred caravan. The Queen of the Caravan City demonstrates and sanctifies her position as ruler of the caravan route, by making such a journey: she too now goes on caravan.

The long, winding train passes through neutral territories, then hostile lands, but by the time her enemies have formulated their makeshift stratagems, she is long gone. The train reaches Jerusalem five months later; this uncanny impulse to move and convey is her kingdom in its essence, her throne's real force and power. It is a power given her by the spirit of the wadi, which in the sister-city Hadramawt they call Syn, and in the others, closer to Ma'rib, they call Ilmuquh. It means the same: the moon god. It is the flood-power of the seasonal waters that brings her to Solomon's arms.

She leaves in late winter, taking advantage of the new fodder for the pack-animals. She will be gone a full year, and will return with the coming of the July rains once again.

Solomon prepares himself, knowing that the Queen of the South is one month, a week, away. She is not the Pharaoh's daughter – that indolent girl sitting still and lifeless on a golden bower hoisted about the garden by four glistening Nubians – this one. No. This one is arriving on a long stuttering train, enthralled by her own power. Solomon cuts himself shaving the space above his lip. His eight hundred wives no longer interest him. The Pharaoh's daughter plays listlessly with her doves.

Everyone in Jerusalem waits.

She is coming.

When the caravan is first seen several leagues from the city, the guard out-posts are relieved and fresh new troops installed, and the watches doubled, then tripled. Not that Solomon is expecting trouble, but he knows that even far-off India is holding its breath, and that what happens now will be the mother of the future. Some counsellors advise the king to stay in his palace, assume the position of the *regnum mundi*, the Oriental despot to whom all things must come of necessity. Solomon, impatient, perhaps only thirty-eight, but certainly no older than forty-two, is young enough to ascend the highest point of the city on foot and watch the advancing cloud of dust himself. He has already heard about the gold; it's the girl he's interested in.

She is unmarried, this nameless queen. But let us call her Bilqis, after the Yemen tradition. Bilqis is smaller than his chunky Syrians and long-limbed Egyptians. Fine-boned, and quick. Her brown-yellow gazelle-eyes notice everything.

"You cut yourself, O King?"

She turns from the window and suddenly asks him this, without warning. He nods, surly – then laughs when she does.

They have dinner. Solomon must accord her a seat at the same height as his own, and he is unaccustomed to the feeling that this equality engenders in his heart. She eats the dates, as he does, nibbling them from her right hand and spitting the pits into her left. They are cousins, they can trace their ancestors back to Noah through three hundred generations in the flicking of an eye. They hardly need the translators who stand by, anxious to authenticate every cough and gesture in the one true language.

He can understand her very well. She has come to him as if from a dream, where you are rendered powerless to act. You merely stand and gaze in awe as the event unfolds before your lidless eyes. The gold comes, the exchange of gifts. She nods off, sleepy at the sight of the heap Solomon's courtiers have brought, her own counsellors are well pleased and very awake. All these ruby pendants! Chunks of Baltic amber. Iron knives with bronze handles in the shape of gryphons' heads.

In front of three hundred highly attentive witnesses, the queen asks Solomon for the truth of his life.

This is nine hundred and fifty years before King Herod and the Romans' logical conundrums; there are no "Jews." No Arabs. The Torah does not exist, and the Old Testament is yet to be written. The tribes of Israel are literally that, a dozen tribes among a thousand similar confederacies, traipsing endlessly over the dry uplands from Egypt to the Peninsula. Like the future clan of the emir of Dubai, these tribes are able to carve themselves a slice of territory that must sustain a limited number of people, holding their positions by sheer wile and desperate tenacity, so it is important to know who is an ally, who is not. Especially since they are lodged between great powers, kingdoms centred on far vaster natural resources.

At 950 B.C., these people know Genesis and Exodus, and Solomon's priests are working on Leviticus; there is peace of a kind in the kingdom, and time for speculation and scholarship. Both Solomon and Bilqis can

read. The question is, What shall be written? Solomon tells her about the
Ark; it is forbidden for anyone but the priests to look upon it. It is forbidden for any woman to enter the precincts of the Ark. She nods, she has
heard of this thing, a boxwood chest with a scroll inside. She wants to know
not if Solomon's power comes from the Ark, but whether he believes it to
be so.

Solomon has built a great temple, and together they go to see it. His
priests are unhappy with the arrival of this woman. She threatens them and
they tell each other stories, tripping over each other to reach the conclusion
that she is a bitch-dog, unfit for the bed of their king. Solomon hears them
before they speak.

Bilqis bathes. Solomon has sent her select attendants, perhaps his own
wives – all but the daughter of the Pharaoh are anxious to see if the queen
has six teats and hairy legs, as the priests claim. All but the Pharaoh's daughter, who sulks in her chambers and curses her sister, who got to marry her
brother, while she was sent here to this grubby rural kingdom of tribal
no-accounts.

In his bedchamber, Solomon mulls over his answers to Bilqis's riddles
and questions. It is a game literate nobles play, to demonstrate their own
power over words, words that carry the great force and conviction of chants
and incantations.

"Y.W.H." Solomon says, or maybe he writes it out for her, showing off
his hand on a papyrus scroll. "This is God; the others are demons."

"Even the gods of the pharaohs, your father-in-law?" Bilqis prods.

"It is so," Solomon says simply.

"And Ilmuquh, who brings us water with the New Moon of Thunder?"

"Y.W.H. *spoke*." Solomon looks at her. "He spoke to Abraham, He spoke
to Moses . . ."

"And has he spoken to you?" Bilqis asks.

Now they are talking in low whispers, and Solomon knows that he has a
witness to his life who is his equal in every way, save one: faith.

"If He chooses to, He will."

"You cannot ask Him?"

"I can ask Him for anything except proofs of His Existence."

"Oh." She is impressed. Not by the Temple, but by Solomon's proud knowledge of all its details, the pride of a man who is building a kingdom from scratch like her own great-great-grandfather did, fifteen generations earlier.

Her seers tell her that Solomon is a skilful magician; they themselves have seen visions of him, as he flies across the countryside with his djinns and animal powers, master of the winds.

"If it is so," she tells them, "it is his own God who gives him this power." She knows the men of his line were able to turn rods into serpents and that truly, unlike the other peoples in the known world, these tribes do not offer human sacrifice, claiming their God told Abraham to offer a ram instead of his child. Their power does not reside in spilled blood. She thinks about the sacrifices she has presided over, the screaming and the fainting and the odd burning smell in the air after, as if an invisible fire had erupted and fed itself on the victim's death throes.

What did Solomon's God want? she asked herself as she fell asleep.

It is the evening of the seventh day, and Solomon's bath attendants have told him that the queen is clean and ready for his visitation. But who shall come to whom?

Solomon wants her now, but there are eyes everywhere, her attendants, his attendants, his own eyes and those of God's, invisible and all-seeing. He suspects she wants a child with him, and he knows that she knows when that event will be most opportune. He has seen her seers casting bones and burning clouds of incense as if they were making signal fires. His own priests mutter aloud, but the whole kingdom depends on trade with others and they all know it. So he devises a simple plan to meet her halfway, and he believes she is working on the same plan.

He builds her a model of her kingdom in the new wing of his palace, from fresh cedarwood, alabaster, copper rivets; it is erected quickly, with the advice of traders who have been to Ma'rib many times, and the craftsmen move the walls and reposition the toy palaces to their final satisfaction.

"Is it right?" Solomon asks, wondering at their indecision.

"It is perfect," the traders tell the king. "Except for one thing. Where is the sweet lake of water that lies above the great dam?"

"Of course." Solomon shakes his head at his craftsmen. Saba is nothing without its shining waters, the silver head of the wadi. He tells his men to prepare a lake, several cubits wide, but to use silvered glass instead of real water, and he is pleased to see the traders nod in agreement with his commands.

Finally the hour comes. Solomon tells Bilqis, "I have made it possible for you to return home to your kingdom without leaving my palace."

"What sort of magic is this, O wise Solomon?" Her eyes take his for a quick dance, and he wonders crossly if she has already ferreted out the secret of his surprise.

"Just an amusement for a king who enjoys building temples," he jokes, to show his indifference to her feelings for him. When they enter the wing, and she sees what he has wrought, she claps her hands in delight.

"Welcome to my kingdom!" she says gaily, and skips across the lake of mirrors in her bare feet. Now they see each other as they are, both real and reflected, and know their desire.

At once. At last.

If Solomon *did* get a visit from an oasis queen – and why not, since it was obviously technically possible and in the best interests of two trading partners to solidify their relationship with gifts and palaver? – why did this story gain such enormous currency over the literary imaginations of so many cultures?

Because she chooses him . . .

Bilqis holds Solomon with the force of her earth-knowledge. The power of the Serpent is the power of water, coursing invisibly through the landscape of Time and seeking its reign in subterranean profundity. She is alert to its presence, to its workings in the human dimension, an adept trained since birth and the high priestess of the cult of Il, the equivocating presence who is sometimes Moon, sometimes Sun. God, and Goddess. Polysexual as the mysterious Asian deities were wont to be. Perhaps she even becomes his daughter, Al-Lat, during lunar eclipses or other auspicious times.

So the mystery remains, for her: What power does this naked man Solomon claim for himself? It is the key.

"Your God, if He does not seek human sacrifice, what does He demand of you instead?"

Solomon smiles.

"You have three more nights to tell me."

On the first night, Bilqis stares into the eyes of Solomon, which shine like basalt stones covered with fine rain. She knows she can divine the answer from strict attention, for Solomon neither conceals nor reveals.

On the second night, Bilqis reads Solomon's palm, and studies the fine grain of his life without surcease. The lines go everywhere. And nowhere.

On the third night, Bilqis falls into his arms, throws herself out of his arms and into his arms. Now she feels it, a kind of terror overtakes her, and suddenly she is no longer Queen of the Black Storm and High Priestess of Ilmuquh, she is a nothing, the pitiful core of a half-eaten apple. The smoke after the fire has gone out.

"I am alone!" she thinks, not daring to speak it aloud.

Solomon nods, and smiles enigmatically. Now she understands; his God is more terrible than anything she could have imagined. It demands annihilation, the sacrifice of every secure hold the senses can conjure up, in favour of a silence more profound than midnight space.

"Can you fly?" she asks Solomon.

He nods. "I held you in my arms long before we met."

She leaves just before the rains fall. Rams and cattle are sacrificed for a safe journey south. Solomon is alone with his eight hundred wives and his God.

He will die alone, as if everything was just a dream, a memory without a trace on the waking pillow. He too will vanish without a trace. In the future some historians will even claim Solomon did not exist, they will point to the lack of monuments and buildings and gold ornaments associated with his reign. "Surely such a great king would have left remains," they will point out, not thinking it beyond strange that Solomon and his realm and his lover all disappeared into a story, the way a flock of birds disappears into a cloud.

Chapter 20

This Way to the Dormitory of the White Eunuchs

"The *black* eunuchs," the Topkapi guide at the Turkish sultan's palace grounds explained, "were used to guard the sultan's harem. The reason for this was that their operations were done in Egypt, and if the procedure did not work successfully, and a child was born to one of the four hundred concubines, they would know if it was a black eunuch's. The *white* eunuchs, usually Slavs from the north shore of the Black Sea, Romanians and Ukrainians, typically, were used to guard the *outside* of the harem compound . . . This is the way to *their* dormitory."

The crowd of twenty nodded, and dutifully followed him through the narrow, chilly passageway. I was somewhere in the middle, listening to comments.

"What did they do with all the testicles?" an Australian fellow in shorts mused aloud. He told me he was a retired mining engineer from Adelaide. I pointed to the pebble-inset path that led to the sultan's mother's bathroom.

"Baked in an oven and set into concrete," I ventured.

He barked a laugh and snapped another picture with his enormous Canon. An anachronism from the Antipodes. Most of the crowd were well-heeled Germans and Japanese, who had forsaken the still camera for the mini-video with its built-in flatscreen monitor; they kept busy, panning over the captioned wall-posters, to save themselves the trouble of closing in to hear the guide's pitch. The stone passage into the harem was narrow and damp; it quickly induced feelings of claustrophobia and anxiety in our little collective. You could hear subaudible demurrals and unhappy groans (*Sheiss!* – Sorry!) echoing through to the high ceilings of the next room.

Our escort this afternoon was a slight young man in elevator shoes, who had wrapped himself around several times in a fake Burberry scarf and topped it off with a pair of thick tortoiseshell eyeglasses and a green melton hat, *á la Anglaise*. He seemed to enjoy provoking these anxious *frissons* in his European audience, underscoring his comments with a fey smile.

"Here is where the eunuchs could *not* go; only the sultan himself could pass beyond this gate, and even the musicians who entertained him here, were *all women.*"

We peered soberly at the old pianoforte visible through the hand-blown glass windows, as if it could divulge something audible about those lost times. Several giant mahogany grandfather clocks had stopped ticking at around nine o'clock, but in what year they halted, impossible to tell. Overall, a queasy, tasteless decor. I had been to film parties in places like this.

"When the sultan died, it was finished for everyone living in the palace. Wives, concubines, even the eunuchs had to go. And the sultan's mother too, the *grandmother* of the new sultan! She had to leave her forty rooms forever!"

The guide showed us the golden grillwork set in a wall, where the sultan could hide and watch his women, panting away unseen. Everything was hidden, recessed, doubled and tripled with mirrors and fretwork.

Clandestine, in a word.

"Perhaps you have noticed all the fountains everywhere, and the brass spouts." The guide pointed to a marbled recess in the blue-tiled wall. "This was so the sultan's words could be hidden by the sound of water. These were his private rooms, and no one was permitted to disturb his privacy."

No one except for four wives, three hundred concubines, and his mother, I thought. And his children and eunuchs and untold numbers of provisioners and handymen. ("Two thousand men were employed to bring

firewood continuously to the palace," the tour guide offered us another statistic.) So this was Turkish civilization, its headquarters.

A huge psycho-sexual machine-apparatus, and all for what?

Judging from the sick looks of the crowd (The men: "My *balls* cut off!" The women: "Enslaved forever in these cold halls, a *piece of meat* in cold storage!), this abnormal psychology still worked on us moderns at a deep level; we viewed the Muslim world as an empire based on symbolic sexual dominance, and Ottoman Turkey as the showpiece of this culture. Black Nubians from the far south of the Turkish Empire. Castrated. Blond Slavs from the far north. Castrated. And the all-too-heady smorgasbord of foreign women, kidnapped from every corner of the empire. Light-skinned Egyptians dancers, the celebrated blue-eyed Circassians from Georgia, strapping Montenegro lasses. Maybe the odd Italian or French redhead, captured by coastal pirates. One of *your* ancestors, hey? But no odalisque dark-skinned lovelies, apparently, for they would spoil the stratagems of Ottoman racial guard-deployment.

No, even today, eighty years after the harem closed its doors forever, there was no real titillation running through our crowd. Just this dumb and cowed silence, the shuffling of dragged feet. An uneasy and disturbing sense of familiarity with the whole, insanely detailed operation. Fear of the Oriental

Despot twittered through the audience. Was this how King Solomon ran his palace? It seemed likely, for this was how all the oriental despots worked. Despotism was simply another Middle East technical innovation, like elephant-armies or wadi-waterworks. And we understood it, this perverse business, for this was how the big boys all worked: cut to the genitals.

This was how the American slaver South might have finally organized itself: vast-slave plantations, pure white-lily lineage-mothers, educated octoroons and sectaroons, breeding farms, a whole society organized around the recognition and distinguishing of racial and gender characteristics – had not northern commercial enterprise repealed sexual gymnastics in favour of the Presbyterian techniques of auto-repression and subliminal persuasion. Now of course, it was the advertisers who were the sultans, who claimed all the beautiful women, virtually locking them away behind their latest products. Now we would see harem-girls only on the runways and TV commercials, applauding their emasculated keepers or stroking their commercial wares with a warmth they would never bestow on any mortal man. Commerce's agents eagerly snatched up all the young lookers they could find, too, from the age of twelve onwards, to feed this machine. Straight out of their childhood homes. And worse, told us the ones we managed to keep to ourselves were not worth the candle.

"Schnitzel-hagen!" Dietrich said to me. "*Gender-hate*! That's what we have in Germany today!"

I met Dietrich back in my hotel lobby. We were drinking Nescafés at the little bar, both too saturated from a case of ABS (Australian slang for "another bloody site") to see more, too bored to stay in our rooms and read our badly chosen books. My Bowles was still irritating me, but I hadn't found anyone who had a decent trade for it, and Dietrich read only–Well, that's part of the story.

I had spent the better part of the hotel morning ignoring his friendly overtures; his Buster Brown haircut with its evenly trimmed yellow bangs and his hidden red jug-ears looked slightly suspect on a forty-five-year-old man with a big broken nose and weather-ravaged skin. It suggested a moneyed twit at best. I relented when the saucy Spanish-looking woman I had been keenly eyeing got up and left with a black man. So.

Dietrich.

He told me that he was on his way back to Hamburg from Africa, returning slowly, for he was in no hurry to get home. His country was too depressing, it was complete bullshit. He had just climbed Kilimanjaro with an especially rabid Japanese, both fighting to the last gasp to be number one. The final two hundred metres took the pair over three painful hours to crawl up. No air, no oxygen. Willpower.

"The Americans *quit*. I gave them my gloves and hat, but they *still* couldn't hack it."

A fanatic's lust gleamed in his eye. Without further ado, Dietrich pulled out a colour photo of a young black woman from his wallet. Nude.

"My wife. I met her in Papua New Guinea when I was working there. Fifteen years."

"I was there too. A month."

"A month?" Incredulous. "What could you see in a month?"

"Enough. They shot at our Jeep with poisoned arrows," I said primly.

"Arrows," he snorted. Yes, Dietrich was clearly a maniac. I studied the photo. Here she was, his dusky harem of one, with her pouty springboard breasts and long pointy nipples, and that woolly topiary hairstyle of the island Melanesians, but lighter-skinned than the deep-purple villagers I knew from New Guinea's interior.

"From the coast then, your wife?" I asked.

"Yes. Lae. I was looking at a Second World War aircraft sunk in the battles with the Japanese. These are my children."

He took out the usual school photos of his two girls, who proved to be much lighter than their mother and sweet-looking in their starched uniforms.

"Very pretty," I commented. "You must miss them."

"The joy of my life, my children. Wives, you know . . . I don't mind being away for one month, three months, it's all the same to me. My wife is home-loving, doesn't want to see the world, but I take my daughters on long trips. Last year we drove all through East Germany, to show them how the other half lives."

"So you made a good marriage, then? Your wife's happy?"

"Of course. My friends all married woman from countries far away from Germany. Kenya, Thailand, Papua. Why? You can't live with a German woman, they give you nothing. I won't even speak to them, if I see them travelling and I am sitting next to them, like that woman who was sitting here a few minutes ago."

"You mean the girl who just left with the black man?"

"Yes, she was German. And that's how desperate they are, because German men won't even *look* at them now. So they go out with blacks, and they must pay. Cash. For me, they have absolutely nothing they can offer me, and when they throw themselves at black men, they are *less* than nothing."

He was getting testy.

"But surely *some* German guys marry German women, otherwise there'd be no German children!" I did not point out there was a certain obvious sexual symmetry to this phenomenon of racial exogamy, as he had demonstrated with his own marital move.

"My children *are* German," he said, fixing me with a look. "But it's like this. My sister? She is forty-eight now, too old to have children. *Ha!* She deserves this! She went from disaster to disaster, she even tried to marry a Yugoslav, but of course he beat her. Now she has crossed the line, and now she must live with her complete failure as a woman!"

He was crowing, a little family triumph. He asked the waiter for more coffee; it was clear he was just getting warmed up. I asked him about his parents, wondering how they had reacted to his marrying a New Guinean fifteen years ago – or who was only fifteen at the time, it was not clear to me which.

"My father is dead. I don't speak to my mother, she gives me nothing. For ten years. Not my sister either. My family is rich. I live in the house my grandfather built, twenty rooms. I renovate room-by-room, as I go. I have one room for my computers and graphic design." He gave me a coloured business card that showed yet another naked black woman, only this one was pure African it seemed. "Another room for all my photography equipment. I have over a hundred thousand slides, all dated and labelled and scanned into a cross-indexed subject file. How do you organize *your* pictures?" he asked suddenly, staring at my camera under his heavy bangs.

"Well, I don't really . . . I just sort of pull out the ones that I like and put stickies on them."

"Stickies? What is this?"

"You know. Those little yellow Post-It notes with the adhesive backs?"

"Yes, yes," he nodded impatiently. "In my system, I can go to any date and time and pull out a picture and know exactly all the technical details about it. I make slide shows for my friends."

I blinked at the thought.

"So you're really into photography," I said stupidly. This is not what I meant, of course, but he was a river tumbling fast off its source high in the oxygenless mountains, and it would be a long time before it slowed sufficiently into meandering pools for self-reflection and philosophy. If ever. It seemed we were leaving race-and-sex behind.

"No, I have *many* interests. I have my workshop for my metal fabrication, another for wood and cabinet-making. I take two trips a year, mountain climbing, hiking, and so on. I have nothing to do with German women, and I laugh when they try and compete with you, on any level whatsoever."

"But Dietrich," I importuned, "you are – how old?"

"Forty-eight."

"Forty-eight. You are part of the postwar baby-boom generation, no?"

"Yes. I was born in the New Economic Miracle times, the 1950s."

"Surely the younger generation of German men, they are *used* to this new woman? They pick up the diapers and help with the housework and so on. They must have a different attitude towards women and the proper relationship, for the last twenty years or so."

"No. It's bullshit. I teach karate? Aikido? In a club. Three, four times a week. There are at least twenty young German women who come to the club to train, every week. I hear them complain all the time, they have no boyfriends. Nobody wants them!" This last said with a malicious grin of pure delight.

"Well, the impression we have in *my* country," I went on. "The so-called Swedish model? It is that the European man gets three-months' pay and leave from work to look after the baby – "

"*What* baby? The birthrate is declining rapidly, it's now in freefall. No one is having children unless they marry outside. German women *hate* children!"

I immediately thought of his mother. In bombed-out Germany, trying to build her life again from ruins. Was this collective postwar denial a syndrome, construed by its children as a refusal to nurse them?

"So Günter Grass, his novel, *Headbirths, or The Germans Are Dying Out.* This was true, not fiction?"

"I don't like him. All that vomiting, the nausea. He's not a writer, he's just sick."

"So who do you like?"

"I read and reread Kant. *Pure Reason.* Also Goethe."

"And the contemporaries? Thomas Mann, Hesse?"

"Hesse, no. Thomas Mann, he's okay."

"And Herder?" Another early-nineteenth-century German philosopher, this the epitome of *Ur-Weltenschalt.*

"Yes, of course." He opened up his camera bag. "Is it okay if I take your picture? This was an interesting conversation, I'd like to remember it."

"Sure, go ahead."

Dietrich was less interested than relieved, I thought. As he fiddled with the lens, I asked him the key question, the only theological question relevant to our blue-screened age, a question only sci-fi flicks like *The Matrix* and *Dark City* dared ask openly.

"But Dietrich. All these pictures. Do you ever worry that they *replace* your memory?"

"Never. They help me remember."

Clickety clack-clack.

The camera shutter opened and shut repeatedly. I think he was automatically bracketing me, compensating for the dim sidelight of the restaurant, and the uncertainty of getting a proper exposure of my face against the dark-red curtains behind me. Germans and Germany had not given Dietrich what he needed; he was carefully reconstructing his own version of a life, room-by-room from the ground up, and trusting no one but himself to get it right this time.

I thought about him and his rage for a long time afterward, the rage of the misbegotten son. Germany was changing radically, from the inside, and no one was watching.

§⁊

I was obliged to think constantly about Germans, because, of all the peoples of Europe, they had been so prominently self-declaring and persistently modern on my travels through these less-than-modern milieus. They were *us* in Europe, we North Americans, if we had stayed in the Old Country or gone back home without regressing into idle folkdom and smelly cheeses. The British on the whole were *not* us, for they were disappointingly parochial and klutzy when touring abroad, goofing about in their badly fitting shoes and ridiculous hats. Always keen, dressing for the part, the British. *Playing* the tourist, as it were, mawkish and embarrassed by the past because they used to run that show . . . whereas the Germans, well, they would always reach the flinty apex ahead of the pack, wouldn't they?

Even in Turkey the German tourists outnumbered North Americans by a factor of three or four to one. I could understand the reason for these relative numbers in Yemen, for the State Department had specifically warned Americans off the country as a result of the *Cole* incident, when the Arab terrorists bombed the U.S. navy's vessel in the Aden harbour. But as for the crowds queuing to get into the Hagia Sophia or the Blue Mosque, so many were German (with a healthy sprinkling of Japanese) that it made one think. Americans, conspicuous by their cheeseburger-chunky bodies and dental-friendly smiles, were festooned about those lines like the olives in a cheap café's feta-salad special: highly visible, but few in number, and a little vinegary to boot.

Why were the Germans so big on archeology? Much of what I read about Turkey testified to the allure of ancient history for the average Deutschlander. I was surprised to discover that even Heinrich Schliemann, who had proved Homer right with his discovery of historical Troy on the Turkish coast, had never been anything like the erudite director of the

Bavarian State Volksmuseum or some such thing, but merely a Californian 49er who made enough loot in the goldfields as a wholesale merchant to set himself up for a few big digs in the Middle East. He ended hauling the Mycenaean stuff he supposedly found in Troy back to the Fatherland, where his tomb-booty now sat like a reconstituted ur-totem to the mysterious wanderings of the prehistoric Goths and other Germanic tribes. Today placards in the National Museum of Archeology in Istanbul must make their apologies to millions of visitors yearly: *Unfortunately all the capitals were removed to Berlin except this one.*

And still the Germans come!

Because they must. In an odd way Turkey is their home. North Americans – Mexicans, Americans, and Johnny-come-lately Canadians – can be forgiven for not realizing that they all belong to older nations than the Germans do. Metternich only succeeded in engineering a confederation of petty states in the 1870s, a full century after the American Revolution and well into the Electric Age. Herder, the Grimm brothers, Schiller, these classic German intellectuals were all products of the anti-intellectual Romantic Age, not the Enlightenment that preceded it. This was an era when the contemplation of ruins signalled a deliciously artistic pessimism and an *arriviste*'s thumbs down to the effete charms of Reason. The Germans – unlike the tweedledee French and their tweedledum British opponents (or was it the other way around?) – did not know who they were. You can only go so far with *Vir-not-Slavs*. German philologists invented the concept of Indo-European, or *Wiro*, as a label for the bewildering hordes of Alans, Goths, Vandals, and Saxons who had traipsed through the Rhineland, leaving slightly different pottery shards in their wake, and *ancient* history to replace the real history they so obviously lacked. The Germans would become experts on the volk, the etymology and philology of a people in its eulogistic aspect, untroubled by the rancour of personal ambitions and counternarratives.

Such an enterprise depends naturally on first principles: that there is such a thing as an original volk. This premise has been questioned and repositioned in various ways. Even the base Indo-European linguistic substratum has been called into dispute. The eulogistic story places a discrete tribe of cattle-herders near the Caspian Sea around 3500 B.C., happily using *milk, honey, beech trees*, and *salmon* enough times that these root-words remain lodged in the brains of their many-tongued descendants (Slavs, Teutons, Persians, Indians) for centuries after. The other story, as we have seen previously in Professor Garbini's thesis, suggests that nations come and go into being, dialectically, through the heightened creative energies given off by paired oppositions forming around a logical conundrum. (Such as, who is the rightful heir to the throne?) Admittedly, the latter is a theory based on Idealism.

But language analysis can only tell us so much about this process, whatever it is, because native speakers don't necessarily speak the language of their genetic ancestors, nor do adversarial relationships necessarily derive from diverse ancestral gene pools: witness the Crips and Bloods. Or, in the case at hand, the Germans and the Turks. The Germans found their true Germanness in Anatolia, and the Turks, presumably, their modern identity behind the wheel of the new Mercedes they helped build.

These two peoples really need each other.

Ancient history is hard to let go of, precisely because it offers up hope for the future; the dark soil is always assumed to harbour a great secret. The Ark, the Grail, Lascaux, and the Sphinx are but types of this singularity, absolving us of all our sins in the great wash of revealed meaning, transcendant purpose, final destiny. Ancient history was the defining program of the nineteenth century, the European nineteenth century, a century looking back over its shoulder and already growing uneasy, sensing that the next one would prove itself terrible. They were not stupid. It was for us in the Americas to discover the joys of excavating the future, Americans who first believed with Henry Ford that the secret of our group existence lay in the opposite direction. We are the moiety, the other half, *opposed* to bunk, we the declared enemies of tradition. North Americans are not uptight, we're into it. Which is probably why the Americans were not here, but at home, on their computers. For somewhere out in hyperspace Rachael waited, the perfect woman from *Blade Runner*, waiting to be freed. Not here in this ancient dirt, covered with cobble. And signs telling us where to walk.

But for Dietrich, as for some of his nation's male peers, apparently, a tribal or a village woman was essentially more German than – and infinitely preferable to – those modern harridans who displayed every symptom of the taint of rootless wandering and cultural permeability.

Hordes of one, in a phrase.

Chapter 21

A Postmodern Circus

A Sunday afternoon. The sun is mild, the air moist with Marmara Sea mist. We need jackets when we sit looking out at the Golden Horn, the busy harbour to the east, but not when we walk down busy Kennedy Cad roadway, watching the fishermen cast their enormous rods into the hopeful blue. What year is it in Istanbul?

Judging from the grotty old zoo in the ravine park below Sultan Ahmet's Palace, I'd say about 1952. The cages are all rusty and battered, the brown bear (*Ursus arctus*) has about five metres of square cement floor to do his thing. A chewed-up flock of ducks and exotic chickens occupy the central compound, as if the populace were counting on the zoo to feed them in the event of a foreign blockade or civil collapse.

No less than a dozen cages are given over to races of the domestic cat. *Syam* is empty, but *Felix domesticus* proves to hold two alleycats busy licking off a little girl's ice-cream-sticky fingers. Street vendors offer pink popcorn, *borek*, a meat patty, pistachio nuts. For a million lires or so (about seventy-five cents), I can fire a pistol at a bedsheet festooned with coloured balloons, punch a plaster dummy right in his soft gut (a lifesized mix of Elvis and

Stallone), or get my fortune told by two Rhode Island Red hens. There are good-looking and smooth-talking Turkish men everywhere, cruising around. Going nowhere special, spitting sunflower seeds into the wind with a certain style.

One is passing at this very moment, a leather-coated Marlon Brando boy, with a cellphone and what I take to be his foreign, pregnant wife, a strawberry blonde in a tight pea-jacket.

On closer inspection she proves to be a stout tourist from Bavaria, her guttural instructions to him – *Hurry, ve don't have all day* – give the game away. She's running the show, and the meter is on, judging from his studied indifference to her prattle.

Then there is the whole other kind. A misshapen and asymmetrical substratum of Turks that defies easy generalization, seems to make this dank and mossy park their daily home. These lumpens do not hustle the foreign ladies. They barely breathe. They sit on their broken park benches and drink their tapwater slowly from reused pop bottles, squinting hard against the March sun whenever it peeks out from behind a cloud, and starting at the peacock's raucous shrieks. They scare the children in the park too, so it's not just me. A young army draftee sits beside me and offers up a sip of his *ayran*, a watered yogourt that tastes agreeably like fresh buttermilk. He is normal, but his hirsute companion is a troglodyte. Heroic Gilgamesh and hairy Enkidu. I want to photograph the forehead-challenged troll for further study, for I believe a weird gene has gone awry somewhere here.

It's the facial asymmetry, and it's astounding, as if two men have been cut in half and then glued back together, a Small Medium stuck to an Extra-Large. I don't want to offend the draftee, so I take his picture too. Everywhere you look there are more extraordinarily homely men, one-offs with bad haircuts, swollen foreheads, a collection of facial wens, welts, and wales. Raw and dripping noses. And above all, a doughlike lack of animation and absence of character, as if they were put aside for baking and then forgotten on the stove. No yeast. Are these simple farm labourers, village simpletons, dumped into the suburbs and shocked into complete catatonia by the caprices of the cruel city? Rural wretches discharged from decades of field-bondage? What chance do they have against the leonine city-slickers prowling back and forth, these smooth hustlers in their bootleg Boss jackets and Wellington half-boots?

The local women too are exactly dichotomous, either unduly plain or sexpots. The plain are suspect, however, divided as they are between the authentically plain and the ideologically homely, for the New Muslim Woman is everywhere much in evidence. She wears a dull grey shawl and long draping skirt, no makeup, and horrible sensibly flat shoes, and she appears afraid of nothing, least of all a national government that frowns on such overt expressions of religious sentiment in the secular sphere. Especially in the universities, which were always Ataturk's special hope for producing the New Turk. He got one, all right, but I'm guessing she wasn't what he imagined.

You would think that the slave-engineered eugenics and the genetic booty of the enormous Ottoman Empire would have raised the beauty bar a little, or is it my prejudice showing? I admit it; I prefer fire to phlegm and sensitivity to truculence. Still, I would like to know: where did all the ugly fellows come from? Were these layabouts slumped on the benches *chaff*, the cast-offs of a conqueror-society? Or were they *grain*, the product of deliberate human engineering, winnowed from a nation that needed gargoyles at its gates, and which kept a place in the ranks for mute obeisance and stalwart drudges? Are they *taught* the limited repertoire of the security-goon? These stumpy facial expressions, the surly glare, the blank stare, and the angry glower? The guidebooks say never get into an argument with a Turk. They don't understand arguments. They just reach for their knives. I recall with fondness the Anglo-French tendency to escape the box and run for the Casbah – Richard Burton, T. E. Lawrence, Arthur Rimbaud, Grey Owl. Playing the native, great fun. And is not the ability to turn around and contemplate your own society, as coolly and indifferently as a stage actor sizing up his audience, the first hallmark of a truly civilized man? That's my prejudice, I admit it.

The irony is that the Turks have guarded the treasures of the East and the West from each other far too long. And in doing so, they seem to have lost their innate stagecraft. In the hotel this morning the deskman became agitated after a guest from Saudi Arabia, wearing the traditional white *gembaya*, the full Gulf robe, and a stencilled *buffin* headpiece, chaffed him about the correct way for a good Muslim to dress. The Arab, to make his point, directed the clerk's attention to the picture hanging over his head, a coloured engraving of six or seven sultans in caftans.

"That was a long time ago," the Turkish clerk retorted. (They were speaking English.) "And that's how he dressed at home!"

The Gulf tourist sniffed at this weak argument and eventually departed, leaving the hotelman fuming.

"We're *Turks*, not Arabs!" He looked to me for understanding.

Still, the first thing that one sees on walking into the pre-Islamic wing of Istanbul's Archeology Museum are the South Arabian artifacts: the same elongated alabaster women's heads, the identical incense holders with the sign of the crescent moon and solar disk, and the multiple bull-headed friezes and leaping ibexes that I had seen in Yemen, long weeks ago. They were displayed, *ex sui generis*, in priority to the much earlier Hittite and Babylonian finds. I think they enjoyed pride of place because they were authentically (and linguistically) pre-Islamic, and ancestral in some unstated but critical way to the Turkish nation itself.

It was partly the crescent moon, of course. The national flag of Turkey was a blood-red field, with the yellow crescent moon enveloping a five-pointed star. The Sabean icon had transposed into this national idealogy symbolized by the flag, and I was not sure what the five points symbolized, but probably the five cardinal directions (including *up*, as one), which would serve the aims of an expansionist state nicely.

The amount of material in the museum was staggering. Catalogues never reveal the scale and the profusion of these exhibits, the giant Beses and Zeuses, the stelae and lifesized torsos ranging beyond number. Outside, under the green trees of the sculpture garden, the same prolificacy reigns. Eroded heads regard the tourists in mute alarm, decapitated snakes continue to writhe thousands of years after the fatal blow, unfinished statues found at the bottom of the Ionian Sea now stand high and dry, golems waiting to take over the world. Beside them perfect bums and breasts shimmy invitingly for the casual street onanist, more real and tangible than anything he could find in a nightclub. A recurrent tale: One Artemis was so delectably rendered she is often found wet between the legs by her keepers at morning. Next to them, unvarnished plinths of purple marble and cobalt-grey granite reach for a different kind of perfection, abstract and unassailable.

It is an antiquities clearing-house, a gigantic marbles-mall. There's too much of this stuff around, and the Turkish style, this suffocating compendium of hookahs and urns and oil lamps and water jugs and brass coffee sets and thick rugs and heavy jewellery and enamelled pictures and overstuffed cushions and leather hassocks and gilded mirrors and the whole ponderous *chose-luxe*, this is the nineteenth-century style we have misrepresented for decades as Victorian. Was this style born of the great Anatolian digs? Or of the *impulse* to dig?

It doesn't take an archeological genius or even a duffer like Heinrich Schliemann to find and start digging up the stuff, for anybody with a shovel and a permit could produce something complicated and timeworn out of the rubble, visible here on the surface everywhere. The story was always the same: A farmer is ploughing his field, that is, trying to plough his field, when *clunk*, he hits something hard that won't give way to his plough. Guess what? It's the past, and it refuses to budge.

The sultans who brought back linen-wrapped mummies from Egypt and celadon porcelains from China and lifesized silver fowl from Venice and brass serving platters from India and artillery cannons and silk pyjamas from France only added to this show, but they had the benefit of limitless storage space in their walled seraglios. The rest of us are not so lucky.

We tourists have to make way for it all.

One goes for a walk in the afternoon, and the sidewalk suddenly narrows and then disappears altogether at the edge of a crumbling battlement wall, and now the traffic whizzes by, mere inches away. It has no other place to go. You go for a stroll at night and great earthworks, hunks of mortar, stony lozenges, loom out of the dark, the grade changes drastically, a depression appears, a hole, a ring of ancient cobble – an old well? A

sunken turret? Across the Golden Horn, a single black slab of modern glass stands alone against a blurry sea of red-tiled roofs, Taksim's sole contribution to the Modern Movement. What legal permits, what disputations to history were wrought by its erection? You can hardly *move*.

It's not the traffic, it's the inherited legacy. The whole country is chockablock, an overcrowded warehouse full of other people's stuff. Moving the stock back and forth requires broad backs and stocky limbs. And amazingly, the Turks have complied.

In this postmodern circus, nearly everyone plays the strong man.

§§

Cybele is what I came for, and Cybele is what I found. The seated goddess, the Anatolian earth-mother of the world. From a few pictures I had seen, there appeared to be certain affinities between the carvings of Cybele and the statuettes of some unnamed female divinities I had seen back in Yemen's National Museum, in Sana'a. But it wasn't easy, for the main attribute of Cybele's divinity was a mysterious and elusive gravity. Ernest Klein, whose *Comprehensive Etymological Dictionary of the English Language* I habitually kept beside me at my home, had this to say about the origin of the goddess: "**Cybele**. Goddess of the earth and mother of the gods. Name of uncertain origin."

The ancient Greek historian Herodotus was no better. He recounted only how a Scythian traveller vowed to make sacrifice to this Mother of the Gods, if he should be permitted to return home safely through the Hellespont. Finally reaching his own country, the wayfarer duly engaged in his propitiation by beating a drum with "images fastened on his dress," and he was shot dead by a Scythian overlord for impiety.

I found four representations of Cybele in the archeological museum in Istanbul. A small marble carving of a seated woman (headless) with her feet supported by a scowling leopard, or possibly a lioness; another headless woman inside a small box, likely representing a cave-recess; a headless woman seated, with great flowing folds in her long garment; and a capped woman wearing a Phrygian-style garment, set within a framework of limestone.

All small effigies, all portable. Suggestive, and roughly carved too, as if roughness and incompleteness was part of their power and charm. They generated the same primitive emotions that rude Orthodox icons painted by rural folk artists do, first arousing a direct devotional response and then transferring one's gaze beyond the surface of things into the other realm. The box enclosure, the cave-recess, was a *portal*. These were not the works of master craftsmen, hired on commission and showing off their skills in the play of light on polished curves. These were self-declaredly *archaic*.

My four little Cybeles had five elements in common:

Each goddess was enthroned and faced outward; her throne and body were one, inseparable and indistinctly carved; her bare (?) feet were raised from the rough base; her hands were held forward and gripped something (a grain stalk?); and in contrast to the static rigidity of her pose, the folds of her robe rippled voluminously, as if she were facing out a windstorm.

The last detail struck me as particularly significant: the Phrygian artist *circa* 1100 B.C. had achieved something not seen before this in Western art; the explicit depiction of Chaos, or the Play of Form. Chaos was something his audience would have witnessed first-hand. The Phrygians and their Indo-European cousins, the Dorians, had initiated the worldwide wars of the twelfth century B.C., setting off a series of domino-slaughters that culminated in the Sea-Peoples' attacks in Palestine and Egypt. What set them off in the first place? *Panic*, according to egyptologist Dr. Leanne Mallory of the University of Toronto. Bubonic plague and its attendant famine hit the Mediterranean basin in thousand-year cycles, and the population's first response was always to flee the dying cities and attack the places still uncontaminated, but of course they took the pathogen (rats and lice) along with them. This was the time of troubles in Egypt, reported in Exodus, with its plagues and unearthly destruction. For the Greeks this was the era when Atlantis disappeared under the sea forever, as recounted by Plato. Major plagues like these struck the ancient world in 2300 B.C., 1500 B.C., 1200 B.C., A.D. 862, and A.D. 1232. The calamities of 1200 B.C. were particularly deadly. They likely killed millions. These violent eruptions ushered in a Dark Age that lasted four hundred years in the Aegean, but they also weakened the previous balance of power sufficiently that Semitic federations in the Middle East could once and for all extinguish their ancient rivals, the Sumerians. Hundreds of thousands of people who built the first civilization all disappeared forever from history in the lands we now call Iraq. Among the new winners were the Aramaeans, whose language was that of Jesus a millennium later. Plague-ridden Egypt also lost her Apiru, the Hebrews, who were suddenly free to move to Palestine but now had to contend with the fierce Philistines, coastal warrior-invaders from Greece and Crete, who forbid them the use of the very discovery that had expedited all this bloody action: iron.

So this is the situation around 1000 B.C., the background to our Solomon and Sheba story, and the era when these museum Cybelline cult objects were likely made, but certainly already set in their alcoves, carried aloft, and worshipped. A cataclysmic bloodbath had just extinguished some of the oldest empires in the world and threatened most others, killing perhaps a third of the population. The new miracle weapon, iron, once worth forty times its weight in silver, was growing cheaper by the decade; the Bronze Age chariot that gave rise to the heroic warrior-class was defunct, and the great warrior-tombs of Mycenaean Greece abandoned; and pillaging warriors on horseback began to show up in the newly composed historical records, with grave consequences for the next twenty-nine centuries.

The Hero was replaced by the Horde.

The earliest known depiction of Cybele was from Catalhoyuk, the "first town" in the interior Anatolian plateau near present-day Konya, Turkey, dating to before 5000 B.C. This is seven thousand years ago, close to the end of the last Ice Age. This stone statuette depicts a pendulous naked matron, squatting, giving birth. Cybele's persistent survival as a cultic figure through long millennia poses serious questions about myth and culture.

What does she represent? To put it plainly, what *function* does Cybele serve? Why did generations of devotees keep her image intact, through the countless wars of conquest that this fertile and accessible country attracted to itself? Why was she still there, four thousand years later, when the world had changed so drastically with its mass migrations, iron weapons, and saddled horses? Was she a totem of *sub rosa* aboriginal identity? The graven focus of a national bardic myth? The focus of a widespread but mysteriously silent and invisible fertility ritual? A Neolithic archetype that simply refused to die? Was she there simply to be worshipped as object, or did she perform some function?

What did experts say of the real purpose of myth and cult?

Ernest Cassirer, in his opus *The Philosophy of Symbolic Forms*, spoke of myth as having its "own mode of *necessity* . . . its own mode of *reality*."

G. S. Kirk, in *The Nature of Greek Myths*, discounted the Jungian emphasis on mythic archetypes, on the simple basis that very little material *was* actually repeated. There was no archetype; if one actually looked closely at comparative mythologies, their interest lay precisely in the complex flow of unique details and their unpredictable storylines. Moreover, Kirk found the intrusion of *history* at the origin of such myths as Demeter and Kore, the basis of the secret Eleusinian rites, a history at once compelling and unavoidable. Demeter the Corn Mother weeps and wails, for her daughter Kore has been taken below by Hades as his bride, and the Greek people are suddenly left starving for lack of bread:

> The famine that afflicts the whole earth and the unexpected terror and submission of the gods comes as a surprise. . . . [I]n Mesopotamia, however . . . occasional great droughts and famines, like periodical floods, were part of ordinary experience.

If history wounds the gods, tumbles them down like Demeter and Kore from their high places, and almost swallows them whole, then the gods, too, are subjects of the myth, subjects like us, and not authors of it. The myths come from somewhere else, somewhere *on the other side* of history. Maybe the gods are mere actors like we are, actors swept along in the tide of history, doing their best to resist, and deny, its ultimate power over us. In the flatlands of Mesopotamia, the life-giving rivers themselves change course, favouring one city-state, then another, and the dynasties can rise and fall along with their gods in a single season.

Arguing against the Freudian-Jungian tradition, that archetypes exist, and that myth is explainable as a subjective dream-state made explicit by a code of symbols, Kirk made two more interesting points about their function. Generally, myths are something "in which inconsequentiality plays its part," and moreover, "they are a response, by direct apprehension, to certain striking aspects of the outside world . . . the resemblance [to dreams] depends on their striking oddity and inconsequentiality."

By the term *inconsequentiality*, Kirk suggests that myths go their own way. They do not seem to be *directed* by men, nor, as we have seen from the above example, by the gods either. They serve other purposes, their own. They act, alive in their own right, or as Kirk concludes, they arise in a "mysterious vacuum."

Okay, so they are just *there*. But if we don't know how they came to *be*, can we at least find out what they *say*?

The Seated Woman, Cybele, what is she telling us? That she sits *on* the throne at the portal, and appears to mediate between pure ephemera (the undulation of her robe corresponding to the waves in the sea or the winds blowing the curtains of Time) and the absolute fixed door of Eternity. She appears to be an elaboration in the round of the simple ideogram of the crescent moon and solar disk, as sophisticated as anything the Buddhists or Marxists might have produced.

The week I was writing this (March 2001), the BBC reported that the Taliban junta in Afghanistan had announced its firm commitment to destroy the Buddhist cliff-statues along the famous silk route, considering them an offence to Islam. In 1998, the head of a ten-metre statue was blown off by a grenade launcher, and the BBC now led the outcry against the renewed desecration of the world's ancient heritage site. The past holds special terrors for Islamic fundamentalists, as for anyone claiming election. The cup must be raised above the waves, the tumuli sidestepped. The dense layering so evident in places like Troy, and not just Troy but the various sites of Troy I through IX, and not Troy I, but Troy IA and IB – these reveal the plasticity and thinness of the topmost layer we call the present. Fundamentalists are not made happy by these persistent reminders of their own relativity.

Speaking of Troy, I have arrived at the bus station of Canakkale, a town on the Aegean coast, to take the dolmus, the mini-bus, to the modern village of Truva, where the fabled site lies, and the diesel-filled garage is filled with small-sellers of every description. Here is a large mustachioed Turk sitting by a set of pink bathroom scales on the sidewalk. He charges fifty lire (five cents) for the privilege of weighing oneself before (or perhaps after) the journey. A pile of brass coins attests to his morning's custom. I take his picture, to record his undeniable *gravidas*, the frank stolidity of his posture. He sits like a field stone on his stool beside his apparatus. He doesn't pose either. He merely inclines his eyes towards the camera and his centre of awareness shifts for the briefest moment, then he returns to his obdurate position. The Arabs of Ma'rib were quick, agile, and voluble. The Ethiopians of Axum, a loping nation of long-legged striders, given to weekly marathons and nocturnal hikes. Once the Turks were nomads too, coursing horses across the Asiatic steppes, but that was in the misty Then. Now they sit and weigh things.

Try to find a single representation of a Turk on horseback in the town squares and you will fail: that's not the past they're interested in these days. Ataturk, whose bronze statues and bust dominate the squares of all provincial towns including Canakkale, broods alone, as stiff and flat as Bela Lugosi waking up after a long day's night in Transylvania. *This* Turk is not going anywhere, he seems to be saying, so don't get any ideas about *that*. The custodian of a heap that's *his*, because he's not the type to argue.

The trip to the site is too short; the countryside, too delightful. In Troy, the depredations of Heinrich Schliemann the Despoiler are made clear to the average tourist. "He made the site a molehill." Here we are, we Turks, so careful with all our stuff, and then along comes this idiot who hacks out a trench right through the middle of Sites II and III, messing everything up. And here is an aquatint photo of the Treasure of Priam he succeeded in squirrelling out of the country. The so-called treasure looks like household laundry turned into copper sheets, a fairy tale gone bad. Schliemann salted the site with loot from other sites, the story goes. Reading between the lines, it's clear our adventurer did not have any trouble scuttling off with his spoils to Berlin because the local authorities at the time didn't much care for Greek history. Contrasts between Greek and Turk are set out in the official Troy guidebook, painted as a conflict between economic expansionist Greek colonists and the indigenous peoples of Anatolia.

> The Trojans were certainly not Greek-speaking peoples.
> Although not proved, we shall go on believing that the
> Trojans were "native people of Anatolia" until archaeologists
> find tablets in future proving to the contrary.

This sentiment that holds Greeks as proselytizing specialists and the locals as laissez-faire generalists finds fuller expression in Turkish literature.

Ayvalyk is a small port on the Aegean 120 kilometres south of Troy, about twelve hours by express bus from the capital of Istanbul. The four-hundred-year-old Greek fishing village is the setting for a current novel by Ahmet Yorulmaz, *The Children of War*. Yorulmaz is the son of Cretan Turks who were forced to evacuate their island home in the great exchange of the two populations, between 1922 and 1925, after the Treaty of Lausanne redrew their international boundaries. Two million in total were dispossessed; Greeks from hundreds of villages and towns in mainland Turkey, Turks from islands like Crete and Lesbos, left for home countries they had never seen. The Greek population of Ayvalyk was forced to leave too. Yorulmaz's novel features a Doctor Sekip, who like Dr. Zhivago witnesses the tumult of his times from the perspective of a decent professional trying to fashion a meaningful private life. A lover, books, patients. Helping his patients beyond the bounds of ordinary duty, Sekip artificially inseminates some infertile patients and thereby gets himself into a foreshadowed predicament. He ends by shooting himself. ("Get my revolver," the narrator's father had declaimed in the Chapter One. "This time the fire will spread!")

I met Yorulmaz's German translator, Annette Steinhot, a tall ash-blonde in her early forties, who had been working on the novel for six months. In the book's view, the Greeks are the perpetrators of the diaspora, the original and fecund colonialists. The Turks, whenever their side wins a round in the contest, keep their "quiet joy to themselves."

Annette played Bach and Schumann in the anteroom of her peaceful whitewashed guest-house, set in the cobbly back lanes of old Ayvalyk. Three Turkish guests came for tea at 4:30 and departed sharp at 5:15, two women and a man who spoke in delighted whispers and ignored the pestering shouts of the village kids knocking a ball just outside the door. It was obvious to me that, just as the British were inclined to favour the mercurial Greeks and Arabs, the Germans favoured the Turks. These affinities had built up over time, and just as America now snatches the brains out of the world's research labs, so too the Ottoman Empire must have attracted certain types to its shores, in this case perhaps immigrants disposed to brokered commerce and the joys of collecting heavy iron keys.

After taking coffee with Annette, I ranged the narrow bumpity streets of Ayvalyk, pressing myself flat against damp alley walls to make way for buzzing motorcycles and clumbering horse-carts. No cars: the town's steep upper streets were far too precarious. Even the taxis waited several blocks below. No life stirred in the dusty warehouse-shops and the signless clutter-bins. Had this still been a Greek town, I told myself, their proprietors would have been lounging outside, watching the sparrows flit away against the moving walls of evening, or betting on the tomcats preparing to fight, *anything*.

But the Greeks had left the shops decades ago. Now their Turkish proprietors sat motionless in their solitary gloom, their stock impossible to fathom from the street outside. Cardboard boxes, ramshackle silence. Ignoring their wares, oblivious to traffic, as still and dull as overkept winter vegetables, the storekeepers waited in dust and silence.

Waiting for something, for history maybe, to reclaim them.

Chapter 22

Characteristics of the Puma

"Turkey faces two possibilities of destruction," Harun said, "the Kurdish problem and the Islamic fundamentalists. And a third, one even more difficult to overcome."

We were sitting in Annette's cozy living room, drinking the local Telhibg white wine, and the poet Harun and his wife, Deniz, had just arrived from their native Istanbul, where they had recently returned to live after their school years abroad in New York and Toronto. Deniz, an attractive urban woman in her early thirties, made her living as an executive with Cisco ("empowering the future," etc.) after obtaining her degree in industrial engineering. "The soft science of making people work better," she called it. Her husband, with his intense eyes and leonine hair and bushy beard, looked like a Turkish beatnik.

He also worked at making people better; he told us he was a *practising* philosopher, part of a movement that began twenty years ago with the German philosopher Aschen, of Freiburg University, who taught that it was not only possible but necessary for people to ask themselves the hard questions of life in an ongoing search for wisdom, *sophia*, over technical knowledge, *epistome*. Harun explained the country's recent history.

"We are a people cut off from our roots, traumatized by change, our identity gone. In the reforms of 1923, Ataturk changed everything, clothes, language, cut us off from our past. Not just the language, making Arabic defunct in place of Roman lettering, but all Arab and Parsi words were taken from our vocabulary. 'Now we are Europeans!' It's as if you North Americans one day all of a sudden had to wear laptops, high-heeled sneakers, and speak digitally, and drop all Latin-based words from your vocabulary. By law!"

"We do!"

"We can't even read our own past, even the gravestones of our ancestors are unintelligible to us now. And the clothes, the role of women, they were given the vote before they asked for it – even time itself! The calendar changed, so we don't even know what year it is now!"

"It was like the French Revolution," I nodded. "The top-to-down revolution that spares nothing."

"Yes, like the Jacobins. Seventy-five-years later, we still feel cut off, the ache of the invisible loss stays with us. There is a teacher near here, he gives classes in Ottoman Turkish, writing and reading, and slowly we make contact with this great lost world."

"And what about the Greeks and the war? The book Annette is translating says the Greeks are interested in their history, but not the Turks."

"No, it is not that we Turks are not interested. It is that for so long there has been an official silence, and people were unable to talk freely of their past, of what happened to us as a people."

"What is there to talk about?" I needed to get at the root of the matter. "The big question?"

"For one, Turkey rejected the role of the leader of the Islamic world that other countries wanted us to assume. We weren't interested, so there was no leader. So what *is* Turkey's role in the Islamic world? That is an unanswered question. Secondly, who shall modernize Islam, which country will create a new vision of Islam that fits into the modern world? Egypt and other countries may be more advanced *theocratically* in this regard, but Turkey leads the way in *practice*. We are far ahead of the other countries in putting modern Islam into our daily life."

"So what about your neighbours? Iran, Syria, these must be difficult relationships?"

"Of course, every country has its peculiar dilemma, its unresolved predicament. Ours is to sit between Europe and the Middle East, and to try to develop our identity when all our neighbours are constantly pushing us to go one way or the other."

"Here you are working for Cisco," I turned to Deniz. "Do you feel part of the American expansion?"

"We're selling 'the Future,'" she laughed. "At least that's the slogan. I've been with the company only a month, so we'll have to see what the future brings, in time."

"How does this 'philosophical practice' of Harun's come into play in your own lives?" I wanted to know.

Deniz answered. "Well, I have asked Harun questions, about work, and we have had hard thinking – he makes me think very hard – and the sessions I found very useful."

"It's analogous to psychotherapy." He paused and looked up to his left, as if the answer would come from the wings. We waited. "You consider your presupposition carefully . . . Take emotions. The emotional life . . . It's considered irrational, these emotions, they just come out of nowhere and flit away again. But if you examine these emotions, their source, you will find that they have a basis in rational perception. This does not mean rationalization. For example: You become angry, enraged. Yet clearly when you examine the process you understand that you feel threatened. And justifiably so, and a part of that feeling *is* therefore emotional."

He cocked his head upwards to the right now, awaiting further questions.

I wondered at the man's interest in practical Greek *sophia*. *Sophia* was one of the seven geniuses that informed Greek thinking, along with others like *epistome*, *arete*, and *letheia*, each more than just words difficult to translate (they signified concepts like wisdom, science, willpower, sacrifice, divination, healing, and mystery). Why choose wisdom?

"So are you both pure Turkish, in whatever way that means?"

"Pure Turkish, yes. An oxymoron," Deniz smiled knowingly. "There is a story my family name is Gushi, *blue eyes*, and my father *has* blue eyes. We came from the south of Turkey, where the Knights Templar once came to live."

"As for me," Harun said, "my mother was Albanian. From the Balkans."

"And you write poetry in Turkish?"

"Yes. A volume of my poems was called *Characteristics of a Pooma*. Is that what you would call it?" He looked at his wife.

"I don't know," she laughed. "What would *you* call it?"

"I'm not sure, in English."

"Puma?" I asked. "Like the American mountain lion?"

"Yes," he nodded, and Annette clapped her hands in glee.

"He *looks* like a lion," our hostess sprang up to her library. "Wait."

She returned with several old books and began flipping through them. "See? He looks like this German architect from the 1920s!"

Indeed the resemblance was striking. The formal bearing, the erect chin, the eyes focused on an unseen horizon. That leonine beard again.

Jason Langford, my Welsh friend, would have been relieved to finally see his lion. We studied the pictures and looked up to compare them with the real thing sitting before us. Even his wife, Deniz, found Harun something of a mystery, judging from the interest with which she followed our questions.

"And your name now," I said. "Is it a Turkish name? What does it mean?"

"Harun? It's from the Quran," he replied evenly. "I don't know what it means."

"Of course," said Annette, "it's in the Bible, like a lot of names from the Quran. It's Aaron."

"Really?" Harun seemed pleased at this and stroked his luxuriant locks thoughtfully.

"Yes, *Aaron's Rod*," I joined in. "A novel by D. H. Lawrence."

We drank some more of the Telhibg white wine and Annette opened another bottle, fussing a little over her laconic guest. An attractive couple, I thought. Confident, well travelled.

"Would you like to hear some jazz? It's great!" Annette fiddled with a 1970s-style portable stereo, a chrome job with too many dials.

Blues came pouring out. Not jazz, but John Lee Hooker, and for the first time in my travels I felt homesick. For that space improvisational music always created. Nothing else like it in the whole square world.

"We went to New York," Deniz was saying, "and wanted to go to the Copacabana to hear some jazz, but we were in the lineup, and the doorman came by, and he looked at our feet, and said, 'I'm sorry, I can't let you in, wearing the sandals.'"

I resisted taking a quick look at Annette's reaction.

"Were you wearing socks or just bare feet?"

"Bare feet, no socks. But we went to another club and they let us in."

"Jazz, yeah, New York, yeah," I began. "Heard Junior Wells, way back when, Doctor John, he's Louisiana blues as opposed to Chicago, ever heard of him?"

"I think so," Deniz said doubtfully.

"Yeah," I continued, riffing, "yeah, the Village Vanguard, Sun Ra? Sun Ra thinks he's from Mars or somewhere. I collected all the LPs. At the end I was listening to Eric Dolphy, and that guy who played nine saxophones at the same time. What was his name?"

They all looked at me. Wondering what I was talking about.

What I was talking about was this heavy dose of European classicism I was picking up from this outpost of Europe. While I ruminated on my wineglass, Annette's Turkish painter-boyfriend dropped by – a tall, shaggy, blond guy in his late forties. He told us he'd been helping out at the Dinosaur, a big music club on the island across the bay. His ears perked up when the subject of music reached Pink Floyd and Led Zeppelin.

"Led Zeppelin, yeah!" He gave a thumbs-up to general approval.

"Man, it's thirty years later and its *still* Pink Floyd and Zeppelin!" I shook my head. From the grinning nods I realized I was in a swarm of unrepentant 1970s rockers. Annette told us how she'd been married several times and was driving into Germany with two-ex-husbands once in the car, and the police surrounded the vehicles with drawn machine-guns, intent on arresting one of the men.

"And what was he arrested for?"

"He was a member of the Marxist-Leninist Communist Party, a Maoist. This was at the time of the Red Brigades and the Bader-Meinhof gang. He got five months. Unfair."

"And where is he now?"

"He's a sociologist, like all my ex-husbands." She shook her head. "I don't know why they are all sociologists."

"So how is it living in Turkey, running a business here?"

"Well, the newspapers are bloody awful. They show pictures of dead people, blood running from their mouths, all the time!" She pounded her fist. "It makes me so mad!"

"But still," I said, "this is a nice place, Ayvalyk, I mean. Comfortable, like this Ottoman furniture here. Once you sit down . . ."

I paused, and included the others in my look.

"There was this guy I met in Ethiopia, he was seeing a wonderful sweet girl who had lovely parents, they lived on the Welsh Downs. Perfect, healthy, and she loved him. So of course he ran off to Africa and hardly looked back!"

I was thinking of Jason and they all laughed.

"But what I am saying is, do you ever think this is a nice trap? The stimulations of the world are waiting for you, and it's dangerous to the spirit to linger too long in one soft place?" What I was thinking about was futility. The futility of action, the futility of thought. What was left? The imagination!

"Well, I drove up and down the coast of Turkey for many months," Annette spoke first, "and in the winter, when things were at their lowest, to see where the best place for me was to live."

"The rational approach," I said. I looked to Harun.

"For me, I think, the centre is where I am, so perhaps it does not matter."

"I see," I nodded. "The *conscious* approach."

"But tell me, what book are you writing?" Harun looked at me with curiosity.

"Well, you know, I was in Yemen. In Ma'rib, I learned that the queen of Sheba was in Ethiopia too, and they both competed for the queen, the way the Greeks and the Trojans contested over Helen. They kept reinvading, colonizing each other, for over a thousand years. Using war-elephants instead of the Trojan Horse. It seemed too coincidental, this polarized relationship. Ethiopians and Yemenis. Like the Greeks and Anatolians. There must be something more to it."

"And so you think that the queen is not a queen? Something more?"

I watched Harun's index finger, it was pointing upwards, out the window into the clear midnight sky bathed in the fine light of an unseen moon.

"Yes," I spoke slowly. "Something more."

"Cybele," he said, without further ado. "Of course."

I stared at him. *That was quick.*

"Yes, Cybele," I agreed. "I'm going to Ephesus tomorrow to see . . . what I can see. And then on to Catalhoyuk perhaps."

"Yes, she is Cybele," Harun nodded, as if he'd been reading my mind before I knew what was in it. "The mother of humanity."

We drank some more wine; Annette put on a tape of Zeki Müren, the celebrated Turkish drag-queen diva who died with her stilettoes on, performing one last time her repertoire of wildly desperate love songs before keeling over on stage.

"*Hallal, hallal!*" The guests all joined in the chorus.

"Doesn't hallal mean *good meat*?" I asked incredulously. I studied the cover picture of a big fellow wearing careful eye makeup and a golden Liberace-style robe.

"Yes, exactly!" Deniz cried aloud, and they laughed and laughed. "Oh, Zeki! He's so great! He's saying, 'You're perfect, 100 per cent okay with me!'"

"No problem!" I offered.

"No problem!" She agreed.

"How refreshing!"

"Well, it's time we withdraw," Deniz got up.

"Withdraw? How about 'advance and attack'?" Harun smiled.

"I got to pick up my daughter," Annette's boyfriend said.

After they all left, Annette shook her head. "I was without a guy for almost seven years, and now suddenly I have a boyfriend again. I don't know if I can handle it."

"Well, what are Turkish guys like? Is Harun a typical Istanbul *entel* [intellectual]?"

"No, no, not at all." She waved her hands in the air. "He's someone out of the 1970s with that suede coat of his, that long hairstyle and beard."

"So he's not typical of his generation? Maybe getting into philosophy as a consolation for the failure of contemporary Turkish politics?"

"No, he's his own person, this is what I think." She downed her glass.

Annette's boyfriend soon joined us again, and now he noticed the pile of books on the copper table-platter. She explained to him in Turkish about our earlier researches into Harun's physical antecedents. He nodded and began flipping through an account of a German expedition to Bergamon in the 1930s, and said something and tossed the book down.

"No, no," Annette answered him in English. "The Germans did *not* 'steal' the relics. They had a legal agreement with the pasha to take 10, 15 per cent of what they found. It was all fully legal, and they put all the pieces together."

"The fucking pasha?" He glared at her. "Who the fuck was *he*?"

He stood up, the words fairly flaming out of his mouth. "They belonged to Turkey, not Berlin."

"They were burning the marble for *lime*, for mortar! The Germans found burnt marble pieces, and put them together again!"

The argument flared like a gasoline fire, and I left them to it. The next morning I woke up with a splitting headache. The Telhibg white, I remembered sourly.

I watched a bread-seller come up the narrow cobbled street, the sunlight glinting hard on the fresh loaves balanced on his head, wincing every time he yelled out for customers.

"*Ekmek chi!* . . . *EKMEK CHI!*"

Chapter 23

The Ruins Are the Story

Harun's fateful words ("Cybele, of course, the mother of humanity") rang in my ears all the next day on the bus to Selcuk, a pretty little town another 150 kilometres south down the coast. For a spiritual rationalist, his powers of intuition were rather acute. It was as if he had already penetrated the core of my research, extrapolating the answer from a few gestures and hints on my part, all over a few glasses of the rough local wine.

And I also thought it more than odd that Annette – quite spontaneously – felt compelled to mention a certain Isabelle Eberhart, who had dressed up as a native boy and wandered about the Maghrib of North Africa back in the early 1900s, entering mosques and outpost souks at will, and talking freely with the imams for nine years, before an avalanche buried her alive at the age of twenty-eight. She sounded remarkably like the Irish trekker who walked bleeding over the Ethiopian plateau from one end to the other, the aspiring martyr whom Jason Langford had told me about. Or for that matter, the ultra-marathon runner who got lost in the South African desert and had visions of spectral Bushmen, the young woman Chad Ulansky had competed against in the Namibia Eco-Challenge. What was this about? Who were these barefoot girl-avatars?

Did these lands all possess presiding daemons? A female presence who consecrated her domain with blood and tears and prophecy? Was it coincidence, or something more that led me to make these investigations? Everything to date had gone like clockwork, and now here I was headed for the ancient pilgrimage site of Ephesus – without a clear idea of why I was going there. Frankly I was as mystified as I had been in Axum, armed only with this compulsive intuitive sense that I was supposed to go. That all would be explained in the fullness of time. Ephesus had been a major centre of pagan worship for long centuries; and more, the Virgin Mary had gone there to die. Like Axum with its Ark, it was a place loaded with heavy occult symbolism.

So here I was on the long-distance bus to Selcuk, with my bag of sweet Izmir oranges bought for a dollar and squirting sticky dark juice. The countryside was breaking into bloom everywhere.

I sat up by the bus driver, watching the blue remnants of the receding Aegean on my right. The road dipped into the interior, then out again. Dark green and bright blue followed each other. On the left, larger and larger mountains collected thickly around us, with their reforested slopes sticking out like the coarse hairs on stubble-bearded street hustlers trying to close a hot deal. Vigorously healthy farm women, with freshly pressed headscarves tied around their sunburnt, meaty faces, hoisted string bags aboard, and their obedient children followed, some, blessed with red hair and blue eyes as dazzling as the peacock tiles of Topkapi, smiled guilelessly at the other passengers.

Sunlight poured through the windows and into our hearts, someone sang and sang, loud enough to be heard, soft enough not to wake the day-sleepers among us. It was going to be okay, I told myself, all I had to do was hang in here and make it to my destination.

And be ready for anything.

&

"Bad hand." My *batak* coach shook his head, confirming the round was hopeless. "You can't win too much."

Over the card game the smoke rose thick as the moaning wraith in *Hamlet*. I was in Selcuk, staying at the famous Ozkan brothers' hotel across from the Roman aqueduct with its migrating storks. Off-season, and with a sudden financial crisis that was shaking the Turkish banking system, there were few tourists in this town of about a hundred thousand. I was invited as a fourth for the nightly game of *batak*, a national preoccupation. Cem ("Jimmy") Ozkan was telling me a sad story of loss and redemption, to console me while I was losing.

"This American couple had no children after many years of trying. So they came here to Turkey and took a baby, a boy, from a farm couple who were poor. This was almost twenty years ago."

"I see," I said, nodding as my good cards disappeared. A queen. I was really getting slaughtered. "How much did they pay?"

"I don't know . . . Anyways, last year? He comes back."

"Who, the baby-stealing American?" Not a single spade! I'd better watch them shuffle more closely next hand.

"No, the baby."

"The *baby*?" I had another sip of sweet cherry wine from Sirince, knowing I would pay for it in the morning. The room was billowing with eye-ripping smoke, and the disembodied grunts of the players now shot through the fumes like card-seeking missiles: *Ugh! Echg! Uugh!* A whole litany of strategic imprecations.

"No, yes. The boy. He grow up."

"He's twenty?"

"Yes. He finish school. He come to look for his parents. He stay one hour."

"One hour?"

"Yes. He say, 'Now I must go back to America. Goodbye.' That is all."

"That's the story?"

"Yes."

"It takes longer to tell, than what happened."

I lost a king to an ace. "So he never saw his parents again? Do you know?"

"Maybe he did, I don't know. It was my uncle, his friend. My uncle works for NATO. The village life is different from the city in Turkey. Maybe he will come back again, to see his mother. Who knows? . . . It's difficult. Now he works for Philip Morris; NATO is closing."

"Who, the boy?"

"No, my uncle's friend."

"Philip Morris is closing too, Jimmy, and soon. No one smokes in America any more except thirteen-year-old girls and dead people."

"In Turkey? Everyone still smokes."

"So I've noticed." I picked up a new hand. Loaded with spades, kings, and aces.

"Five," I said, betting on the rounds I would win.

"Good, good," said my coach, massaging my shoulders like a boxing trainer, getting his boy ready for the third, pace-setting round.

§₺

"Did you hear about the man whose wife began speaking a foreign language?" they asked me.

"Tell me." I sipped at hot apple tea from a small clear glass, with puckered lips. I had expressed an interest to the card table in urban myths, in the contemporary Turkish folktales of sudden transformations, something like Ovid's *Metamorphoses*, with local accounts of persons who unwillingly evolve overnight into saints or vice versa leading the way so far. Like the queen of Sheba, who kept changing her role. But the story of Jennet was different.

"Jennet means *paradise* in our language. They were married for two years, I think, and her husband, Kargun – Kargun, it means like a black bird that we have in our country."

"A crow?"

"Like a crow but not so big."

"Starling?"

"Bigger than a starling."

"Okay. Go on."

"So, this Kargun, he is in the shower room one day, and he hears his wife Jennet say, 'Remember to wash your pants well. They are not clean.' 'My *pants?*' he asks. 'What do you mean my pants? I am taking a bath!' 'Pants! Pants!' she yells through the door. 'Wash your pants!'

"He shakes his head. He finishes. They go shopping later. She tells him, get in the bar and wait for me. Five minutes!

"'The bar? I don't want to go to the bar!!' 'Bar, bar! What's wrong with you? *Go!*'

"He sits in the car and watches for her with his ears. His eyes are full, looking at the past. But she comes and does not say anything. They get in the car and drive home again."

"She was having a speech problem? Brain tumour? *What?*" I love guessing at endings. Jennet meant *heaven*. This one, I figured, would have Jennet gone to jennet, and Kargun flying off to find another lady crow.

"No. More words come out. Every day mix-ups. They go to a doctor. The doctor is Mustafa Achmet, good doctor. The husband thinks she is crazy. They fight all the time, always about the words. He knows what she mean, but she yell when he ask her to say the right word. He doesn't like to call his hands, *pants*. His clothes, *milk. Sut*, I mean. I say like this so you understand, but these are not what she says, really, you understand?"

"Yes, they were talking Turkish, not English."

"Exactly . . . so the doctor, he makes CAT scan, you know what that is?"

"Everyone in my country have the CAT scan."

"Really?"

"Only joking. Go on."

"Dr. Mustafa tell the husband she is not sick. She's Persian."

"Poisoned?"

"Persian. She speaks Farsi, Iranian."

"I see. Why?"

"They think that, when she was small child, something happen. She forgets, then she remembers again."

"Her parents were Persian? Her real parents?

"Who knows who her parents were? Lots of people in Turkey come from other places. The Caucasus, Iran. Solonika, in Greece. They forget much, remember much. What's true?"

"And the man? He was happy?"

"He buy a book of words, in Farsi. Is okay."

"A dictionary?"

"Yes."

"Every man needs this for his wife. This one was lucky, to find her book!"

"Yes, yes. This is so." My words were immediately translated into Turkish, and a knot of smoking chins bobbed up and down in studied agreement with my sentiments.

෯

In the sparkling morning of the next day – the cherry wine was not as insidious as I feared – I ate my breakfast on the open roof terrace of the hotel, overlooking the Roman aqueduct, with great heaps of sticks piled atop each of a dozen or so ancient brick columns. The fabled stork nests.

Breakfast took a while to arrive, since Cem insisted on bringing up the whole production – fresh orange juice hand-squeezed by Cem's father, sheep cheese, black olives, tomatoes, *simici* (warm sesame bread), bananas and honey, coffee, and chocolate cake. I studied the rooks, as *kargan* proved to be, negotiate loudly over a table scrap in the street below. They were see-sawing away at each other until one bold attacker feinted, forcing the claimant off the throne. Then a third rushed in to plunder the prize and took off to a tragic chorus of shrieks following close behind him. They sounded like rusty bedsprings as they took up new positions around the victor, and then the whole production started all over again.

A kilometre away, across the town's red terraces and palm trees, stood Ayasoluk Hill, an ancient archeological site, topped by a medieval walled fortress that loomed larger than life against the violet hills in the horizon. The fortress flew the crescent flag; it was patrolled by soldiers and off-limits to tourists. Below the fortress lay a major ruin, the Basilica of St. John, allegedly marking the grave of the Apostle, who left Jerusalem in A.D. 40 and, as the story goes, travelled here to Ephesus in the company of the Virgin Mary Herself. This is the same John, it was claimed here, who wrote the Book of Revelation in Patmos, a small Greek island across the Aegean Sea. But again, the dates were wrong by centuries. Revelation was written after A.D. 200.

This John certainly got around, I thought, studying the impossible spring greens and yellows that saturated the ruins. Cem arrived with a Turkish newspaper. The front page showed men hauling bodies out of a flood that had hit southern Turkey the night before last. I remembered the terrific offshore winds that chopped up the sea bay in Ayvalyk and rattled the windows all night. We had caught only the edge of the storm's tailwind. Annette had spoken disparagingly of the Turkish propensity for front-page blood and guts, but for me these awful pictures only aroused a holy terror and gratefulness, not a whit of prurient interest in the morbid details of instant death.

"See this man?" Cem's finger drew my attention away to the inside page. "He covers his head?"

"He's arrested? What for?"

"He and two friends, they steal many things from houses, but the police don't catch them."

"Burglary gang?"

"Yes. But one day he drops his telephone card on a job. So the police, they only have his phone number, nothing else. So they phone him up, and he answers hello, and they say, we are the phone company. Special promotion. You are lucky customer that wins five hundred million lire for your phone-card number. Please come to collect your prize."

"And he stupidly thinks it's true?"

"Yes. There he is, up on the fence, trying to get away. But the police have official photographer ready, and everything . . ."

"They knew his name?"

"Yes, but lots of people have the same name here. So the police, here they are very smart. They know people, how they think."

"I wonder if that accounts for the success of the Turkish empire for so long." I looked up at the brooding fortress above us, flying the scarlet flag and still visibly much in use. Awaiting customers for its guns.

"Maybe so."

The eerie milkiness in the sky unaccountably increased as the sun rose. The middle distance was sharp and green with new grass, and the orange and lemon groves stood tall and lush, fanciful with bright fruit. But the horizon now showed the soft, worn fluster of an old carpet, mousey browns and faded greens and streaks of rust in the underbelly of the clouds.

"It's the sandstorms blowing off the Sahara," someone at the next table decided.

Another disagreed. "Turkey's too far from the desert . . ."

I wondered how my friends Peter Boehm and Jason Langford were making out now, crisscrossing Africa, kicking up the dust of forgotten kingdoms. More than enough madmen and missionaries to go around for everyone, a jumble of lost cultures, and for what? Everybody wanted to be American now and go to the moon, right? I did. I'd read a piece in a week-old copy of the *Herald Tribune*. The Russian correspondent had discovered late in his career that the cosmonauts' little chrome suitcases, featured so prominently in the newspaper photos of the 1960s, were filled with bags of their own orbital shit.

"Usually it rains and is cold at this time of year," Cem said, breaking into my savage thoughts with a warm smile. "You are lucky to have such good weather."

The man at the next table spoke up. He wore a baseball cap with a red rooster on the crown and a pale-blue Polo shirt. An American preppy in his early sixties.

"I've been to Turkey twenty-five times, usually in the spring, and this weather is glorious."

"You must like it then."

"Love it. The people couldn't be nicer."

"What's the best thing about it?"

"Well, I'm a medieval scholar, Princeton originally. But now I deal in carpets. And this is the place for carpets."

RobRoy McCampbell, the originally-from-Princeton man, was from Minnesota, and spoke exactly like Garrison Keillor, whom he claimed to know and love. ("He always gets it right," he said. "It's Jenny's Motel *and* Bake Shop, if you know Minnesota and Wisconsin.") How I wished we had developed name brands like these in my country, brands to proclaim to strangers who we were exactly. In two seconds or less. Instead of having to *think* of things to say all the time. It was a lot easier, this Oxford, Harvard, Chanel, Cote d'Azur thing. Where was I? Oh, yeah, McCampbell was talking about Caucasian carpets being the cream of the Oriental rug world:

"Oh, you *hear* about the Iranian carpets, the Tabriz and the silk Ishfehans and the like, but for my money the best in the world are the Caucasians, tight weave, real nomadic carpets made on portable looms, last you hundred of years, natural dies from indigo and rose madder and some plants that only grow in the Caucasus – Sotheby's has an auction, and a three-by-five old Caucasian will go for half a million in the blink of an eye. When I first came out here, twenty-five years ago, you could find them everywhere. Now they're all gone . . ."

He looked into the same timeworn horizon I had been searching hard a few minutes before, and then he absently placed a dozen pills on the table and asked for an orange juice. I recognized the ginkgo biloba and ginseng, but not the others.

"So, did you ever run into a problem dealing carpets here in Turkey?"

"A problem? Yes, with a friend of mine who was my friend for two years. I used his shop in Istanbul to store the carpets I bought, $150,000 worth of inventory collected over many months. The day came to ship them back, he calls a taxi, we pile the carpets into the cab, and he says, 'Look, there's a paper back in the store I want you to sign, come back in the store,' and I do, when we come out both the taxi and my carpets are gone.

"We go to the police, and they immediately handcuff my friend without a word and start beating him up. I say, 'Stop, stop! He's my friend, the cab driver did it!'"

"They look at me like I'm stupid, but they let him go, and would you believe it, I see the cab driver standing at a stand, a few blocks away.

"'Akbar, look! The taxi driver! It's him!'

"'No, that's not him,' Akbar says, but his face gets tight.

"'It's him, I tell you. It's him!'

"I run and get the police, and they interrogate the driver. He tells them that he took the carpets to the Ottogar like he was told to. A man had come out of the office next to the shop and told him the plan was changed and the American wasn't going with the taxi.

"The police immediately grabbed Akbar again and this time showed him no mercy; all the carpets had been shipped to his other store in another city, and when they came to the police station they made him carry all the carpets up all the flights of stairs, hundreds of pounds, and back down again, when they released them to me.

"After he got out of jail, he disappeared from Istanbul forever, but if I had not spotted the cab driver, it would have been the end of my business."

I thought about the odds of this. "There must be a million cab drivers in Istanbul."

"Yes, at least that number. But only one who was important to me."

RobRoy got up to meet the cruise ships at Kusadasi, the cheesy new tourist port. He took it upon himself to help his local friends in the carpet business get some tour business. "You get a lot of lower-middle-class Americans on these cruises," he sighed, "so it'll probably be a waste of time."

He finished his coffee and strode purposely to the dock. It was obvious that the carpets had got into his blood, and he couldn't quit the chase, even if the Caucasians were all gone.

I was left alone to contemplate the scattered ruins of St. John's Basilica once more. Ayasoluk Hill was a hot green platter, turning its offerings over to the midday sun. I was thinking.

Thinking it was all a matter of luck. A man's luck either held or it didn't. There was no way of telling either way, unless you went directly to the edge of the sky and looked down, at the point where the clear meets the murk. The ruins tell the story, whatever it is. The ruins *are* the story. I would have to go and read them, and find out what they said.

Chapter 24

Inside the Water Palace

I t was mid-afternoon by the time I slowly trudged my way up Ayasoluk Hill, hurrying past a family of bright-eyed gypsies whose children approached me with half-hearted requests for money. There were two major sites in town; this hill was the first of them and easier to comprehend. Ephesus, the huge pilgrimage ruin, was a twenty-minute taxi ride through the mountains, and needed a full day just for a quick gloss. Here, beyond the gates of the basilica wall, lay an archeological site of four or five parklike acres.

It was all enclosed by a sturdy barbed-wire fence, but I immediately spotted an American trekker in the characteristic bandanna and Columbia gear who had found his way through a secret exit hole and was now climbing resolutely up towards the forbidden castle, despite the stern warnings posted everywhere. A different guidebook, I reckoned.

A few black-and-white storks circled overhead, checking us out, we, the latest newcomers to invade their ancient homelands, flapping hard in the still air, as ungainly and prehistoric as our pelicans back home, but with a grave solemnity few other birds could match. They were African, and they came to the town every year on the same dates, roosting atop the Roman

279

aqueducts and other abandoned promontories. Their nests must have presided over the ancient civilizations from the onset, for their ancestors had shared this valley with the Ephesians of three thousand years ago, and others before them.

I spotted the tomb immediately. It was overgrown with new grass, a carved marble sarcophagus sitting squarely on the ground, something that might have been mistaken for a horse's water trough. A *sarcophagus*, Greek for "consuming the flesh," so-called because in Greece, where they were invented, the stone coffins were deliberately made of a limestone that literally ate away at the flesh of the dead person. In fact, the one lying before me had the same proportions as the bull-headed water troughs I had seen back in Ma'rib, but bigger. I pushed the grass away and tamped the weeds down with my feet, for a better look.

Yes, here it was, all right.

The crescent-moon-and-solar-disk insignia.

It was carved at the end piece of the casket. I walked around the box, and there it was again, the same portent on the other end. The casket was only

about five feet long, sixteen inches high, and a foot and a half wide. Custom-built for a small corpse. Still, it must have weighed twelve hundred pounds or more. Other than being carved of grey marble, not alabaster or some other local Sabean stone, it was something that would not have been out of place twenty-five hundred kilometres to the south.

Now what was this insignia doing here? Here, in this Asiatic Greek temple-city, this South Arabian motif announcing the Marriage of Time and Eternity, this distinctive religious motif that I had never seen on any of my travels through Greece? It was clear that this casket itself once held a small adult, or more likely a child. Its location in the heavy grass at the south end of the basilica precincts gave no indication as to its age or provenance. Had it belonged to the original and local Temple of Artemis, the Greek name for the Mother of the Gods, the Queen of Wild Things? Had it simply been dragged here for safe storage? And how could one date this stone, except from stylistic rendering? It was impossible, I knew.

Archeologist Dr. Leanne Mallory, who specialized in Egyptian basaltic funerary vessels, had warned me that secure dating was virtually impossible when it came to stone relics. There were stylistic details that would give you only an approximation. Then all you could do was collate any written records available with the atomic signature of known quarries, to reach an approximate date – if you had the records, which was unlikely here.

I wandered the field, stepping over fallen columns and more architectural salvage than there existed foundations to support it hereabouts, and soon located another sarcophagus, this one much larger than the first. This had been constructed for a giant or a man of great public estimation, for the granite tomb was over six and a half feet in length, and four feet high. It too held the Sabean symbol at both ends, the crescent moon and solar disk. Now, as I turned and looked about the field, I realized there were more sarcophagi like these two, and those that didn't have the simple disk-and-crescent symbol had elaborations of it, with round human faces and bowers of draping vine, in place of sun and crescent moon. Opposing and conjoining Logos and Life. Variations on the same theme.

Confronted by the implacable evidence of my senses, by the proofs of cold hard stone, I began speculating, and my mind raced. Was it possible that this archaic symbol was Cybele's sign all along? Was Cybele the original goddess worshipped at this site before the Greeks and Romans and the early Christians, the immigrants who came along with their successive layers of new sins and old salvage? Was it even possible that *Sheba* and *Cybele* derived from the same word? Linguists said the origin of the name Cybele was unknown, meaning that the language it derived from was also unknown. So was the origin of the name Artemis. Saba, Sheba, was related to Arabic for *morning*. The Beginning. We knew that Artemis and Cybele were both Asian goddesses, not indigenously Greek. We knew that the Cybele-cult was present with the appearance of the first irrigated town in history, Catalhoyuk in the interior plateau of Anatolian Turkey, seventy-five hundred years ago. We also knew that ancient peoples were often named after their gods, especially in the original homeland of the Semites and their Sumerian neighbours, where the ancient cities like Ur and Kish and Babylon (Ba'al's city) belonged to those very gods. We knew that the Sabeans had migrated from the north to the fertile valley of the Wadi Qataba.

How far had they come in their wanderings? Or rather, how far had their religious conceptions travelled? From the heartland of the Anatolian valleys? What had they brought with them in the way of religion and its constructs from this riverine cradle of civilization?

I had been on a quest to discover the origin of what I originally thought to be a local queen. One that seemed native to Yemen, Ethiopia, now Anatolia. But it takes more than a queen to appear simultaneously in so many places. For me, the most compelling part of the essential story was that the queen of Sheba had appeared at the court of Solomon, not the other way around. She came, he stayed. In *all* the accounts too: Biblical, Quranic, Ethiopian. A prince out in the world hunting for his princess was nothing, common fodder for fairy tales. This story was different.

This core idea, the princess who comes to the prince, was a reversal that reminded me of something I had seen in the East, in a mountainous land where ancient cultic goddesses still walked the earth. Or rather, where they were carried about in litters, high above it.

In Nepal, I had seen the Tantric Hindus of Katmandu, with their thirteen-year-old girl-goddess held high in a litter, worshipping the incarnation of the Goddess, whose presence was invoked by chanting, ritual, and priestly indifference to marketplace matters. She could appear at any time, the Goddess. The costumed girl was her medium, her instrument. This was the spectral apparition, the Goddess who in her various incarnations and under a plethora of names might appear to mendicants and merchants alike, but spontaneously and fleetingly. Stories abounded in the sacred literature of yogis and monks having such visions. She might appear as a traveller, disguised as an old woman or a young girl, and asking directions. You had only one chance. If you did not recognize Her immediately and comply with Her requests, you never got a second chance. She would be gone for another lifetime.

The Biblical story told us that Solomon knew exactly whom he was meeting, and complied. He rose to the occasion, when "she proved him with hard questions," as it says in I Kings 10.

Here, in this ruins-ground at Ayasoluk Hill, the association of this ancient symbol was only with *death*. Coffins, as far as the eye could see. Death, and only death. There was not a single use of the disk and crescent on anything in this salvage-field except these grandiose sarcophagi, monuments that must have been fabulously expensive to procure, given the time it took to carve a two-ton monster from marble or granite or limestone with archaic hand tools. Did the dying worthies who commissioned them anticipate that they too might be granted a vision of the queen in their last moments, as they walked through the final Portal of Eternity?

I hastened across to the Selcuk Archeological Museum, which was only a few hundred metres down the road from the grassy St. John's ruins. The modern little museum housed the more valuable local finds from the major site of Ephesus, ten kilometres away, in the interior. Centuries of silting had left the original port eleven kilometres from the present seashore. Here in the museum I quickly spotted no less than five cultic effigies of the great goddess, including a Cybele seated on a throne with her feet supported by twin leonine creatures, likely the extinct Anatolian leopard.

Again these effigies were carved on the same scale as the alabaster figures in Yemen, no more than sixteen inches high and six or seven inches wide. Their faces had been mutilated, scored off, possibly by early Christian or

Muslim iconoclasts, over the years. On the other hand, the nose and other
fine facial features would have been the first to go in an earthquake or flood,
and these statues had all survived dozens of such natural disasters, besides
the arrival of rival religions, beginning with Christianity in A.D. 464.

It was in the great cult-city of Ephesus, which derived the bulk of its
income from the offerings of itinerant Artemis worshippers, that the final
showdown between Paganism and Christianity was fought to the death.
Not only St. John but St. Paul himself, the heavy gun of the militant faith,
descended on Ephesus to claim the city for the followers of the cross. Paul
risked martyrdom to preach and convert the populace, and went out of his
way to specifically deny the divinity of Artemis, so the silversmiths who
depended on the custom of the pilgrims organized a riot and drove him
from the city, according to Corinthians.

The city survived Paul nonetheless, and in the fifth century A.D. it
remained effectively a sanctuary for runaway Jews, escaped slaves, crimi-
nals. And, judging from the large number of brothels and graffiti that still
remained intact fifteen hundred years later, it also served as a playhouse for
sexual adventurers of every description. Paul's strategic retreat proved
effective in the end; the Basilica of St. John was one of the largest in
Christendom when completed by Emperor Justinian in the sixth century. It
lasted until 1402, when the Mongols, like their spiritual descendants the
Taliban Afghans, taking the nomads' dim view of architecture, razed it
along with everything else with four walls that they ran across.

A temple of Artemis itself once stood only a few hundred metres below
the Basilica – there was a lot going on here in this smallish tract. Was this *the*
Temple? Impossible to say. It was the same question as with Axum's Palace of
Sheba, only here the temple was specifically dedicated to Artemis, and not
just conjecture. But here again I searched in vain for any statuary or other
device in which the disk and crescent played its part.

The temple precinct was overgrown with weeds; it had been abandoned
to the village's stray dogs. This was originally set by a famous spring, now the
spring had run dry. The classical world was drying up, the ancient ports were
all inland now. I walked around the flattened trail carefully, holding a heap
of stones in my hands, listening for growls and watching for snakes in the

long grass. The temple priests of Artemis had ceremonially been made eunuchs, and their testicles figured in a complex iconography, so a specific feature of this religion had survived until modern times in the standard mutilation of the male attendants to his Sultanic Majesty. I found nothing on the surviving material of any interest. The disk-and-crescent symbol had only the coffins on the hill as its home.

Why was this symbol confined to grave rites in the long centuries before the final Christian ascendency in A.D. 464? I returned to the little Selcuk Museum a second time, a pleasant walk of a few hundred yards made more than pleasant by the abundant spring bird life, and a new idea began to emerge. It was abundantly clear that the enthroned Cybele images were of a scale to encourage portability; they must have been intended to be carried in a procession at seasonal celebrations. Or perhaps they were the effigies of a mobile people, traders, caravaneers. Otherwise, they might have been kept at the back of a natural depression in rock or other cave-sanctuary, where they would be glimpsed, revered, adored, and spiritually apprehended, but not scrutinized or studied. They were emotive, not intellectual. The oldest image of them all, in Catalhoyuk, was crude, lewd, and rude. Ultimately, profane and sacred come to the same thing. I contrasted this with the mannerism of the celebrated Artemis marble, the goddess wrapped in her bull-testicle girdle, the town's famous showpiece, which was kept here in the Selcuk museum. This pink polished marble statue was indeed a *showpiece*. A demonstration of the consummate skill that had completely mastered its medium and served only to encourage admiration for the artist, and for the civilization that engendered him. It wasn't religion at all, but technique for its own sake. High art, effete spectacle.

Did these two images – the rough, crouching, semiferal earth-Cybele and her testicle-adorned beauty-queen Artemis – coexist? Undoubtedly, but the difference lay in their practical function. People came *to see* Artemis, the central-casting showpiece. The flashy exhibit. Cybele on the other hand must have been a processional goddess, with a portable effigy that represented her power, moving freely through her territory and consecrating her domain. Authorities on the Iron Age Doric period, such as Professor H. J. Rose of Oxford, identified Cybele with Rhea, the mother of the gods, who had tricked Kronos (Time) into spewing them up from his belly. Like Cybele, the word *Rhea* also came from a lost language. And like Ilmuquh, the bisexual god of Ma'rib in South Arabia, Cybele too was a hermaphrodite:

> Cybele sprang originally from the ground, and was bi-sexual, until the gods reduced her by surgical methods to a female. (Here at the very beginning, we find the Asiatic fondness for beings who were both god and goddess.)
>
> – H.J. Rose, *A Handbook of Greek Myth* (Methuen, 1928), p. 170

She was mistress of a people who still relied on the vagaries of nature, hunting and opportunistic pastoralism, supplemented by agriculture. By "opportunistic pastoralism," I mean the permanent activities of cattle raiding, trading, and seasonal war, where the object was simply to acquire loot instead of more territory.

Cybele was a land goddess in every sense of the word, a goddess born of the earth, who ruled the deserts, moraine, tablelands, and hilltops. For the coast would always belong to the next fleet of pirates, whether they called themselves Philistines, Dorians, or Trojans. The coast was where the new gods came and went, like island-hopping tourists, Isis, Dionysus, Mithra, and the rest. Cybele would be relegated to the afterlife because, when one dies, one goes *to meet one's ancestors*, and Cybele was clearly ancestral to all the gods and men, according to her honorifics. Death was the Country of the Past for pagans. She was always there to greet the traveller at the Portal, the doorway between life and death.

She *sat*, and waited.

Early the next morning I took a farmer's horse-cart to the staggering multi-acred site of Ephesus, a league distant from town. Preserved on the same scale as Heraculum, the famous Greek ruins were reached by a pleasant paved avenue framed with plane trees, a route that soon turned into an open country road, winding its way through pink peach blossoms and freshly cut fields of spring hay. There were acres of fat, red, innocent flowers, which tugged at my memory – Turkish *poppies*, of course! Dozing village dogs on the road pulled their tails away from the wheels at the last second, blue woodsmoke from a charcoal pit skated across the road in lazy spirals; strands of birds too quick and bright to identify flitted from orchard to orchard. The farmer driving the horse-cart was happy. He was making five dollars for taking me through the glistening morning, and he began a little song under his breath, then caught me listening and shut up, thinking perhaps that I considered vocal music out of keeping with his retainer.

His mare was one of those sturdy beasts that grew shaggy coats for the Turkish winters; now it was spring, and her coarse hair was falling off and birds were snatching it up for their nests and donkeys were braying love-calls and irate roosters were strutting over the gravel shoulders in search of phantom rivals, pumped, so pumped with it all. Oh, the juice of life. Here was the place to die with a full heart.

Wasn't a local life expectancy of fifty-seven, and an early death from pleurisy or pneumonia in full view of these almond trees, worth the candle? The red earth was friable, the summers cogent. Winters perfect for reflection and solace. You could see at a glance why they came, the Phrygians, the Hittites, the Greeks, Romans, and Turks. Seven thousand years of farming later, and the Anatolian countryside was still brimming with crops and fruit trees and the promise of another harvest, better than the last one.

The entrance to Ephesus was through an iron gate. Despite the complaints in the guidebook about "gross commercialization," there was nothing in evidence but a few souvenir shops arranged before the wicket. I left my driver chortling over his haul of deflated Turkish lire-notes and walked through the gates, continuing a tradition that was three thousand years old. The threatening "masses of tourists" had disappeared from sight for the moment. I was free to wander slowly through the marble roads and poke into the weedy crevices at my leisure. The day was sunny and the light grew intense against the play of polished stone walls: "Marble, marble everywhere, and not a shadow to rest." I sipped frequently at a litre of

Turkish mineral water in anticipation of a sweat that never came. This was mountain air, and this was March. The temperature in the shade was markedly cooler than in the sun; I found it pleasant to sit on the front stoop of an ancient bordello and contemplate what it was that I did not like about the place.

Unlike Troy and Bergamon up the coast, citadel-cities both, Ephesus was as intact as any site in the Mediterranean could be, and left less to the imagination than most. It was impossible not to recognize that much of it was unreal, overblown, and artificial from the beginning.

This was not merely bad reconstruction. The German expeditions had left their self-congratulatory notices everywhere, in German and Turkish only, bold-as-brass signs dating back to the less-than-lovely 1970s. They might be accused of imposing a Wagnerian Götterdammerung theme on these soft old marbles, certainly; but these congregations of tourists from the Bible Study Group of Minneapolis, with their blue plastic tractor caps, and these coveys of infantile Japanese women in their white gloves, taking mincing little Geisha steps (one actually had the effrontery to wag her gloved finger in my face for taking a telephoto picture of her collective, all of whom were sketching the same column, when everywhere around us her compatriots were shamelessly sticking their cameras into other peoples' faces, including mine), these beefy, gasping arterial-sclerotic Australians, and these knots of tight-lipped Midwestern appliance-dealers in their powder-blue leisure suits, they were all doing a pretty good job of wrecking the joint too. Oh, yes, I was looking for trouble despite the clement weather and the fine breakfast. And then it hit me:

I knew where I was.

Las Vegas.

Yes, I'd been to Ephesus before, many times. Zip City, the place where all good pilgrims come, century after century, looking for a chance to part with their money in exchange for a quick fix. In its heyday after the eighth century B.C., when commerce really took off in the eastern Mediterranean, the city's reputation grew exponentially. The Ephesus elders travelled in trade missions to other Mediterranean ports to ferret out economic information, and hustle up new business for their town, just as big cities do

today. Ephesus was not an ancient town, but a strip. And much of what I was seeing here today was not architecture at all, but *signage*.

There was no depth or feeling of entry, once you were inside the marble portico. A false-front western town, but in marble. And the buildings were all originally designed to be "shallow," for each had its preferred "vantage point" from which best to view it, as the tour guides were loudly declaiming in their various tongues. It was a bazaar, a mall of storefronts. They were designed for fast traffic, to get the pilgrim in and out of his spiritual shopping-experience as quickly as possible.

"McDonald's is good, in case you don't like Turkish food."

The tour guide was explaining it to his U.S. group, "So, in the eighth century we too had globalization here in Ephesus, with new markets appearing and new surpluses creating more demand. People were beginning to talk the same language, and there was even a wage-shuffle, especially in the transportation industry, after the wars were eliminated. The Roman empire was a direct result of this commercial activity, this need for economic stability."

Next, I thought, he is going to talk about the ancient antecedents of the cellphone and the spreadsheet. Indeed he had a cellphone dangling from his belt, and I wondered idly if Ephesus was in wireless range. (I later discovered that indeed it was.)

"Now here is a city of two hundred and fifty thousand people that needed an *infrastructure*." He paused and looked around. The group was silent and staring off into the nothingness between the carved rocks and dust devils, most of them. "They would have consumed around two hundred million litres of water a day. That's *a day*. And eighty thousand loaves of bread."

I quickly worked that out. He was figuring on eight hundred litres per person. Why? On what basis? After more spurious statistics to bolster his claim for a supply-side eighth-century economy, he went in for a bit of titillation.

"Those egg-shaped things in the pillar? Those are wolf-testicles, to show the power and authority of the state. And those zigzags, running along the side? That's the *real* River Meander, behind the hill here. It shows long life, as well. You have the same word in English?"

"Oh, yeah, *meander*." A capped man worked it out for himself in a broad New York accent.

"Well, Tom, I sure figured out what the business was to be in *those* days." The fellow turned to his similarly capped companion, and there was the grim profile of American Gothic on holiday, in duplicate.

"What's that, Ed?" Tom's lips barely moved.

"The column business. These fellows sure cleaned up in this market."

At least the guide knew *his* market, I decided, as I strolled away to a quiet corner labelled the Water Palace. It must have been musical with water at one time. A cascade of rippling, bouncing, splashing, and crashing timbal-sounds. There were other fountains at Ephesus, but the water had run out for all of them. Over the hill I could see the flat green plain shimmering in the afternoon heat. The harbour that once brought Alexander the Great and a host of other luminaries to its shores was now a flat and dry part of the Anatolian interior.

Cybele had reclaimed her stony realm.

Chapter 25

The Last Days of the Queen of Heaven

The coffin business was a big business along the coast of Anatolia, judging from the immensity and variation in the number of sarcophagi to be found at all the sites. And by studying them even a casual observer could discern repeated themes the ancient peoples had explored in death.

It was natural that pre-existing gods should inhabit the afterworld, for the most obvious theme carved on the stone crypts themselves was the Deceased One Meeting the Ancestors. This was conceived as a figure going forward towards a female figure, who herself was emerging from a coffin (similar to the coffin the relief itself was carved on, a case of infinite recession like the picture of a Coca-Cola bottle on a Coca-Cola bottle). In one such coffin, which sat outside the Selcuk museum, apparently imported from a workshop abroad, the inscription said merely that the deceased young man was twenty-eight. The museum's own caption queried why the figure in the coffin-image was a woman, when the two figures standing by were both men, and clearly the male middle figure was the deceased youth himself. The answer was simple to me. The woman emerging from the crypt-image had to be none other than Cybele, she whom the Anatolians called Ana Tanrica, the Mother

Goddess, coming awake to reclaim her progeny for his *ancestral* family. This was not the only stylistic problem, however.

"What's this business with all these testicles, Cem?" I asked my Turkish host. "The tour guides in Ephesus claimed they represented wolf testicles, but I know the thing he said about the zigzag design being the Meander River was wrong, because I've seen the same symbol on Hittite carvings from hundreds of miles to the east, and those were much older."

"I don't know for sure," Cem began, "but there is a story of the Always Unlucky Man."

"The Unlucky Man?" We were sitting outside drinking coffee, happy to ignore the descending chill of evening after the long day of tomb-roaming.

"He was always unlucky, until one day he won a free trip on an airplane. He was sitting on the plane thinking, 'At last my bad luck is over.' But the plane has a big problem, they must throw all the luggage out or they will go down. And the unlucky man is sitting. Waiting, sweating.

"Sure enough, they say, it's not enough. One passenger must jump out of the plane too. Unlucky man *knows* he will pick the wrong number, and sure enough, it is him they choose by lot to jump from the plane.

" 'Wait, wait!' says Unlucky Man. 'Give me one last chance!' He knows he can reverse his life of bad luck if he uses his head; this is his chance."

"His *only* chance," I interjected.

"Yes. So he says, 'I will pick one man from all of you, and then ask you a question, and it will be a very simple, easy question. And if you get it right, I will leave the plane. If you get it wrong, the other man goes.'

"They all agree. So he chooses another man, and he says, 'Stand beside me here . . . Now, how many eggs do we two men have between us?' "

"*Eggs?*" I interjected, making sure of the word.

"Eggs, yes. So they say, 'That's easy. You have four!'

" 'Wrong,' says Unlucky Man. And he pulls down his pants and shows them. 'See, I am different, I was born with *three* eggs. That makes *five*.' He smiled, for now he has outwitted Fate at last.

" 'I am sorry, my friend,' the other man says. And he pulls his pants down. 'I too am different. I have only *one* egg – '

"Four eggs! They take him away –

"And that was the end of Unlucky Man!"

After we stopped laughing I wondered how old this tale was; it must have started life aboard a leaky oxhide boat, and the passenger who had to lighten the load might have been the butt of a thousand variations leading to the same sorry end.

"He's like the perpetual tourist," I said.

"Yes, always the outsider," Cem agreed.

"You have lots of tourists here. I wonder about the Japanese. What do they get out of coming here to a place like Ephesus?"

"The Japanese are very nice. They must work very hard in their country. Once, a Japanese man came to a party we had. A typical party, music, food, dancing. He started to cry. I said to him, 'Why are you crying? Are you not having a good time?'

" 'Yes,' the man said. 'I never had such a good time in my life. This is wonderful; everyone is so friendly. In Japan I was so lonely, my whole life. Until now.' "

Ephesus was not the only site that drew foreign visitors. Like Axum, which had supposedly attracted to it the Ark of the Covenant through some mysterious osmosis, a supernatural form of gravity, Ephesus too had pulled a heavenly body from the Christian cosmos. The Virgin Mary had supposedly followed the Evangelist John out of Jerusalem, after the death of her Son, to spend her last days in Meryem Ana, a small stone house set by a natural spring.

This site was a heavily treed hilltop ten kilometres inland from the St. John Basilica. The chapel of the Virgin was called Panaya Kapuli, and a steady stream of international pilgrims made their way to the place where the Queen of Heaven had spent her last days. It was from these cedar groves that she had been taken up to heaven.

By now I had fallen into a routine – big breakfast, Turkish newspaper translation, and then the cab's here, let's go! – that would put me in a taxi again the following morning, whether I wanted to move or not. So today I found myself waving the usual pungent cigarette smoke away from my face, and dutifully driving up into the monastic hills, although my interest in the whole enterprise was fading fast. The world was a lonely enough place without more Las Vegas–style retreats offering ersatz spiritual comforts at rates you could afford. On the way, I thought of the unhappy Japanese and his doppelganger, Unlucky Man.

The church cost ten bucks to see. Well, *not exactly*; it was the Municipality of Selcuk that was charging the nice admission to the grounds, the *church* itself was free. Okay, here's some more million-lire notes, the pink ones, yes. More than yesterday, when is this crazy inflation going to stop? With the wheelbarrows to carry the cash? I grimly took the handout and proceeded to the chapel grounds, while my gold-toothed driver joined the other cabbies under a huge cedar tree for a gleeful discussion of their fares so far. The yellow stone church itself looked no more than a hundred or so years old. I looked at the handbill. It reproduced a prayer addressed to the Virgin:

"Most Holy and Immaculate Virgin Mary, who followed the Beloved Disciples into Asia and who was proclaimed Mother of God at Ephesus, protect the Church of Smryna, sole survivor of the Seven Churches of the Apocalypse . . . Our Lady of Ephesus, Queen assumed into Heaven, you who are the Mother to all Mankind . . ."

On the other side was printed the highly scary chapter 12 from the Book of Revelation. As I carelessly scanned it, without warning, it came alive, suddenly and with alarming force, after all my months of research:

"A great sign appeared in the sky, a woman clothed with the sun, with the moon under her feet, and on her head a crown of twelve stars.

"She was with child and wailed aloud in pain as she laboured to give birth.

"Then another sign appeared in the sky, it was a huge red dragon . . . it pursued the woman who had given birth to the male child.

"But the woman was given the two wings of a great eagle, so she could fly to her place in the desert . . . far from the serpent.

"The serpent, however, spewed a torrent of water out of his mouth after the woman, to sweep her away . . .

"But the earth helped the woman, and opened its mouth and swallowed the flood.

"Then the dragon became angry . . . and went off to wage war against the rest of her offspring. . . . It took its position on the sand of the sea."

It was obvious to me that this woman was the same deity worshipped at Ma'rib and Axum, and that the addition of the twelve stars to the sun and moon referred to the twelve signs of the zodiac, and she would have been generally understood as a mediating reality between Absolute and Relative Time. The association of the great serpent with the water-course could not have been more transparent either. The woman *was* the Water-Dragon, and the two were inextricably bound up as inseparable aspects of one Reality: Nature bestowing, and destroying.

The academic specialists were less keen to see a big picture like this; but in my view they were blindsided by the residual nineteenth-century dogma that held myth and cult as structured allegory, and not as encapsulated accounts of cataclysmic events. Was this story of the water-spewing serpent something more than symbolic shorthand expressing our existential predicament? Was there a *folk-memory* hidden in this esoteric text? Was the author, John of Patmos, speaking of eschatology, or giving an encrypted historical text? For it was clear that earthquakes and flood had repeatedly claimed the Anatolian plain around me. The whole region around Yemen, Ethiopia, and Turkey was a vast earthquake zone, ripped apart repeatedly by titanic forces. The question was, how far? How long, how well remembered? Were these events *encoded in the cultures*? I had seen the foolish tilt of subsiding temple foundations, felt the great marble heads lolling on their brows like so many marbles scattered by an idiot's child, talked to the survivors of the 1999 earthquake that rocked all of Turkey at 3:02 a.m. on August 18.

"The newspapers said twenty thousand died, but we know it was at least forty-five thousand," a Turkish designer from Istanbul had told me. "I was lucky. I wanted to stay in bed with my girlfriend in the south, because if I got on the road that night, back to the city, I wouldn't be here talking to you now."

Natural disasters, as anyone who has survived them knows, happen with the force and speed of a disaster movie, not the slow ebb and flow of theoretical plate-tectonics and seasonal tillage. Was it possible that Revelation, rather than a vision of the future, reflected the story of a cult that had fled to the highlands of Yemen after the great floods of 6000 B.C. had covered the entire sea coast, turned the former sweet lakes of Marmara and the Black Lake into salt seas, and connected them to the Aegean, turned the Bos Valley into the Bosporus Sea, and drowned Neolithic villages all over the Middle East, so many that dredging companies regularly turned up soggy posts and antique dreck in their scoops and buckets?

The torrent had pursued her, but the woman had made her escape in the interior, because the earth had swallowed the flood. Then the flood took its position on the sand of the sea, the primeval power receded, the shorelines of this new maritime world settled down. The world after 6000 B.C. was a vastly different place from what went on before, it had an unsettled climate and brand-new geology. Humankind would have to begin anew. The first lesson was how to tame the water. It was not impossible that the secret of how to tame this water was accorded a woman, a woman who was remembered long after the marvellous mystery was first revealed.

From the stone church – which like the ruined temples at Ephesus was designed for quick entry and exit, consisting of an entrance passage into a narrow transom, a wooden chapel, and an exit door to the left – there descended a series of stone steps leading to the spring waters.

There were three taps cut into the face of the rock before the house, and a strange relief of the Virgin overlooked the scene. I drank the water.

It was clean and cold.

Epilogue

A late Sunday afternoon, bleak December. The phone rings. It's Fipke.
"How's it going?"

"Hey, Chuck. What's doing?"

"Not much," he says. "Got some guys interested in my Yemen gold project."

"Yeah? Who?"

"Bahrain. The Saudis too. Bidding."

"That must feel pretty good."

"Soon as it gets wrapped up, I'm headed off."

"Oh yeah? Where?"

"Mongolia. Trekking with pack horses."

"Mongolia? What are you going to find there? Gold? Diamonds?"

"Who knows, hey?"

Selected Reading

1. Breton, Jean-Francois. *Arabia Felix from the Time of the Queen of Sheba*. Notre Dame: University of the Notre Dame Press, 1999.
2. Fakhr, Ahmed. *An Archeological Journey to Yemen*. Cairo: Government Press, 1952.
3. Frolick, Vernon Mark. *Fire Into Ice: Charles Fipke and the Great Diamond Hunt*. Vancouver: Raincoast, 1999.
4. Magnusson, Magnus. *BC: The Archeology of the Bible Lands*. London: The Bodley Head Ltd., 1977.
5. Mallory-Greenough, L., J. Greenough, and C. Fipke. "Iron Age Gold Mining: A Preliminary Report on Camps in the Al Maraziq Region, Yemen." *Arabian Archeology and Epigraphy* II, 2000.
6. Pritchard, James B., ed. *Solomon & Sheba*. London: Phaidon, 1974.
7. St. John Philby, H. *The Queen of Sheba*. London: Quartet Books, 1981.

Acknowledgements

The author thanks the many people who made this book a reality. In Canada: Steve Wilson, my agent Joanne Kellock, editor Pat Kennedy, and publisher Doug Gibson, who all trusted me to come back with my manuscript, or on it. And Dr. Leanne Mallory. In Yemen: Chuck Fipke, Chad Ulansky, and all the people at Canadian Mountain Minerals (Yemen) Ltd., Iqbal Jailani, Ahmed Mossoud, Abdul Razzaq, Abdul Shybani, and especially Ahmed Mossen; Dr. Yusuf Abdullah, director of Sana'a's National Museum (who first suggested the secret of Sheba's gold); the Taiz poet Al-Hakimi and the staff of the *Yemen Times*. In Ethiopia: Jason Langford, whose mystical Welsh bent proved itself on the road to Yeha, Aklilu Berhane of the Africa Hotel, and Johannis Aychew, the perfect travelling companion. And in Turkey: Annette Steinhof, Aydin Can, and Cem and Cunet, the Ozkan brothers.

And thanks to Rosi Zirger, who spotted the tomb first, and Vern Frolick, who knew all along something was out there.